SAGE ANNUAL REVIEWS OF DRUG AND ALCOHOL ABUSE

Series Editor:
JAMES A. INCIARDI, *University of Delaware*

Other Books in this Series:

Volume 1: *Street Ethnography*
Robert S. Weppner, Editor

Volume 2: *Drugs and Suicide:*
When Other Coping Strategies Fail
Dan J. Lettieri, Editor

Volume 3: *Addicts and Aftercare:*
Community Integration of the Former Drug User
Barry S. Brown, Editor

SAGE Annual Reviews of Drug and Alcohol Abuse
Volume 4

DRUGS and the YOUTH CULTURE

FRANK R. SCARPITTI
SUSAN K. DATESMAN, Editors

 SAGE PUBLICATIONS   Beverly Hills   London

For information address:

SAGE Publications, Inc.
275 South Beverly Drive
Beverly Hills, California 90212

SAGE Publications Ltd
28 Banner Street
London EC1Y 8QE, England

Printed in the United States of America

Library of Congress Cataloging in Publication Data

Main entry under title:

Drugs and the youth culture.

(Sage annual reviews of drug and alcohol abuse ;
v. 4)
    Includes bibliographies.
    CONTENTS: The contemporary drug picture:
Richards, L. G. The epidemiology of youthful
drug use. Stephens, R. C. The hard drug scene.
Johnson, B. D., and Uppal, G. S. Marihuana and youth. [etc.]
    1. Drugs and youth—Addresses, essays, lectures.
2. Drugs and youth—United States—Addresses,
essays, lectures. I. Scarpitti, Frank R.
II. Datesman, Susan K. [DNLM: 1. Drug abuse—In
adolescence. 2. Social problems. W1
SA125TD v. 4 / WM270 D7957]
HV5824.Y68D78   362.2'9'088055   80-11613
ISBN 0-8039-1103-3
ISBN 0-8039-1104-1 (pbk.)

CONTENTS

PART III. PREVENTION AND CONTROL OF DRUG USE

PREFACE

As we begin the decade of the 1980s, drug use and abuse among young people continue to be subjects of considerable concern in American society. It is important, however, that this concern not be exaggerated or distorted by misconceptions and misunderstandings that may adversely affect the formulation of policy regarding drug use. The formulation of an enlightened drug policy for the 1980s requires a clear understanding of the current drug situation. In this volume, we have attempted to provide the reader with such an understanding. Current usage is discussed as well as recent trends in youthful drug use. In addition, the effectiveness of various prevention, education, and treatment programs is assessed.

We would like to thank the authors of the chapters in this volume for their contributions, and for their patience and cooperation in making suggested revisions, all of which were minor. We would also like to thank Carol Anderson, Marie Gregg, and Claire Blessing for their secretarial help. Finally, we appreciate the assistance of James Inciardi in preparing this volume.

–F.R.S.
S.K.D.

7

INTRODUCTION

FRANK R. SCARPITTI
SUSAN K. DATESMAN

Considerable concern is still being expressed in American society about the use of various drugs by adolescents and young adults. Popular communication media convey the image that a sizable portion of the youthful population smoke, drink, and use various drugs; college administrators complain about excessive drinking, especially of beer, on campuses; and scientific research continues to investigate, and to substantiate, patterns of substance abuse among youths. Indeed, our concern for, and knowledge of, each behavior is probably greater today than at any previous time. That does not mean, however, that there is a great deal of agreement on the appropriateness or inappropriateness of drug use. Indeed, debate continues not only on the nature and extent of youthful drug use, but also on its consequences and acceptability. Some even question the role of the state in attempting to control and prevent illicit substance use (Szasz, 1972).

The fact of the matter is that the existence of any social problem, including the use of alcohol and drugs, depends to a great extent on certain social definitions held within a society. These definitions in turn depend on social attitudes and behavioral norms which are often reflected in and reinforced by law and government regulations. Currently, considerable conflict exists within American society concerning the appropriate use of drugs, and this conflict is manifested in a lack of consensus about the very nature of the drug problem.

A portion of the disagreement over the proper use of drugs and alcohol, by both adults and youth, is a reflection of our social attitudes and values. Americans use chemicals in great quantity. We smoke, we drink, and we take pills at an ever-increasing rate, usually for the purpose of allowing ourselves to experience alternative psychic states. In spite of such use, at least one study has shown that a large majority of the population disapproves of the use of drugs for nonmedical purposes. In response to a survey conducted in New York some years ago, 90.3 percent of the people interviewed disagreed with the statement that "everyone should try drugs at least once to find out what they are like" (Chambers, 1971: 3). Furthermore, some 76 percent also disagreed with the statement, "People can find out more about themselves through drugs." Similar questions asked of college students in a more recent survey also elicited a large percentage of negative responses (Inciardi, 1978). Only 11.9 percent of the male college students and 3.8 percent of the females agreed with the former statement, while only 14.8 percent of the males and 11.5 percent of the females agreed with the latter statement. One might gather from this that attitudes concerning "appropriate" drug use appear to be related more to how a drug is obtained and the purpose for which it is used rather than to its effects.

The public definition of appropriate use is also a function of the type of people who use drugs. In the past, when the majority of illegal drug users belonged to outcast groups such as criminals, prostitutes, nonwhites, and the urban poor, the drug laws reflected and reinforced public attitudes that illegal drug use undermines moral restraints and leads to crime, violence, and other forms of deviance. In the 1960s, however, illegal drug use spread to the middle and upper classes, particularly to the youth of these classes. Not only was there a startling increase in awareness and alarm concerning the new "drug problem," but the new users also created some changes in social attitudes and definitions. For many people, appropriate drug use has been redefined and extended to include the use of marihuana and has resulted in a call for change in the drug laws. Yet others continue to consign the young who use drugs to stigmatized groups of law violators.

The use of drugs for inducing changed mental states is not confined to any particular society or historical age. For centuries, American Indians used peyote, a type of cactus that grows in the Southwest and Mexico, in their tribal religious ceremonies. Peyote was considered the most powerful and sacred of the various hallucinogenic plants in common use among the tribes for healing, prophecy, and divination.

Opium was used in Asian countries for centuries and became a serious problem in China in the early 1800s. Although many Chinese immigrants brought the use of the drug with them to the United States, opium was not unknown in America. It was the major ingredient in many nineteenth-century patent medicines. Morphine, an opium derivative that was not at first thought to be addictive and was considered a miracle drug when introduced as a pain reliever in the early 1800s, was widely used during the Civil War in the medical treatment of wounded soldiers.

Prior to World War I, there was an estimated 200,000 to 500,000 drug addicts in the United States, many of whom had become addicted through the use of patent medicines containing morphine (Clausen, 1976: 144). These medicines were widely advertised and available over the counter in any drugstore for the cure of "female troubles" and many other diseases. A large proportion of the user population was white, middle class, and female. *Long Day's Journey into Night,* an autobiographical play by Eugene O'Neill, dramatizes his mother's addiction and the family's hearbreaking attempts to deal with it (O'Neill, 1956). The users of laudanum, as morphine was called, were often not aware it was addictive or that they were addicted. Narcotic drugs and addiction were not yet viewed as a personal or social problem.

New addicts in the 1920s and 1930s were largely white males who frequented areas where illegal drugs could be purchased—the disorganized areas of the largest cities, characterized by overcrowding, crime, and other social problems (Winick, 1961). In fact, narcotics use may actually have declined during the period between the two world wars.

THE POSTWAR ERA

Recent decades have witnessed the emergence of drug use as a significant factor in the seemingly ever-changing structure of the American youth culture, however. Both popular history and social commentary suggested a generation ago that the widespread use of drugs among juveniles first occurred during the 1950s, and such drug use was essentially addiction to heroin. By the early 1950s new population groups, primarily blacks and Puerto Ricans, were taking up residence in the slum areas where illicit drugs had long been available. Adolescents and young adults thus had access to drugs in their home neighborhoods. It was a central-city problem which was confined to the half-worlds of the urban ghetto or the periphery of the jazz scene, and it was viewed as some kind of malignancy that might be expected among the populations who were only marginal to the mainstream of American social life. By 1960, in some neighborhoods as many as 10 percent of all males sixteen to twenty years of age were officially recorded as drug users (Clinard, 1974: 416).

Yet curiously, the then conventional images of youthful drug use appear to have been continually jaded by the specter of prejudice and bias, combined with a folklore generated by ignorance and the influence of both mass media and the contemporary popular arts.

By the time that the post-World War II era had begun, conceptions of drug use had already been scarred by the ravings of Harry J. Anslinger's crusade against marihuana which, beginning in the late 1930s, had attributed to drug-taking a level of wickedness that could only have been matched by the Victorian imagery of masturbation and its consequences. Quite typical of Anslinger's scenarios were his descriptions in *American Magazine* of the brutalities which he attributed to marihuana use. For example:

> The sprawled body of a young girl lay crushed on the sidewalk the other day after a plunge from the fifth story of a Chicago apartment house. Everyone called it suicide, but actually it was murder. The killer was a narcotic known to America as marihuana, and to history as hashish. It is a narcotic used in the form of cigarettes, comparatively new to the United States and as dangerous as a coiled rattlesnake [Sloman, 1979: 34].

Or similarly:

> An entire family was murdered by a youthful addict in Florida. When officers arrived at the home, they found the youth staggering about in a human slaughterhouse. With an ax he had killed his father, mother, two brothers, and a sister. He seemed to be in a daze. . . . He had no recollection of having committed the multiple crime. *The officers knew him ordinarily as a sane, rather quiet young man; now he was pitifully crazed.* They sought the reason. The boy said he had been in the habit of smoking something which youthful friends called "muggles," a childish name for marihuana [Sloman, 1979: 63].

Linked to the already celebrated stories of marihuana as a dangerous "narcotic" drug, images of drug use in the 1950s also included descriptions of heroin addiction as part and parcel of the ghetto. In his renowed work, *America as a Civilization,* distinguished author and journalist Max Lerner (1957: 666) summarized in 1957 an image of heroin use that was common during that time:

As a case in point we may take the known fact of the prevalence of reefer-and-dope addiction in Negro areas. This is essentially explained in terms of poverty slum living, and broken families, yet it would be easy to show the lack of drug addiction among other ethnic groups where the same conditions apply.

Lerner went on to explain that addiction among blacks was due to their rapid movement from a depressed status to the improved standards and freedoms of the era. But, of course, Lerner was benignly mistaken, and not only about "reefer addiction" but also about the prevalence of drug use in other populations—rich and poor, white and black, and young and old.

Or consider the images of heroin addiction offered in 1955 in the United Artists production *The Man with the Golden Arm*. The film was controversial in its day, for its producer, Otto Preminger, had touched upon a prohibited subject. But in its actual content, like most films during the comfortable, conservative, prosperous, classless, and consensual paradise of the 1950s, it reflected majority attitudes and served only to confirm established versions of reality. Cast in the role of a would-be professional musician, Frank Sinatra was the hero of the story. He was plagued by the evils of heroin addiction, only to be saved by the help and understanding of his girlfriend Molly (Kim Novak). As with other media images of the drug scene, only a contorted view was offered, nor did it probe beyond the surface of basic issues.

As might be expected, most explanations of the drug addiction of this era focused on young heroin addicts in urban ghettos. It was believed that the addict was either psychotic or neurotic and that drugs provided relief from anxiety and a means of withdrawing from the stress of daily existence in the ghetto. Perhaps the most definitive study of heroin use among adolescents in the 1950s was Isador Chein's *The Road to H.* Concerning youthful addiction in New York City, he (1964: 14) concluded:

> The evidence indicates that all addicts suffer from deep-rooted, major personality disorders. Although psychiatric diagnoses are apt to vary, a particular set of symptoms seems to be common to most juvenile addicts. They are not able to enter into prolonged, close, friendly relations with either peers or adults; they have difficulties in assuming a masculine role; they are frequently overcome by a sense of futility, expectations of failure, and general depression; they are easily frustrated and made anxious, and they find frustrations and anxiety intolerable.

Thus, this comprehensive work leans heavily on the notion of psychological predisposition to drug usage. Chein's discussion revolves around such terms as "weak ego functioning," "defective superego," and "inadequate masculine identification." Most of these so-called predispositions can be traced, Chein implies, to the subject's family experiences. If the subject received too much love or not enough, or if the parents (usually the mother) are overwhelming in some way (love, affection, indulgence), then the child will develop inadequately. This means that the child is likely to be unable to withstand pain and discomforts, will be unable to cope with a complex world, will incorrectly assess reality, and in general, will feel incompetent around children with more varied social experiences. This type of child is thought to be much more prone to trying drugs than the child with a more conventional family life.

The portrait of addiction in the 1950s was that of passive adaptation to stress, in which drugs allowed the user to experience fulfillment and the satiation of physical and emotional needs. This view of drug use was supported even by sociologists attempting to explain the broader concepts of deviance and delinquency (Merton, 1957; Cloward and Ohlin, 1960). Cloward and Ohlin (1960: 178-186) concluded, for example, that ghetto youth who experienced double failure, those incapable of succeeding in the gang subculture or in the legitimate larger culture, turned to drugs as a way of finding a place for themselves in society.

THE NEW DRUG USE

A major change in drug use patterns occurred in the mid-1960s, when young people, particularly white middle-class students, began smoking marihuana and taking nonnarcotic drugs such as barbiturates, tranquilizers, amphetamines, and hallucinogens for their euphoric effects. The boom in psychedelic drugs began as early as 1954 with the publication of Aldous Huxley's *The Doors of Perception* in which he described his visions and insights under the influence of mescaline. "Beat" writers—Allen Ginsberg, William Burroughs, and Ken Kesey—began writing about their drug experiences. At Harvard University in 1960 Professors Richard Alpert and Timothy Leary began using mescaline, psilocybin, and LSD in a research project, for which they were later dismissed from the university. Leary established a psychedelic cult, declaring it was time to "tune in, turn on and drop out." By the late 1960s and early 1970s, in addition to the increased use of nonnarcotic drugs, the consumption of heroin and cocaine had risen, including very high use in the armed services, particularly among troops in Vietnam.

During the 1960s when the use of drugs seems to have spread from the urban minorities to the white middle-class and to the college campus, it was often seen as a characteristic of a "new left-wing" cohort of adolescents and young adults who were both irresponsible and unwilling to participate in the roles and relationships of the normal-conventional social world. Youthful users of "hard" or addictive drugs continued to pose a problem for American society. Although there is no evidence that this form of drug use diminished significantly, it did receive less attention in the public press as well as in the professional literature. Instead, the various media focused their full attention on the new use of "soft" drugs by high school and college youth.

Coming from "good" homes with "good" parents, and possessing all the opportunities denied to impoverished youth, these middle-class drug users could hardly be described as entrapped souls responding to intolerable environmental conditions. Nor did anyone suggest that they possessed unique psychological predispositions to drug experimentation and use. In short, this type of user did not seem to fit any of the explanations heretofore offered. It was obvious that new explanations were needed.

In the drug literature of this period, such familiar terms as "narcotics" and "addicts" were augmented by the terms "dangerous drugs" and "users" which connoted new problems and new life-styles in the use of drugs. The new drugs being used and the different levels of effects suggested that many of the new users were increasingly concerned with the sensate, with manipulation of the body and mind to achieve new physical and psychological experiences, rather than with withdrawal, escape, and narcosis—numbing which characterized traditional heroin users. Not only were different substances being used, but different groups were using these substances with unknown degrees of exclusivity and overlap. That is, opiates were used more frequently by members of the lower class and LSD users seemed to originate in the middle and upper classes. Other drugs, especially marihuana, were more often used across social classes. To compound the problem further, many were sporadic users who switched from one drug to another, seemingly as the fashion changed (Scher, 1966).

With the rise of white middle-class drug use, alternative explanations of the drug scene began to take form. One group of such users was characterized as normal adolescents conforming to an adolescent culture which emphasized defying rules, seeking "kicks," and pursuing pleasure at almost any cost. Another group, however, was thought to use drugs as a form of purposive dissent, protesting through their use all that was "wrong" with society and its institutions. As one commentator put it:

First, there is a type of substance use, particularly of marijuana and the hallucinogens, which is extraordinarily prevalent among middle- and upper-class teenagers today. This is conformist adolescent use, and it is *not* associated with psychiatric disorder. Second, among many older adolescents and young adults, drug use is but one facet not of rebellion, but of dissent; not of social irresponsibility and immorality, but of adherence to a set of rational and humane tenets, quite like those upon which, in theory, our democracy is founded, but which are not infrequently rather contrary to the way we actually do business. There is, in addition, an almost total lack of knowledge about the understanding of this phenomenon on the part of those of us not directly participating in it [Brotman, 1967: 43].

The conformist drug user was thought by some to be part of a new breed of young people who conformed to a "hang-loose" ethic, first described by Simmons and Winograd (1966: 12).

One of the fundamental characteristics of the "hang-loose" ethic is that it is irreverent. It repudiates or at least questions, such cornerstones of conventional society as Christianity, "my country right or wrong," the sanctity of marriage and premarital chastity, civil disobedience, the accumulation of wealth, the right and even competence of parents, the schools, and the government to head and make decisions for everyone—in sum, the Establishment.

Observing that the youth of the period talked about smoking pot socially, the fun of breaking society's rules, and the kicks of doing something dangerous, Suchman (1968) believed that youth had accepted a "hang-loose" ethic. He made the point that the more this ethic was internalized the more likely youth would be using drugs. Suchman demonstrated that much youthful drug use was only one aspect of the overall scene and that one had to understand what that scene entailed to appreciate the meaning of such behavior. Rather than being a mark of alienation, Suchman believed that drug use was an overt manifestation of a contemporary philosophy and a rejection of the old Protestant ethic. Although many drug users saw a great deal wrong with our system, they were not necessarily apathetic or withdrawing from the system. And, in a final plea that the "hang-loose" ethic and drug use be seen as a legitimate response to the social order, Suchman (1968: 154) concludes that, "while there can be little question that the 'hang-loose' ethic is contrary to the Protestant ethic and spirit of capitalism, and may be socially disapproved for that and other reasons, the issue, it seems to us, should be openly faced and debated as one of conflicting social values and not of crime or health."

Keniston (1968) agreed with Suchman's contention that drug use was still a subgroup phenomenon. In the 1960s, though, the subgroup had changed; it involved a new morality and philosophy. Keniston pointed out that there were at least two types of new drug users, "heads" and "seekers." On the one hand, "seekers" were better-than-average students who were determined to find some meaning to life. On the other hand, "heads" referred to those genuinely alienated from society, at least for the present.

Keniston noted that drug users seemed to be found most often in certain types of social settings, such as high-pressure colleges, and that drug use might be a reflection of an experimental counter culture with a focus on the here and now. In Keniston's (1968: 129) words, "the experimental subculture stresses genuineness, adventure, spontaneity, sentience and experimentation. Since the past is seen as irrelevant (or 'exhausted') and since the future seems profoundly uncertain, the real meaning of life must be found within present experience." Thus, his and others' suggestion that middle-class drug users may be reacting against the intense pressures of modern society is not so far removed from earlier ideas of heroin use which explained it as an adaptation to a social system that was overwhelming the users. The difference between these forms of behavior appears to lie in the user's objectives. The new users of the 1960s seemed to be seeking meaning and stability from drug experiences rather than an escape from reality.

RECENT DEVELOPMENTS IN YOUTHFUL DRUG USE

As we enter the 1980s, there appears to be, broadly speaking, two types of youthful drug users. On the one hand, there are the urban, largely minority, street-users who remain committed to using various drugs. More recent studies of drug use in urban settings have found that many different patterns of use exist, however. Many habitual users avoid addictive drugs or are weekend users. Because the street dose of heroin is relatively low in potency, many addicts are able to control their habits. They may work or attend school and must exhibit energy and resourcefulness in order to support their drug use. Today, drug use is an integral part of the lives of many young urban residents who respond to the goals and beliefs of their drug subculture and in so doing gain status.

On the other hand, middle-class drug use continues to abound (Green, 1979). Investigations of the more recent upsurge of drug use among middle-class youth have found that the majority tend to avoid hard drugs such as heroin and cocaine, generally come from stable homes, and are not psychologically disturbed. For these people, drug use appears to be a response to their environment, a way of dissenting from middle-class values and life-styles and of affirming their own values. A middle-class youth who is an illegal drug user may reject the values of society. This rejection may be either a result or a precondition of illegal drug use. But whether antiestablishment values encourage drug use or result from it, drug use probably reinforces these values.

But the middle-class drug use of the late 1970s was not the same as that of the 1960s and early 1970s. Unlike the drug use of "hippies" and others who were attempting to expand their consciousness and experience new levels of understanding and communication, contemporary middle-class drug use appears to be motivated by self-indulgence, boredom, and what Lasch (1979) has called the culture of narcissism. He contends that "to live for the moment is the prevailing passion" (1979: 30) and that "people today hunger not for personal salvation, let alone for the restoration of an earlier golden age, but for the feeling, the momentary illusion of personal well-being" (1979: 33). The boredom and self-indulgence of contemporary middle-class youth, perhaps exacerbated by their prolonged exposure to the mass media and the opportunities provided by affluence, take on added importance when they combine with the traditional problems of adolescence. According to Erikson (1963), the central task of the adolescent period is the establishment of a consistent identity. The adolescent attempts to fit his or her many roles into a unified, coherent whole. The individual makes strides in the direction of increasing autonomy by making more and more decisions independent of other family members.

However, the adolescents' roles are not clearly defined for them. Many of the roles assigned to them in our society are marginal at best.

No longer children, not yet adults, adolescents are put in a holding pattern for a number of years. They are required by law to stay in school until 16 and are encouraged by a tight labor market to remain there even longer. Adolescence is the period when society, primarily through the family and school systems, makes its final attempt to bring the person into line with adult standards. Yet, even for those who conform perfectly, the privileges of adulthood are denied. Adolescents are barred from the economic sector by the inability to find full-time employment. They are barred from the political sector by the inability to vote. They are barred from the sexual sector by a society that frowns on such relationships among people their age. Though they are banned from engaging in many of the activities of the adult world, adolescents are expected to be able to present a rough draft of what they want their adult life to look like (Elder, 1968).

The process of "pulling up roots" and establishing a life relatively independent of parents can be long and drawn out. Some people enter this period at 17 and do not exit until 22 or later. Others do not even begin until 21 or 22. But in all cases, the problems of the transition are similar. They revolve around the issues of locating ourselves in a peer-group role, a sex role, an anticipated occupation, and an ideology or world view.

During the transitional period to adulthood, individuals are frequently overcome with the sense that the lives they have been leading are not part of the real world. They feel that their families have shielded them from participating in this world and so they try to forget past associations. Some choose to join strict authoritarian groups that command the individual to break off all ties with the past. Others defy parental authority by using drugs and participating in a drug culture. Most are content with less drastic measures. Moving away from the parents' home for short periods of time, to college or to the army, is a more common form of escaping the parents' influence. Such steps can be seen as preliminary inquiries into life in the adult world that allow the adolescent the opportunity to examine possible career lines and life-styles.

Although most young adults struggle to establish a firm identity for themselves, the majority accomplish this without undergoing a major personal crisis. According to Erikson's (1963) scheme, they must face the issue of establishing close, intimate relations (sharing oneself with another person) or of remaining somewhat isolated (incapable of such intimacy). In dealing with the issues of identity and intimacy, young adults fall into one of four broad categories. Persons in the "moratorium" group are unsure of the identity and level of intimacy that they desire. Yet they struggle to find the right combination. They delay finding solutions but feel that delaying is only making matters worse. Persons in the "identity-diffused" group are also unsure of what values or identity to attach themselves to, but they do not attempt to define or confront these issues. Either because of attitudes of inferiority, alienation, or fatalism, people in this group allow things to pass as they are and do not see themselves in any major crisis. The "identity-foreclosed" group includes those who have passively accepted the identity designed for them by their parents. There is no struggle or crisis for this group either. Finally, the "identity-achieved" group has endured a crisis and succeeded in obtaining a clear identity, value system, and philosophy of life. It is possible for individuals to be members of all of these groups at some time or other during the young adult stage, and even to belong to one group at two different times.

Adolescence is a time for experimentation and attaching great importance to one's peer group. In this period of personal turmoil and identity uncertainty, played out in the culturally accepted context of self-gratification, it is not difficult to imagine youthful drug use as a means of enhancing personal experience while identifying with one's peer group. Hence, one study of drug users in a southeastern university found that the strongest indicator of use was found, not in social background characteristics or in feelings of alienation, but in subcultural factors within the university environment. The more integrated students were into the student subculture, the more likely they were to use drugs (Thomas et al., 1975). Findings from a survey of junior and senior high school students revealed that the single best predictor of students' use of drugs was whether their friends used drugs (Schulz and Wilson, 1975).

CURRENT USAGE AND RECENT TRENDS IN YOUTHFUL DRUG USE

Accurate figures on the number of persons using drugs in this country are notoriously difficult to obtain for the obvious reason that penalties for drug violations are severe and users wish to avoid detection. Most estimates in the past have been based on arrest records and the number of persons treated in rehabilitation and detoxification centers, but such figures represent an unknown percentage of the actual drug-using population. For about the past decade, the extent of drug use has also been ascertained through the use of large-scale surveys based on representative samples. This section will rely heavily on two such surveys. The first is a series of five studies based on national samples of households that span the period from 1971 to 1977 (Abelson and Fishburne, 1976; Abelson et al., 1977; Cisin et al., 1977). The second is a series of four studies of national samples of high school seniors conducted annually from 1975 to 1978 (Johnston et al., 1977, 1979).

Both studies indicate that drug use is widespread among youth and young adults. For example, the 1978 high school survey reports that drugs are now used by a majority of high school seniors, with between six and seven out of every ten reporting drug use at some time in their lives. This accounts for about 64 percent of the seniors and represents an increase over 1975, when about 55 percent of the sample reported using drugs at some time.

The most commonly used drugs among youths and young adults are not illegal—i.e., alcohol and cigarettes. Most recent studies have shown that alcohol is the drug most frequently tried, and the one most heavily used by young people. For example, a study in New York State revealed that 82 percent of the high school students had experimented with alcohol, while 27 percent were classified as regular drinkers (Kandel et al., 1976). In the household survey, alcohol was the most widely used drug among youth aged 12 to 17 years and young adults aged 18 to 25 years. In the most recent survey, 53 percent of the youth and 84 percent of the young adults reported alcohol use at one time or another. The use of alcohol was even more extensive among high school seniors in 1978: 93 percent had tried alcohol and 6 percent reported daily use within the past month. Alcohol use has increased only slightly among high school seniors since 1975, when 91 percent reported use at some time; additionally, daily use has remained about the same. Longitudinal studies also show that the first use of alcohol is occurring at earlier ages. One such study indicated that in 1969 about 11 percent of seventh-grade males in San Mateo County had used alcohol within the past six months; by 1977, the figure increased to almost 23 percent (Blackford, 1977).

Since alcohol is easily obtained and the penalties for its consumption are mild relative to those for other drugs, alcohol is considered a safer high and is the most popular drug among teenagers. Drinking among adolescents is strongly related to attitudes and drinking practices of peer groups and parents. If drinking is accepted and engaged in by parents and if it is practiced or even expected by members of peer groups, then the likelihood of alcohol use is greatly increased. There is reason for particular concern with teenage alcohol abuse, for if an adolescent learns to cope with stress by drinking, this may become established as a general pattern for coping with any kind of stressful situation in adult life. Recognizing the seriousness of adolescent alcohol abuse, all 50 states have enacted legislation requiring alcohol education programs in the public schools.

Cigarettes rank second to alcohol in the prevalence of use among American youth. Among high school students in New York State, 72 percent reported having tried cigarettes, and 23 percent reported themselves as being regular users of cigarettes (Kandel et al, 1976). In the 1977 household survey, 47 percent of the youths and 68 percent of the young adults reported having used cigarettes at some time. In the 1978 high school survey, 75 percent had tried cigarettes and 28 percent smoked daily. These proportions were about the same in 1975, when 74 percent reported ever smoking and 27 percent reported smoking on a daily basis. The incidence of cigarette use, however, apparently increased in the household sample: While in 1971, 15 percent of the sampled youths were regular smokers, 23 percent were regular smokers in 1976. Additionally, it has been found that more individuals are becoming smokers at early ages.

The most widely used illegal drug among youth and young adults is marihuana. Of New York State high school students, 30 percent reported ever using marihuana and 8 percent reported regular use (Kandel et al., 1976). In the 1977 household survey, 28 percent of the youths and 60 percent of the young adults had tried marihuana at one time or another. And 49 percent of the high school seniors in 1978 admitted to ever using marihuana, with 11 percent using it daily.

According to several studies, marihuana use has increased substantially among young people during the past decade. For example, a 1967 Gallup Poll of college students revealed that 6 percent had ever used marihuana. By 1974, the estimate based on a poll taken for two national commissions had risen to 61 percent (Goode, 1975). In the household survey, the proportion of youth who had tried marihuana increased from 14 percent in 1972 to 28 percent in 1977. Among young adults, the increase was from 48 percent to 60 percent. In the high school survey, similar findings were uncovered: 47 percent of the high school seniors in 1975 reported having tried marihuana, while 59 percent reported having tried it in 1978. This study also showed a small but steady increase in daily marihuana smoking. In 1975, 6 percent of the high school seniors claimed such use, 8 percent in 1976, 9 percent in 1977, and 11 percent in 1978.

With the exception of alcohol, cigarettes, and marihuana, drug use among youth tends to be very limited. Among the youth in the most recent household survey, only about 5 percent reported ever using hallucinogens and stimulants, 4 percent had tried tranquilizers and cocaine, and 3 percent had tried sedatives. The use of these drugs was generally higher among young adults, with approximately one-fifth reporting some use of hallucinogens, stimulants, sedatives, and cocaine, and about 13 percent admitting to ever using tranquilizers. In the 1978 high school survey, stimulants were the most widely used of these drugs, with 23 percent of the sample reporting some use, followed by tranquilizers (17 percent), sedatives (16 percent), hallucinogens (14 percent), and cocaine (13 percent). Regular use of these drugs is even rarer. For instance, only 1 percent of the New York State high school students regularly used any illicit drug other than marihuana (Kandel et al., 1976). And in the national high school survey, only one-tenth to one-half of one percent of the seniors used any of these drugs on a daily basis.

Trend data from the household survey indicate that the proportion of youth ever using hallucinogens, stimulants, sedatives, and tranquilizers has remained relatively steady, while the proportion of young adults ever using these substances has increased somewhat. Among high school seniors, the proportions ever using these drugs have stayed about the same. On the other hand, both studies show that cocaine use has increased, particularly among young adults in the household survey: 19 percent reported some use in 1977 compared with only 9 percent in 1972.

Heroin is the drug least used among youth. Among New York State high school students, only 3 percent had ever experimented with heroin (Kandel et al., 1976). In the 1977 household survey, heroin had been tried by only 1 percent of the youths and 4 percent of the young adults. Similarly, only 2 percent of the high school seniors in 1978 reported ever using heroin. Moreover, rates for heroin use have remained fairly stable over the past decade. Researchers have also learned that the first use of heroin tends to occur in the later years of adolescence.

It is believed that there is an increasing prevalence of multiple drug use among youth (Green, 1979). Many studies have indicated that there is a correlation between licit drug use and the subsequent use of illicit drugs. In a New York State study, it was found that almost 100 percent of all high school students who tried an illicit drug had previously tried alcohol, and 89 percent had smoked cigarettes (Single et al., 1975). Additionally, there appears to be a relationship between the use of an illicit drug and the development of a multiple drug use pattern: 70 percent of those high school students who tried an illicit drug, tried more than one other. Another related finding is that among those students who have used marihuana 60 or more times, 84 percent have also used pills, 78 percent have used LSD, and 62 percent have used cocaine, heroin, or other narcotics; daily marihuana smokers also tend to be heavy consumers of alcohol.

PLAN OF THE BOOK

The focus of this volume is on adolescent and young adult use of drugs, including alcohol and cigarettes. The chapters which follow attempt to describe and analyze current usage as well as explain the changes in youthful drug use which have taken place over the past ten years. As we have seen, during that time the youthful drug scene has changed from one characterized by drug "subcultures" and hard drug use to extensive interclass use of various substances, especially marihuana and alcohol. Part I, The Contemporary Drug Picture, examines current use patterns as well as relevant explanations of specific types of drug use.

In Chapter 1, The Epidemiology of Youthful Drug Use, Louise G. Richards describes nonmedical drug use today and reviews the recent history of such use. She concludes that the picture of youthful drug use has changed some but not drastically since the late 1960s. Alcohol and tobacco continue to be the most widely used drugs, with marihuana now occupying a fairly comparable status. Drug use has moved from being described as an epidemic (in the 1960s) to being endemic. That is, at this time, it appears to be a more or less traditional or tolerated form of social behavior.

Richard C. Stephens, in this chapter, The Hard Drug Scene, lends support to this argument through his examination of the current extent of hard drug use. He shows that not only are certain types of drug use increasing, but that there is also a demographic broadening in the use of all drugs throughout the country. In Stephens's estimation, there are two dimensions that underlie adolescent drug use: the youth's degree of integration into the society and the youth's perception of his or her primary group's attitudes toward drug use. He concludes that by knowing these two things one can predict the extent of adolescent drug use.

While the extensiveness and pervasiveness of hard drug use may be somewhat uncertain, there can be little doubt about marihuana. In their chapter, Marihuana and Youth: A Generation Gone to Pot, Bruce Johnson and Gopal Uppal show that marihuana use has increased throughout the 1970s. They assert that "current marihuana use now equals or surpasses alcohol consumption among secondary school students in some parts of the country." Not surprisingly, marihuana use has become institutionalized within today's youth culture. Even as it is widely used and its use is becoming increasingly decriminalized, new biological and pharmacological research findings indicate that regular marihuana use is potentially harmful for individual health. While these findings have yet to be verified, they do create doubts about the wisdom of chronic marihuana use.

Despite the extensiveness of marihuana use, it is alcohol which has been shown to be the most widely used drug among teenagers. Various surveys reported by G. Nicholas Braucht in his chapter, entitled Psychosocial Research on Teenage Drinking: A Review of the Past and a Paradigm for the Future, indicate that over half of all adolescents 12 to 17 years of age have used alcohol at one time or another. Of these, a sizable number may be classified as problem drinkers. Braucht also examines the personality correlates of teenage drinking as well as environmental factors associated with such behavior. After reviewing an array of data on youthful drinking and drinkers, he summarizes: "There seems to be a general syndrome of unconventional, nonconforming, social *problem* behaviors among a select group of teenagers in which problem drinking, marihuana and other illicit drug use, precocious sexual behavior, delinquent behavior, and other antisocial behavior patterns are component parts."

In the last chapter of this section, Dorothy E. Green examines Teenage Smoking Behavior. Some of her findings are surprising. For example, she shows that between 1968 and 1979, there has been a decrease in the proportion of teenagers who smoke. This has been especially true in recent years for boys. In addition, by 1979 a larger proportion of girls than boys were classified as smokers. Green also shows that regular teenage smokers differ from those who are not in terms of relevant demographic characteristics, life-style, and attitudes toward the world around them.

Part II of this book examines three topics that continue to be of interest to everyone concerned with youthful drug use. Chapters 6 and 7 deal with the relationship between drug use and crime, and the use of drugs on American college campuses respectively. James Inciardi in Youth, Drugs, and Street Crime reports on research that he and his associates have undertaken over several years with various types of drug users. Within street populations of drug users, he shows that "high volume drug use and widespread criminality go hand-in-hand." Although drug use on the college campus is also widespread, only those students dealing in drugs or using drugs on a regular basis show an unusual involvement in crime. Current trends indicate that these patterns will continue.

Henry Wechsler and Mary E. Rohman also examine Drug Use Among College Students in their chapter. They find that drug use is increasing among college students, with alcohol the most widely used drug. Over two-thirds of the students surveyed reported using other drugs, however, particularly marihuana. College drug use of all kinds appears to be an occasional practice, usually occurring less often than once a week. Significantly, Wechsler and Rohman found that boredom was the only problem area that differentiated among frequent marihuana users, infrequent users, and drug nonusers.

In Chapter 8, Manuel Ramos examines what happened to the "hippies" of the 1960s. This chapter, entitled The Hippies: Where Are They Now?, is especially relevant since it has been about ten years since the height of the hippie movement, the "hang-loose ethic," and the type of drug use that supposedly symbolized a new way of life. Based on his unique follow-up of one such group, Ramos shows why it was inevitable that hippies, despite their heavy drug use, would, as they became adults, abandon drug use and seek conventional pursuits. Reform occurred, he explains, not necessarily because of efforts to "stop the drug problem," but rather because of subtler, more natural processes.

Finally, in Part III, the issues of prevention and control of drug use are examined. Chapter 9 reviews the objectives, methods, and success of drug education, the multimillion dollar attempt to prevent drug abuse. Unfortunately, such programs appear to have met with only limited success. In fact, in the early 1970s, the National Commission on Marijuana and Drug Abuse, recognizing the lack of knowledge regarding the impact of drug education, recommended a moratorium on all such programs until their effectiveness could be evaluated. It speculated that the avalanche of drug education might even be counterproductive by actually stimulating use. Since then, increasing attention has been directed toward the consequences of drug education and this chapter examines the existing evidence regarding its effectiveness. As the author, David J. Hansen, concludes, "the largest number of studies have found no effects of drug education upon use."

What does one do, then, with the youthful drug user? In Chapter 10, David Huberty reviews various treatment modalities that have been used with young users. He illustrates how the history of youthful drug treatment has seen both attempts to control drug abusers as well as varying techniques and programs to help them. Changing public attitudes, laws, and program success rates are traced, beginning with the substituting of heroin to cure morphine addiction in the early 1900s. This chapter notes the treatment landmarks of the establishment of the federal narcotic hospitals, Synanon and the therapeutic communities movement, compulsory supervision of civil commitment programs, and combined alcoholic and addict treatment. Lastly, family counseling, an attempt to see drug use as resulting from an interactive process within the family context, is examined.

As a new decade begins, many mysteries surrounding youthful drug use remain. During the 1980s, it is likely that the problem will continue to be an important one in American social life and that new attempts will be made to understand and control such use. Hopefully, the information contained in the following chapters will allow the readers to understand the state of our knowledge at the present time while appreciating the many complexities that continue to characterize drug use among the young.

REFERENCES

ABELSON, H. I. and P. M. FISHBURNE (1976) Nonmedical Use of Psychoactive Substances: Nationwide Study Among Youth and Adults. Princeton, NJ: Response Analysis Corporation.
––– and I. CISIN (1977) National Survey on Drug Abuse, 1977. Rockville, MD: National Institute on Drug Abuse.
BLACKFORD, L. (1977) "Summary report–surveys of student drug use, San Mateo County, California." (Reported in Green, 1979)
BROTMAN, R. (1967) "Adolescent substance use: a growing form of dissent," pp. 36-43 in Conference Proceedings: Inhalation of Glue Fumes and Other

Substance Abuse Practices Among Adolescents. Washington, DC: Department of Health, Education, and Welfare.

CHAMBERS, C. D. (1971) "Drug use in New York State." Special Report 2. New York: New York State Narcotics Addiction Control Commission.

CHEIN, I. (1964) The Road to H. New York: Basic Books.

CISIN, I., J. D. MILLER, and A. V. HARRELL (1977) Highlights from the National Survey on Drug Abuse, 1977. Rockville, MD: National Institute on Drug Abuse.

CLAUSEN, J. A. (1976) "Drug use." pp. 143-178 in R. K. Merton and R. Nisbet, Contemporary Social Problems. New York: Harcourt Brace Jovanovich.

CLINARD, M. (1974) Sociology of Deviant Behavior. New York: Holt, Rinehart & Winston.

CLOWARD, R. and L. OHLIN (1960) Delinquency and Opportunity. New York: Free Press.

ELDER, G. (1968) Adolescent Socialization and Personality Development. Chicago: Rand McNally.

ERIKSON, E. (1963) Childhood and Society. New York: Norton.

GOODE, E. (1975) 'Sociological aspects of mariiuana use." Contemporary Drug Problems (Winter): 397-445.

GREEN, J. (1979) "Overview of adolescent drug use," pp. 17-44 in G. M. Beschner and A. S. Friedman, Youth Drug Abuse. Lexington, MA: D.C. Heath.

INCIARDI, J. A. (1978) Unpublished data, available from the author.

JOHNSTON, L. D., J. G. BACHMAN, and P. M. O'MALLEY (1977) Drug Use Among American High School Students, 1975-1977. Rockville, MD: National Institute on Drug Abuse.

———— (1979) Highlights from Drugs and the Class of '78: Behaviors, Attitudes, and Recent Trends. Rockville, MD: National Institute on Drug Abuse.

KANDEL, D., E. SINGLE, and R. C. KESSLER (1976) "The epidemiology of drug use among New York State high school students: distribution, trends and change in rates of use." American Journal of Public Health 66: 43-53.

KENISTON, K. (1968) "Heads and seekers: drugs on campus, countercultures and American society," pp. 118-136 in J. N. McGrath and F. R. Scarpitti, Youth and Drugs. Skokie, IL: Scott, Foresman.

LASCH, C. (1979) The Culture of Narcissism. New York: Warner.

LERNER, M. (1957) America as a Civilization. New York: Simon & Schuster.

MERTON, R. K. (1957) Social Theory and Social Structure. New York: Free Press.

O'NEILL, E. (1956) Long Day's Journey into Night. New Haven, CT: Yale University Press.

SCHER, J. (1966) "Patterns and profiles of addiction and drug use." Archives of General Psychiatry 15: 539-551.

SCHULZ, D. and R. WILSON (1975) "Some traditional family variables and their correlations with drug use among high school students." Journal of Marriage and Family 35: 628-631.

SIMMONS, J. L. and B. WINOGRAD (1966) It's Happening: A Portrait of the Youth Scene Today Santa Barbara, CA: Marc-Laid.

SINGLE, E., D. KANDEL, and R. FAUST (1975) "Patterns of multiple drug use in high school." Journal of Health and Social Behavior 15: 344-357.

SLOMAN, L. (1979) Reefer Madness. Indianapolis: Bobbs-Merrill.

SUCHMAN, E. (1968) "The 'hang-loose' ethic and the spirit of drug use." Journal of Health and Social Behavior 9: 146-155.

SZASZ, T. S. (1972) "The ethics of addiction." Harpers (April): 74-79.

THOMAS, C. W., D. M. PETERSEN, and M. T. ZINGRAFF (1975) "Student drug use: a re-examination of the 'hang-loose ethic' hypothesis." Journal of Health and Social Behavior 16: 63-73.

WINICK, C. (1961) "The drug addict and his treatment," pp. 372-373 in H. Toch, Legal and Criminal Psychology. New York: Holt, Rinehart & Winston.

PART I

THE CONTEMPORARY DRUG PICTURE

1

THE EPIDEMIOLOGY OF YOUTHFUL DRUG USE

LOUISE G. RICHARDS

The epidemiology of a given disease or condition is much like the news. It usually deals with the human element and it answers questions of who, when, where, how, and, to the extent of its methods, why. It is the area of inquiry ordinarily of greatest interest to the general public and to officials and other figures whose responsibility it is to deal with the immediate situation. Epidemiology can sometimes provide a brilliant solution to an intriguing mystery, as in cases like *Eleven Blue Men* (Roueche, 1955) where sodium nitrite poisoning was uncovered in true Holmesian fashion. But primarily epidemiology satisfies curiosity and is a backdrop to deeper investigations of the phenomenon.

The concepts of traditional epidemiology fit the realities of drug abuse imperfectly. A number of terms from the predominantly medical field of epidemiology are *prevalence, incidence, epidemic, sequelae, etiology,* and *populations at risk.* But drug use and drug dependence,

AUTHOR'S NOTE: Views expressed in this chapter are the author's and do not represent the position of the National Institute on Drug Abuse.

and their consequences, are not medical in all manifestations. The phenomena of drug use lend themselves just as comfortably to concepts drawn from the social sciences, particularly consumer behavior, deviance, and cultural innovation (Richards, 1977). At the same time, the phenomena of addiction and withdrawal, and many of the effects (acute or chronic), are truly medical and can profitably be explored with the traditional epidemiological concepts and methods.

Traditionally, the study of epidemiology has centered on concepts of the host, the vector(s) of disease, and the environment, assumed to have independent effects on the cause and spread. In the case of nonmedical drug use, the vector is a drug, but neither it nor the environment is independent of the host. The host seeks the drug and may also seek an environment sympathetic to drug-taking. Only after the development of dependence does the traditional epidemiologic model seem to fit the situation. To meet the special needs of epidemiology in the drug abuse and alcohol fields, a federal workgroup recently recommended a "multiaxial" classification of disorders and related problems for those problem areas. According to the report,

> NIDA [National Institute on Drug Abuse] and NIAAA [National Institute on Alcoholism and Alcohol Abuse] have been reluctant to adopt any of the [medically oriented] classification systems for the conduct and analysis of community surveys . . . their efforts have concentrated on describing community patterns of drug and alcohol use and related behavior, without identifying individuals as having disorders.

> Criteria are necessary for a multiaxial classification of the following:

> (1) [Alcohol, drug, and mental health] disorders or syndromes
> (2) Quantity/frequency of related symptoms and behavior
> (3) Social functioning and adverse consequences of [alcohol, drug, and mental health] disorders or problems [U.S. Department of Health, Education, and Welfare, 1978: 33-35].

Regardless of conceptual fit, the epidemiology of drug use has been of continuing interest to many sectors. When the "new wave" of nonmedical drug use hit in the sixties, the most frequent requests for knowledge were epidemiological in nature: How many were using marihuana, LSD, and the other newly appearing substances? Who were they? Where were they using them? And, of course, many also asked the question of why young people were turning to drugs. The answers to this question were more often than not speculative and unsatisfying to a panic-stricken public.

It was and is natural to want to know the extent and description of a phenomenon before probing more deeply. The full meaning of the new era of nonmedical drug use that began in the sixties has not yet been explained satisfactorily and we still have need for continuing epidemiologic investigation of its major dimensions. We still dare not predict how far nonmedical drug use will spread into the population in the next decade or what new (or revived) substances may emerge next.

The plan of this chapter is to describe the epidemiology of nonmedical (or nontherapeutic) drug use today, particularly among those under 21 years, and then quickly review the recent history of youthful drug use from the early sixties to the present.

"Nonmedical drug use" in this chapter means the use of the substances often labeled as illicit (because of their illegal status in the U.S. Pharmacopeia, in interstate commerce, and the like), such as marihuana and heroin, as well as deviant, unauthorized, or unsupervised use of drugs that have approved uses in medicine. The latter may be prescription or over-the-counter drugs, but, as will be discussed here, their use must have been for recreational, utilitarian, or other nontherapeutic purposes. This seems straightforward enough, but it is not. There is a gray area between nonmedical and medical use that encompasses self-administration of drugs for physical or psychological conditions when it is not medically approved or supervised. This is not the same as "misuse" of drugs, usually used to refer to therapeutic misadventures when use is unintended or hapless, as in misreading of instructions. When it is intentional use unapproved by a physician, it is included here as "nonmedical." This convoluted semantic space is frustrating to workers in the field, and is evidence of the disjunctions in our traditional perceptions brought about by the new drug use patterns.

"Nonmedical drug use" in this chapter also covers inhalation of substances not ordinarily classified as drugs, such as gasoline, paint thinner, and other volatile materials. Again, the use may be recreational or possibly self-administered psychotherapy, but certainly not approved treatment. So the semantics are further confused.

The conceptual theme that ties these various substances and types of behavior together appears to be the breaking away from conventional sources and authorities in the use of a variety of psychoactive agents. Although it seems new and unsettling, it is highly probable that such a breaking away (from roles, settings, and traditions that were sacred in the societies where they were developed or adopted) occurred in the past with the psychoactive substances alcohol and tobacco. That is, the "new" drug use era may be a repetition of age-old processes still poorly understood.

Alcohol and tobacco are not included in this discussion of the epidemiology of youthful drug use, but are dealt with in separate chapters (4 and 5). Some would argue that conceptually they cannot be separated from psychoactive drugs, and should not be discussed separately. However, historical and legal separation between them and drugs, as well as the separate development of their sciences, makes it practical to treat them separately here. Interestingly, one of the by-products of the "drug crisis" seems to be the increasing acceptance by the public of the idea that alcohol and tobacco, too, are "drugs."

Having broadly stated the terms of reference for the subject, description of youthful drug use patterns today and in the recent past follows.

DIMENSIONS OF YOUTHFUL DRUG USE TODAY

It is conventional to describe individual drug use according to the types or classes of substances used, the frequency of regularity of use, the recency of use, the dosage or amount, and the route of administration. These constitute the "quantity-frequency" dimensions described earlier as a necessary part of epidemiological investigations of substance use. In the drug abuse field a pharmacological emphasis seems to have prevailed in much of the analysis of quantity-frequency data. Before the upsurge of drug use in the sixties, it was "heroin addicts" or marihuana users" who were studied. With the advent of sample surveys in recent years, drug users are usually described in multiple separate drug classes, repeating the individual's use for all the classes of drugs chosen for study. It is as if the pharmacological drug class rules the user, rather than the converse. Phenomenologically, an individual's use is not usually divided into depressants, stimulants, hallucinogens, and inhalants. His or her choices of substances, subjective experiences with them, and the observable changes or effects of the choices and experiences (on the user as well as on others) fit the reality of use much more closely. Some attempts to represent this reality for individuals have been made and will be described later.

THE GENERAL POPULATION

The most comprehensive picture of the extent of nonmedical drug use today is found in the results of the 1977 National Survey carried out by the National Institute on Drug Abuse (NIDA) [Abelson et al., 1977]. Rates of lifetime prevalence ("ever used") and current use ("in the past month") are published for eleven classes of substances and a combined class of "stronger" drugs, for three age groups: 12 to 17 years, 18 to 25 years, and 26 years or older. Although the survey cannot provide reliable estimates of the rarer forms of use, such as heroin (because of the sample size), and admittedly underrepresents hard-to-find respondents, it provides a rich panorama of usage patterns by drug type and sociodemographic characteristics. It is a unique source of information on frequency, new use (incidence), and attitudes. In a separate *Highlights* volume, based on the same survey, are portrayals of subjects' acquaintance with users, their opportunities to use drugs, and family patterns of use (Miller et al., 1978).

Lifetime and current experience with the eleven types of substances (plus one combined type) for three age groups were collated by Parry (1979: 382), as shown in Table 1.1. It is obvious that alcohol and tobacco have been most widely experienced among the eleven types. Among the other substances, marihuana (and/or hashish) has been the most widely experienced and heroin the least. Among young adults, whose drug experience is more extensive than either younger or older age groups, stimulants, hallucinogens, cocaine, and the other prescription drugs (used nonmedically) are next to marihuana in extent of experience. It was noted that the use of inhalants is almost as great among youth 12 to 17 years as among young adults.

Summarizing the patterns of lifetime and current use are these statements from the *Highlights* volume:

Lifetime experience with illicit drugs is considerably more prevalent than current use, and young adults (aged 18 to 25) are characterized by much higher rates than are youth or older adults. In contrast, legal substances such as alcohol and cigarettes have been used by the majority of adults of all ages and are currently being used by a majority of all those who have ever used them.

Detailed analyses have shown that people between 17 and 34 years of age are much more likely than others to encounter opportunities to use illicit drugs. This fact accounts for much of

TABLE 1.1 Lifetime Prevalence and Recency of Use by Age, in Percentages, Household Population, 1977

	Youth (Age 12 to 17)		Young Adults (Age 18 to 25)		Older Adults (Age 26+)	
	Ever used	Used past month	Ever used	Used past month	Ever used	Used past month
Marihuana and/or hashish	28	16	60	28	15	3
Inhalants	9	1	11	(a)	2	(a)
Hallucinogens	5	2	20	2	3	(a)
Cocaine	4	1	19	4	3	(a)
Heroin	1	(a)	4	(a)	1	(a)
Other opiates[b]	6	1	13	1	3	(a)
Stimulants (Rx)[c]	5	1	21	2	5	1
Sedatives (Rx)[c]	3	1	18	3	3	(a)
Tranquilizers (Rx)[c]	4	1	13	2	3	(a)
Any illicit drug "stronger" than marihuana[d]	(9)	(e)	(34)	(e)	(12)	(e)
Alcohol	53	31	84	70	78	55
Cigarettes	47	22	68	47	67	39
Number of persons	1,272	1,272	1,500	1,500	1,822	1,822

SOURCE: Parry (1979: 382).
a. Less than 0.5 percent.
b. Includes methadone.
c. Nonmedical use. Estimates based on split sample: N = 623, 750, and 897, respectively.
d. "Stronger" drugs defined as: hallucinogens, cocaine, heroin, and other opiates.
e. Not available.

the difference in prevalence across age groups. However, these differences are further widened by the fact that persons between 15 and 34 years old are also more likely to take advantage of opportunities to use drugs [Miller et al., 1978: 5].

Commenting on demographic factors, the *Highlights* authors summarize the findings as follows:

> Among young persons (youth and young adults) drug use does not, at the present time, appear to be strongly influenced by demographic factors, such as area of residence, race, or even socioeconomic status. To the extent that such differences exist today, those more likely to use or experiment with drugs are white, middle- to upper-middle-class young persons and/or young adults who live in metropolitan areas (regardless of whether the particular neighborhood may be classified as urban or suburban or even rural) and in the West and Northeast regions of the country [Miller et al., 1978: 8-9].

The analysis of new use (in the past year) revealed that it tends to occur at ages 15 to 17 and is virtually absent after age 21. Also, young adults were often found to discontinue drug use as they married and had children; college students tended to quit when they left school and assumed a white-collar job (Miller et al., 1978).

The picture of family factors and drug use from the National Survey was provocative. Teens were found to use both alcohol and illegal drugs if their mothers had used cigarettes, alcohol, and/or one of the prescription drugs (medically). Also, teenage drug use was more common when an older brother or sister had used drugs.

A word should be said about household surveys as a method of measuring illicit drug use. To some, a method whereby individuals are questioned about their illegal behavior in a door-to-door survey is less than desirable. However, after years of repetition of the method, and with some experience in checking validity (Abelson and Atkinson, 1975), many researchers have come to rely on it. Underreporting of heroin use is taken for granted, as is the underrepresentation of persons with no fixed addresses. But the data so obtained agree closely with survey data collected with other methods not dependent on random selection of households. And the characteristics of users found in household surveys conform closely to observations of users in other kinds of studies.

One of the benefits of the series of surveys conducted by NIDA (and before, by the National Commission) is that figures can be attached to a standard set of categories for comparison over time. However, there is a disadvantage inherent in this design too, in that newly appearing or unanticipated fad drugs are not measured over the same span of years. Phencyclidine hydrochloride (PCP) is an example of this disadvantage. In the late sixties it was believed that its use had died out, so it was not included in the 1972, 1974, and 1975 national surveys. After its resurgence in the seventies, PCP was included in the 1976 and 1977 surveys, and since pharmacologically it is neither a sedative nor a hallucinogen, it was placed in a category of its own. On the other hand, rates for other fads such as methaqualene ("sopers") or amylnitrite ("rush" or "locker room"), which have appeared in the mid-to-late seventies, remain buried in the large categories of sedatives and inhalants.

HIGH SCHOOL SENIORS

Before turning to more complex patterns of use, it would be useful to look at youthful rates from another nationwide survey, one focusing on high school seniors (Johnston et al., 1978a). These provide a somewhat different lens for viewing youthful drug use. The respondents are the more fortunate or achieving adolescents who have made it to the 12th grade without dropping out. Often seniors serve as models for younger high school students. And the senior class contains a certain proportion who are college bound. This group is midway between the teenagers and young adults of the National Survey in age, and a group with characteristics of special interest. It should be remembered, though, that their drug use is probably not as extensive as that of their dropout schoolmates.

Lifetime and current (30-day) prevalence rates for high school seniors (Table 1.2) appear for the most part to lie between the rates for teenagers and young adults in the National Survey (Table 1.1). The seniors are more like young adults than teenagers in their use of stimulants, sedatives, and tranquilizers, but surprisingly their lifetime experience with alcohol and cigarettes is higher even than that of young adults in the national sample of households (Johnston et al., 1978a).

The figures for prevalence of daily or near-daily use are especially interesting since they come close to being "abuse." Cigarettes are used daily by more of the respondents than any other drug class, which is

TABLE 1.2   Lifetime Prevalence, 30-Day Prevalence, and 30-Day
Prevalence of Daily Use of Eleven Types of Drugs,
High School Seniors, Class of 1977

	Lifetime Prevalence[a]	30-Day Prevalence[b]	30-Day Prevalence of Daily Use[c]
	(N = 17,116)	(N = 17,087)	(N = 17,087)
Marihuana	56.4	35.4	9.1
Inhalants	11.1	1.3	0.0
Hallucinogens	13.9	4.1	0.1
Cocaine	10.8	2.9	0.1
Heroin	1.8	0.3	0.0
Other opiates[d]	10.3	2.8	0.2
Stimulants[d]	23.0	8.8	0.5
Sedatives[d]	17.4	5.1	0.2
Tranquilizers[d]	18.0	4.6	0.3
Alcohol	92.5	71.2	6.1
Cigarettes	75.7	38.4	28.8

SOURCE: Johnston et al. (1978a: 14, 18-19).
a. Percentage who ever used.
b. Percentage who used in last 30 days.
c. Percentage who used daily in last 30 days.
d. Only drug use which was not under a doctor's order is included here.

probably to be expected. Among the other substances, the authors
emphasize these results concerning daily use:

> A particularly important finding is that marihuana is now used
> daily by a substantial fraction of the age group . . . even more
> than the proportions using *alcohol* daily. . . . Less than 1% of the
> respondents report daily use of any of the illicit drugs other than
> marihuana. Still, .5% report unsupervised daily use of *ampheta-
> mines,* and the comparable figure for *tranquilizers* is .3%, for
> *sedatives* .3%, and for *opiates other than heroin* .2%. While very
> low, these figures are not inconsequential considering that this is
> a nationally representative sample [Johnston et al., 1978a: 3].

Looking at special subgroups among the seniors, the authors summarize their prevalence rates as follows:

> In general, higher proportions of males than females are involved
> in drug use, especially heavy drug use. . . . Despite the fact that
> most illicit drugs are used by more males than females, about

equal proportions of both sexes report at least some illicit use of drugs other than marihuana during the last year.

Overall, seniors who are expecting to complete four years of college . . . have lower rates of illicit drug use than those who are not. . . . Frequent use of all the illicit drugs is even more disproportionately concentrated among students not planning four years of college.

In general, there are not very great regional differences in 1977 in rates of illicit drug use among high school seniors. The highest rate is in the Northeast . . . followed by the North Central . . . the West . . . and the South.

Overall illicit drug use is highest in the largest metropolitan areas . . . slightly lower in the other metropolitan areas . . . and lowest in the nonmetropolitan areas [Johnston et al., 1978: 12, 14-16].

Notice that in the analyses summarized above, Johnston and his associates created a drug use index consisting of three categories: (1) no illicit use; (2) marihuana but no other illicit drug; and (3) any illicit drug other than marihuana. Lifetime prevalence of marihuana alone (category 2) in the class of 1977 was 25.8 percent; and for any illicit drug other than marihuana, 35.8 percent. Thus, a little over 60 percent of the seniors used at least one illicit drug in their lifetime (Johnston et al., 1978a: 22). This kind of integrating measure seems to have more utility for understanding the scope of drug use than separate analyses by drug classes.

DRUG USE SCALES AND SEQUENCES

Several researchers have looked at drug-use patterns and undertaken scaling or indexing as a means of compressing an individual's drug-use behavior into a single measure. Using the data from a nationwide sample of 2500 young men interviewed in 1974 and 1975, O'Donnell and his associates found that use of drugs in any of the nine drug classes analyzed was associated with use in all the others. They found that 78 percent of the respondents were included in ten pure scale types in a progression from no use to any use in all nine classes (O'Donnell et al., 1976: 98-99). They also found, as have others, that heroin represented the heaviest involvement; that is, persons who had ever used heroin were likely to have used all or most of the other drugs.

Data from the 1947-1975 study of young men also were used to construct a Total Drug Use Index (TDU) which could be used to compare different drug-involved groups on a variety of characteristics. Although these analyses could not prove that drug use "caused" those characteristics, or that the characteristics were responsible for the drugs used, the TDU scores produced more succinct findings than examining each type of drug use separately (O'Donnell et al., 1976: 105-117).

Those with high drug-use scores (TDUs) were much more likely to have had unpleasant consequences of use than those with lower scores— conditions such as bad trips, fights, memory lapses, and dependence on a drug. Those with high scores also more often reported problems with health, work, relatives, or friends. High scorers reported criminal activities of all kinds more often and, finally, high scorers were more likely to have been involved in counter-cultural activities and unconventional behaviors than low scorers. In connection with the latter correlations, it should be mentioned that many of these men were in late adolescence or older when the tumultuous events of the sixties were taking place. It is possible that such behaviors and attitudes are not as strongly correlated with young men's drug use today (O'Donnell et al., 1976: 105-117).

Although limited to males and to one slice of history, the O'Donnell study is a treasure house of basic facts about drug use not previously available for a youth sample. An analysis of methods by which the nine classes of drugs were obtained, for example, showed that gifts from friends and purchases (from friend or dealer) were the primary methods, but a small group obtained sedatives and opiates other than heroin from their own prescriptions. Forged prescriptions were rare and the only drugs reported as stolen were sedatives and heroin, and only by a small proportion (O'Donnell et al., 1976: 62-63).

Reported routes of administration were also tabulated by drug class in the O'Donnell study. A few surprising findings were the relatively high proportion (over 25 percent) who used marihuana orally, who sniffed psychedelics and heroin, who smoked opiates other than heroin (presumably opium), and who mainlined cocaine. These patterns were reported for those users who took the drug more than just experimentally (O'Donnell, 1976: 63).

One other type of analysis is the temporal ordering of first use and/or continuation of use of the various substances over time. This has been of interest for many years, but the framework of thinking has changed between the fifties and now. At that time, a number of examinations were made of the order of use of marihuana and heroin in an attempt to test the hypothesis that marihuana use was a stepping stone to harder substances and addiction. The assumption (sometimes unstated) was that marihuana possessed a pharmacological quality that made the user crave stronger drugs. The hypothesis was strengthened by the observation that most heroin users had earlier used marihuana. An article by Ball and associates (1968) went a step further and made two important observations: (1) not all heroin users had used marihuana; and (2) the social situation in which both drugs were used and available could explain the progression just as easily. But the debate went on for a number of years without the benefit of data that could settle the issue—a representative group of nonusers and users of all types of substances, preferably a group whose drug histories could be followed over time.

Today, data bases on representative samples are available and analyses have established the general "scalability" of substance use. It has been shown that substances usually occupy unique, predictable places on a scale of use from the most widely to least widely used. Heroin has been used by the fewest, generally, but heroin users are very likely to have used all the other more widely used substances. The reporting of "pure scale types" by O'Donnell and associates (1976: 99) for over three-fourths of the sample means that progression is common, but not inevitable.

Longitudinal studies looking at samples of the general population over time also have appeared in the seventies, making possible more and better prediction of sequences in substance use. Summarizing a number of such studies, Kandel reported that "*there are clear-cut developmental steps and sequences in drug behavior, so that use of one of the legal drugs almost always precedes use of illegal drugs*" (Kandel, 1978: 14). Four stages were identified by Kandel in two follow-ups of adolescents in New York state: beer or wine; cigarettes or hard liquor; marihuana and other illicit drugs. The order of use among the various illicit drugs was more difficult to determine than those basic stages; a sample of black adults differed from the representative adolescent sample followed previously (Kandel, 1978: 14). Single et al. (1974: 913) reported an interesting corollary of the theory: Regression from heavier to lighter involvement usually follows the same order as progression, but in reverse.

Despite the exoneration of marihuana as the initial stepping-stone to other drugs, most studies support the proposition that a portion of marihuana users do go on to other illicit drugs (Kandel, 1978: 14). They do not necessarily become habitual users, however. And one other generalization is pertinent to the discussion of sequences: The earlier the age of onset of marihuana use, the more likely one is to go on to other illicit drugs or heavy involvement with drugs. The converse is also true—later onset usually means less involvement and earlier cessation.

By now it is well accepted that sequences are typical, that they start with the legal drugs alcohol and tobacco, and those who use the rarely used drugs have probably used other more widely used drugs previously. The pharmacological assumption is not encountered now and the social or group explanation is accepted: Adolescents are exposed to the substances in the company of their peers and tend to adopt some or all types with increasing time. This theory may need further elaboration along such lines as (1) the possible modeling effect of slightly older peers and (2) the local availability of substances. The first point would account for the fact that the substances are adopted in a fairly predictable sequence over time; and the second for the exceptions that are described in some groups. Also, there remains the possibility that certain personality types are predisposed to drug use of any or all kinds, though the evidence is far from persuasive on this point.

Digression into the topic of personality and its relation to drug use cannot be indulged in a chapter on epidemiology, but a few words can be said. In considering the factors or forces that may explain initiation and movement from one substance to another, personality has been of interest to many. A recent book by Jessor and Jessor (1977) provides a middle-range theory of "transition-proneness" to explain the tendency for "problem" adolescents to traverse a range of disapproved behaviors, sexual experience, alcohol use, drug use, and other delinquency. Most of these are adult behaviors not approved for adolescents—they are associated with transition to adulthood. But marihuana involvement as one aspect of transition-proneness was more highly correlated with environmental factors than with personality. The environment of drug-using friends and a comfortable climate of use were more important for marihuana involvement than a particular personality type.

DRUG DEPENDENCE AS A CONSEQUENCE

Up to now, drug users have been described without regard to two important aspects of use: dependence (or addiction) and other consequences of use that cause it to be classed as "abuse" or a "problem." They have been described along quantity/frequency dimensions in much the same way that consumers of a product might be described.

The medical aspects of use—those of dependence, withdrawal, other sequelae, and even the psychological and social consequences of use— have not been studied sufficiently for epidemiological purposes. They are admittedly not easy to study, for several reasons. Drug users who have reached the stage of dependence (or addiction) are less likely to admit to the condition in routine interviews or questionnaire surveys. The concept of dependence is subject to controversy over its referents, and other sequelae are subject to disagreement over causal attribution. (The longer the period between the use and the hypothesized consequence the more disagreement over whether or not the drug use caused the effect.) Also, many are uncertain as to whether all consequences should automatically be considered adverse. These problems are indicative of a large area still in need of development.

The reporting of national incidence and prevalence of heroin addiction (or dependence) has had an uneven history. Disagreement over the assumptions, bases for projection, multipliers, and other means of estimation continue today, but there is consensus on a broadened framework for the debate. That is, heroin addiction (as well as dependence on any other drug) is now believed to be only part of the larger picture of heroin use. Those who are addicted are now considered a subgroup of all users, and addiction a stage in an individual's history of use, not necessarily an irreversible one. Robins's study (1974) of the returned Vietnam addict had much to do with broadening the view.

One attempt at estimation, admittedly an underestimate, is the National Survey's population projection of lifetime experience with heroin in 1977: 2.3 million (within a possible range from 1.69 million to 3.13 million). The estimate of current use (within the past month), because of the sample size, was too small to be confident of its reliability (George Washington University, 1978).

The estimation of heroin prevalence from a national sample has been attempted only in the last few years. The same reservations mentioned earlier from household surveys must be applied even more stringently than in the estimation of other drugs. Numerous efforts have been made to estimate national (and local) prevalence with other methods, but they too have been the objects of considerable criticism. Most depend on indicators or indirect measures, such as drug law arrests or treatment admissions. A publication devoted to heroin epidemiology has described most of the methods and also included the major points in the debates (Rittenhouse, 1977). Two further developments since the publication, described below, have not settled the issue, but may prove fruitful in the future. In this author's opinion, the most credible estimates will have to be grounded in both usage data and indicators.

The Heroin Problem Index (HPI) is a composite measure derived from figures representing five indicators (Person et al., 1977):

(1) admissions to federally funded treatment programs for heroin problems
(2) heroin-related emergency room cases
(3) heroin-related deaths
(4) retail price of heroin
(5) retail purity of heroin

The HPI was used to calculate prevalence figures for 1973 through 1975, projecting from independent prevalence rates of "anchor" cities to the other urban areas for which HPI scores were available. Those independent prevalence rates were not consistently measured from city to city or from year to year, however, and the heroin prevalence rates projected from them to the nation do not seem well-grounded enough to use as a valid series.

None of the above efforts has tried seriously to distinguish heroin-dependent users from others, or to distinguish any users defined as medically dependent from those who merely have used or are using the substance(s). With the difficulties encountered in measuring sheer prevalence of use, this task may seem beyond hope. But there is now in existence a diagnostic interview schedule designed to enable researchers to make psychiatric diagnoses. Among the diagnoses measured are drug dependence and alcoholism (National Institute of Mental Health, 1979). The interview schedule can be administered by lay interviewers (i.e., nonphysicians) as well as physicians and is scorable by computer. With this new development, there is hope that the national prevalence of dependence on heroin (and other drugs) can be measured and placed side by side with estimates of the quantities and frequencies used. Only then can officials be confident about the size of the heroin "problem" and whether it is increasing or decreasing.

The indicator data from treatment programs, emergency rooms, and medical examiners are perhaps most useful for seeing the complications or consequences of drug use. Information on treatment admissions and discharges from federally funded programs is available from the Client-Oriented Data Aquisition Program (CODAP) of the National Institute on Drug Abuse, and other information from the Drug Abuse Warning Network (DAWN), a U.S. Drug Enforcement Administration data system also supported by NIDA.

Among treatment admissions in the latest published summary tabulations (National Institute on Drug Abuse, 1978), 55 percent were because of heroin problems, 10 percent because of marihuana, and the rest distributed in small proportions among other drug categories. (A small minority of 8 percent were admitted for alcohol problems.) Over three-fourths of the treatment admissions were 21 years of age or older, and over three-fourths were male. Most of the heroin abusers were over 21, but the majority of marihuana abusers were under 21. Females tended to be overrepresented among abusers of the prescription drugs. Heroin abusers included proportionally more black admissions than the 34 percent overall rate would indicate. The white admissions (52 percent of the total) were more often among those admitted for a problem with the other substances. Hispanics made up about 13 percent of the total admissions and Asian, American Indian, and Alaskan natives under 1 percent each.

Although the treatment admissions group was primarily an over 21 group, most (72 percent) had started using drugs before age 21. Over a quarter had started using drugs under 16 years of age. At the time of admission, more than 70 percent were unemployed.

About 70 percent of treatment admissions were in outpatient status—almost all the marihuana, barbiturate, and amphetamine abusers. Abusers of opiates, including heroin, were about equally divided among drug-free treatment, (drug) maintenance, or detoxification.

After admission, almost half (48 percent) left before completing treatment, but 22 percent did complete the program. The rest were transferred or referred (16 percent) or discharged for noncompliance (9 percent).

Another source of information on the hazards of nonmedical drug use is the Drug Abuse Warning Network (DAWN), which collects data from emergency rooms, crisis centers, and medical examiners (or county coroners) in 24 urban areas (Standard Metropolitan Statistical Areas or SMSAs) and selected other areas (Drug Enforcement Administration, 1978). "Drug abuse" defined for this purpose includes non-medical use of the substances and suicides or suicide attempts; cases of children under six years are omitted, however, on the assumption that they are accidental poisonings.

The relative frequency of involvement for the different drug classes varies considerably according to whether a case is seen in an emergency room, crisis center, or the medical examiner's office. Table 1.3 shows the proportions of drug "mentions" in each for the last year of published figures (Drug Enforcement Administration, 1978). Tranquilizers are implicated most frequently in emergency room visits, narcotic analgesics (primarily heroin or morphine) in crisis centers, and barbiturates in drug-involved deaths. Cannabis is the second most frequently encountered drug class in crisis centers, but is ninth and thirteenth (or last), respectively, in emergency rooms and medical examiners' offices. Hallucinogens also are higher on the list in crisis centers than in the other facilities.

In applying the figures from Table 1.3 to the drug abuse picture in the United States, several cautions should be mentioned. One is that the areas surveyed are not a strict random sample of the nation. Another is that number of mentions of drugs does not represent individual visits; and "episodes" or visits do not represent unique individuals. (An individual may have visited more than once during the period.) The motivations for use include suicide, not solely "drug abuse" as ordinarily defined. For example, 40 percent of emergency room visits and 5 percent of crisis center episodes were because of suicide attempts or gestures. Also, among drug-involved deaths, a percentage was merely drug-related, not "caused" by a drug; and of the drug-induced (or "caused") deaths, 48 percent were recorded as suicides (Drug Enforcement Administration, 1978).

With the above qualifiers in mind, some characteristics of the patients and decedents in the DAWN system can be described. Emergency room visitors tended slightly more often to be female than male, and there were proportionately more black patients than white. Their modal age range was 20-29 years. In crisis centers, the patients tended slightly more often to be male than female, and their modal age range was 10-19 years. Like emergency room patients, blacks were somewhat overrepresented. Among drug-involved death cases, males were slightly overrepresented compared with the general population; but compared with national death rates, the sex ratio was not very different. Again, blacks were somewhat more numerous compared with national popula-

TABLE 1.3 Percentage of Total Mentions for Emergency Rooms, Crisis Centers, and Medical Examiners by Therapeutic Class, DAWN VI, May 1977-April 1978

Therapeutic class	Emergency room drug mentions	Crisis center mentions	Medical examiners' mentions for drug-involved deaths
Tranquilizers (TC07-08)	23.9%	9.4%	12.6%
Barbiturate sedatives (TC46)	6.2	6.6	20.1
Nonbarbiturate sedatives (TC47)	8.4	5.7	6.5
Alcohol-in-combination	11.3	8.7	12.3
Narcotic analgesics (TC40)	8.3	23.7	18.6
Nonnarcotic analgesics (TC41)	10.0	2.7	12.2
Amphetamines (TC12A)	1.5	6.9	0.6
Cocaine (TC12B)	1.0	4.5	0.9
Psychostimulants (TC11)	3.2	1.7	7.8
Cannabis (TC35A)	2.7	15.2	0.2
Hallucinogens (TC39)	3.0	7.5	0.8
Inhalant/solvents/aerosols (TC29)	0.4	1.1	1.1
All other drugs	13.4	5.5	5.8
Drug unknown (TC35B)	6.8	0.9	0.3
Total drug mentions	100.0	100.0	100.0
Number of total drug mentions	178,410	41,551	6154
Number of total drug episodes	118,517	27,674	3358

SOURCE: Adapted from Tables 2.1, 3.1, and 4.1 (Drug Enforcement Administration, 1978).

tion and overall death figures. The modal age range was in the 20s, which of course is strikingly younger than the mode for overall deaths.

To summarize the patterns of complications or hazards of nonmedical use, the following can be cited:

(1) The rate of induction of dependence among all users is an elusive figure and must await further methodological development and research.

(2) About half of treatment admissions, as measured in federally supported programs, were for heroin problems and a small

minority for marihuana. Most of the admissions were over 21 years of age (except the marihuana clients), but most had started using drugs in their teens.

(3) Emergency rooms, crisis centers, and medical examiners (or coroners) deal with a relatively young segment of the population, peaking in the 20-29 year range. A large minority (30 percent) of crisis center visits are by those under 20 years of age. The primary drug creating the problem varies among the three types of facilities. Tranquilizers, heroin (or morphine), and barbiturates are the most frequently encountered in emergency rooms, crisis centers, and medical examiners' offices, respectively.

This completes the picture of youthful drug use today. With surveys measuring quantity/frequency dimensions of drug use, and indicator data providing evidence of some of the identifiable consequences, a picture of youthful drug use has emerged. It seems clear that marihuana now occupies a status close to that of alcohol and tobacco for transition-prone youth. It is a middle-class student phenomenon more often than one of a lower-class dropout. The other illicit (or illegally used) drugs are reported currently by fairly small proportions, but these are the ones who have the most problems; certainly the ratio of problem users (as indicated by CODAP and DAWN data), to those who have ever used is much higher for heroin and the prescription drugs than for marihuana or even cocaine. This is not to say that users of the latter do not suffer any adverse consequences, but they do not show up as often in the places where other drug users do.

The picture of youthful drug use above has changed some but not drastically since the "drug epidemic" appeared to peak in the late sixties. In the next section, some comparisons of today and the earlier phase are highlighted.

FROM THE "NOW GENERATION" TO NOW

It has been thirteen years since the "Summer of Love" (1967) and eighteen years since the White House Conference on Narcotic and Drug Abuse called by President Kennedy in 1962 (White House, 1962). Many such events of the sixties stamp that decade as the launching point for the current drug abuse era. As a demarcation of the decade, 1970 was the year that the Comprehensive Drug Abuse Prevention and Control Act (21 U.S.C. 801) was passed, consolidating most of the older laws and, from the standpoint of lawmakers, attempting to bring order to the situation. Enough years have passed since then to allow some perspective on recent history.

The epidemiology of drug use has changed its character drastically since 1962, but it is not so different from 1970. Two fairly subtle changes are discernible—(1) a stabilization of rates for most of the substances of concern (except marihuana); and (2) a homogenization of the population using many of them. But there are still elements of surprise and worry—eruptions of fads like methaqualone ("sopers") and PCP, making prediction of the future unsure.

Changes in drug use rates from the early to the late sixties were not documented by epidemiological surveys, but the newspaper headlines did the job. Almost every day the front page carried accounts of a drug bust, a freakout, or the confession of an acidhead. Since the behavior and especially the kinds of actors (white middle-class) were different than past stereotypes of drug use and users, the news was dramatic and much of it exaggerated.

The first nationwide survey apparently was one conducted by Gallup in 1967. College students were queried about their experience ("ever used") with these substances (Dickenson, 1967). Only 6 percent had ever used marihuana and 1 percent had used LSD. Then in 1971 the National Commission on Marihuana and Drug Abuse conducted a nationwide survey on marihuana use and attitudes and it was reported widely that 24 million Americans (14-15 percent) had used marihuana. In 1972 the Commission surveyed the general population again and published rates for twelve classes of substances. This is the survey that provided a base year for subsequent surveys conducted by the National Institute on Drug Abuse. (National Commission on Marihuana and Drug Abuse, 1972).

Through an ingenious analysis in the 1977 National Survey of retrospective reports by those queried about their earlier use, it was possible to reconstruct patterns of use for the period when drug use began to increase (Miller et al., 1978). The authors' summary of trends from the mid-sixties to 1977 was as follows:

> Noticeable changes in the prevalence of illegal drug use began in the mid-sixties with increased marihuana use among youth and young adults, particularly males and those living in metropolitan areas and outside the South. This trend continued in the late sixties accompanied by increases of a lesser magnitude in the use of stronger drugs. During recent years drug use has become more prevalent not only within those groups in which drug use

increases were initially seen, but also among groups who demonstrated relatively low use rates in the sixties. Detailed analyses of recent changes in marihuana use reveal that previously low-use groups are "catching up" to high-use groups. Differences in drug use rates across demographic subgroups are less significant today than in former years. This observation, coupled with the rate and the extent of change in drug use, particularly over the past ten years, raises the issue of whether or not drug use, at least marihuana use, may be in the process of becoming part of the general culture [Miller et al., 1978: 21].

Focusing on high school seniors and more recent trends from 1975 through 1977, these were highlights noted by Johnston and associates (1978b: 17, 22-23, 33):

The past two years have witnessed an appreciable use in marihuana use without any concomitant increase in the proportion using other illicit substances.

There has been a decline over the past two years in the prevalence of hallucinogen use among seniors.

Cocaine, on the other hand, has exhibited a modest but continuing increase in popularity.

The rate of cigarette smoking for females has increased from 16% to 19%, virtually eliminating the previous sex difference.

[There] has been some closing of the gap between the large cities and the less metropolitan areas in the proportions using any illicit drug.

There is no consistent, comparable series of figures to chart the course of heroin addiction. In 1967, immediately preceding the Federal Bureau of Narcotics' merger with the FDA's Bureau of Drug Abuse Control (to become the Bureau of Narcotics and Dangerous Drugs), active narcotic addicts nationwide were estimated at 62,045, based on the number (mainly arrests) reported to the Bureau (U.S. Treasury Department, 1968: 23).

In an attempt to go beyond arrests as a base, Richards and Carroll (1970) estimated the number of addicts in 1969 at more than 200,000, projecting from the number in the Narcotics Register of New York City. Several estimates, official and unofficial, have been published since 1970, but no consistent method has been used and there are numerous gaps during years when estimates were not attempted at all.

One source of information on trends in problem drug users, of course, is treatment admissions. Again, no single series with a standard form is available for more than a 5-year period, and all the data are subject to severe qualifications as epidemiological data because they are affected by funding ups and downs and guidelines for (or restrictions on) program operation. Nevertheless, the demographic characteristics of clients over time can give some hints about changes.

The federal treatment information system in force before 1973 was the Drug Abuse Reporting Program (DARP); after that, the CODAP system described earlier fulfilled the function. Sells (Director of DARP), in a meeting of the NIDA Task Force on the Epidemiology of Heroin and Other Narcotics in 1976, compiled sex, age, and ethnic characteristics of admissions to both systems from 1969 through 1975 (Sells, 1977: 151). The trends can be summarized as follows, complemented by the most recent annual figures in 1977:

(1) Sex differences: The proportion of females increased discernibly (but not dramatically) in the six-year span, from 20 percent in 1969 to a high of 31 percent in 1974. It dropped slightly and in 1977 was 28 percent of total admissions.

(2) Age distribution: In 1969, the majority of admissions were over 25 years old, determined in part by the fact that only opiate addicts were admitted to Federal treatment. Beginning in 1970, the balance shifted so the majority were under 25. In 1972, those under 18 began appearing in greater numbers (up to 21 percent). In 1977, however, the under-18 group was back to 10 percent of admissions.

(3) Ethnic groups: In 1969, black clients were 55 percent of the total, and whites 30 percent; by 1975 the percentages had virtually reversed—35 percent black and 52 percent white. (Hispanic clients ranged between 12 and 23 percent of the total over the six-year span.) In 1977, the proportions were virtually the same as in 1975 (Sells, 1977: 151; National Institute on Drug Abuse, 1978: 4-5).

As seen above, the homogenization appears to have occurred in a minor way among treatment admissions too. The differences between drug clients and the general population in 1969 were not quite so vivid by 1977. To some extent, these trends reflect the admission of a greater variety of drug users to treatment.

IN CONCLUSION

Many are of the opinion that drug use has become endemic, not epidemic as it was described in the sixties. Endemic drug use has been described by Bejerot (1968: 55-57) as the more or less traditional or tolerated social form of drug consumption. As such it cannot be expected to disappear completely from the society. The endemic form also implies that a visible proportion of "normal" individuals, not a deviant drug subculture, will continue to use drugs despite discouragement by parents, schools, government, and other formal social institutions. Judging by trends in the last five years, this seems to be a reasonable conclusion.

History shows that drug use waxes and wanes through different geographic areas as well as through time (Austin, 1978). It remains to be seen whether current endemic use will persist, decline, or perhaps become a base for further increases. These are some forces worth mentioning that may affect the future:

(1) The changing composition of the population, not only fewer young persons but a changed ratio of older to younger persons.
(2) The women's movement, with girls adopting more previously masculine behavior and women subject to more of the effects of the wider society (with perhaps less constraint on deviance).
(3) The possibility of more adverse economic conditions. Since the new drug era emerged only after the Depression and the austerity of World War II, the effects of possible future economic reverses cannot be predicted.
(4) The new emphasis on natural and healthful life-styles, more visible now on the West Coast than elsewhere, and the increase in negative attitudes toward tobacco smoking.

Since some of the above forces might dampen and some might enhance future drug use, it would be folly to make weighty predictions. One thing is sure, however. We need to know much more about how the use of these substances affects humans, both in the short run and over many years, and we need to know how to establish lasting values in the face of new knowledge.

REFERENCES

ABELSON, H., and R. ATKINSON (1975) Public Experience with Psychoactive Substances. Princeton, NJ: Response Analysis.

ABELSON, H., P. FISHBURNE, and I. CISIN (1977) National Survey on Drug Abuse: 1977. Vol. 1. Rockville, MD: National Institute on Drug Abuse.

Alcohol, Drug Abuse and Mental Health Administration (1978) Epidemiology, Health Systems Research and Statistics/Data Systems: Report of a ADAMHA Workgroup. Rockville, MD: Author.

AUSTIN, G. (1978) Perspectives on the History of Psychoactive Substance Use. Research Issues 24. Rockville, MD: National Institute on Drug Abuse.

BALL, J. C., C. D. CHAMBERS, and M. H. BALL (1968) "The association of marijuana smoking with opiate addiction in the United States." Journal of Criminal Law, Criminology and Police Science 59, 2: 171-182.

BEJEROT, N. (1968) "An epidemic of phenmetrazine dependence—epidemiological and clinical aspects," in C.W.N. Wilson (ed.) Adolescent Drug Dependence. Elmsford, NY: Pergamon.

Comprehensive Drug Abuse Prevention and Control Act of 1970 (1970) 21 U.S. Code 801.

DICKENSON, F. (1967) "Drugs on campus: a Gallup poll." Reader's Digest (November): 114.

Drug Enforcement Administration (1978) Drug Abuse Warning Network Phase VI Report. DEA Contract 77-11. Washington, DC: Author.

George Washington University Social Research Group (1978) Supplemental Tables. Population Projections Based on the National Survey on Drug Abuse 1977. Rockville, MD: National Institute on Drug Abuse.

JESSOR, R. and S. JESSOR (1977) Problem Behavior and Psychosocial Development. New York: Academic.

KANDEL, D. B. (1975) "Stages in adolescent involvement in drug use." Science 190: 912-914.

JOHNSTON, L. D., J. G. BACHMAN, and P. M. O'MALLEY (1978a) Drug Use Among American High School Students 1975-1977. Rockville, MD: National Institute on Drug Abuse.

——— (1978b) Highlights from Drug Use Among American Students 1975-1977. DHEW Publication (ADM) 79-621. Rockville, MD: National Institute on Drug Abuse.

MILLER, J., I. CISIN, and A. HARRELL (1978) Highlights from the National Survey on Drug Abuse: 1977. Rockville, MD: National Institute on Drug Abuse.

National Commission on Marihuana and Drug Abuse (1972) Marihuana: A Signal of Misunderstanding. Washington, DC: Government Printing Office.

National Institute of Mental Health (1979) The NIMH Diagnostic Instrument Schedule (DIS). Rockville, MD: Author.

National Institute on Drug Abuse (1978) Annual Summary Report 1977. DHEW Publication (ADM) 78-735. Rockville, MD: Author.

O'DONNELL, J. A., H. S. VOSS, R. R. CLAYTON, G. T. SLATIN, and R. G. ROOM (1976) Young Men and Drugs—a Nationwide Survey. NIDA Research Monograph 5. Rockville, MD: National Institute on Drug Abuse.

PARRY, H. J. (1979) "Sample surveys of drug abuse," pp. 381-394 in R. L. DuPont et al. (eds.) Handbook on Drug Abuse. Rockville, MD: National Institute on Drug Abuse and Office of Drug Abuse Policy.

PERSON, P., R. RETKA, and J. WOODWARD (1977) A Method for Estimating Heroin Use Prevalence. DHEW Publication (ADM) 77-439.

RICHARDS, L. G. (1977) "Role of society," pp. 505-514 in S. N. Pradhan and S. N. Dutta (eds.) Drug Abuse: Clinical and Basic Aspects. St. Louis: Mosby.

RICHARDS, L. and E. CARROLL (1970) "Illicit drug use in the United States." Public Health Reports 85, 12: 1035-1040.

RITTENHOUSE, J. D. [ed.] (1977) "Executive summary," pp. 1-6 in The Epidemiology of Heroin and Other Narcotics. NIDA Research Monograph 16. Rockville, MD: National Institute on Drug Abuse.

ROBINS, L. N. (1974) The Vietnam Drug User Returns. Contract HSM-42-72-75. Washington, DC: Government Printing Office.

ROUECHE, B. (1955) Eleven Blue Men. New York: Berkley.

SELLS, S. B. (1977) "Reflections on the epidemiology of heroin and narcotic addiction from the perspective of treatment data," pp. 147-176 in J. Rittenhouse (ed.) The epidemiology of heroin and other narcotics. NIDA Research Monograph 16. Rockville, MD: National Institute on Drug Abuse.

SINGLE, E., D. KANDEL, and R. FAUST (1974) "Patterns of Multiple Drug Use in High School." Journal of Health and Social Behavior 15, 4: 344-357.

U.S. Treasury Department (1968) Traffic in Opium and Other Dangerous Drugs. Washington, DC: Government Printing Office.

White House (1962) White House Conference on Narcotic and Drug Abuse, September 27-28, 1962. Washington, DC: Government Printing Office.

2

THE HARD DRUG SCENE

RICHARD C. STEPHENS

In this chapter we will explore the use of the so-called "hard drugs" among adolescents.[1] By hard drugs we mean the psychotropic substances other than alcohol and marihuana; hard drugs include the narcotics, inhalants, hallucinogens, cocaine, stimulants, sedatives, and tranquilizers. In reviewing the use of these substances among adolescents, I hope to accomplish several goals: (1) to describe both the current extent of hard drug use and the changes which have occurred over the past several years; (2) to provide some speculations regarding these changes; (3) to review the major theoretical explanations for adolescent drug use; and (4) to attempt to integrate these explanations into a more holistic, sociologically informed explanatory paradigm.

AUTHOR'S NOTE: The author wishes to thank Suzanne Underwood and Alice LeBlanc for bibliographic assistance and Cathy Williams for typing the manuscript.

EXTENT OF HARD DRUG USE

CURRENT PREVALENCE OF HARD DRUG USE

The extent of drug use among adolescent populations is usually ascertained through the use of surveys.[2] Such surveys are sometimes targeted directly at youth and at other times youths constitute only part of the survey sample. I have drawn data from both types of surveys which have been most recently conducted.[3] Two general population surveys have been used here. One study, conducted early in 1977 by Cisin and his associates (1977; Abelson et al., 1977), is a probability sample of 4595 respondents aged 12 or older. The other study, published by Lipton et al. (1978a), was based on a general probability sample of 11,410 New York state residents aged 14 and older who were interviewed during the winter of 1975-1976. Two recent surveys of high school students were also utilized. One is a study of 35,317 New York state high school students who were queried about their drug use in 1977 (Lipton et al., 1978b). The second is the most recent in a continuing series of studies of a national sample of high school students published by Johnston and his associates (1977a, 1977b). His sample included over 17,000 high school seniors. These four studies, taken as a whole, complement one another to provide a wealth of current and trend data on the use of psychotropic drugs among youth.

Tables 2.1, 2.2, 2.3, and 2.4 present data, in part, on the prevalence of drug use ("ever used") among selected groups. As extensive epidemiological data are presented elsewhere in this book, detailed examination of these figures is left to the reader. However, some general conclusions can be drawn. First, these data show that close to half of the adolescent population has used a drug. It is obvious that marihuana and hashish account for much of that use. However, it is also apparent that roughly one-fourth of all high school students have used some drug other than marihuana (see Table 2.4). Use figures for these other drugs range from a low of 1-3 percent for heroin to a high of 23 percent for stimulants. Examination of Table 2.4 shows that, with the exception of heroin, all other drug categories have been used by at least 10 percent of high school seniors. When all four studies are compared, the stimulants, inhalants, and tranquilizers appear as the most frequently used drug categories.

TABLE 2.1   Lifetime Prevalence ("Ever Used") of Drug Use by Age and Year in Which Study Was Conducted: National Sample

	Youth (12-17 years)				Young adults (18-25 years)			
	1972	1974	1976	1977	1972	1974	1976	1977
Marihuana/hashish	14.0	22.6	22.5	28.2	47.9	53.2	52.9	60.1
Inhalants	6.4	8.5	8.1	9.0	–	9.2	9.0	11.2
Hallucinogens	4.8	6.0	5.1	4.6	–	16.6	17.3	19.8
Cocaine	1.5	3.6	3.4	4.0	9.1	12.7	13.4	19.1
Heroin	.6	1.0	.5	1.1	4.6	4.5	3.9	3.6
Other opiates	–	6.1	6.5	6.1	–	11.8	14.7	13.5
Stimulants	4.0	5.0	4.4	5.2	12.0	17.0	16.6	21.2
Sedatives	3.0	5.0	2.8	3.1	10.0	15.0	11.9	18.4
Tranquilizers	3.0	3.0	3.3	3.8	7.0	10.0	9.1	13.4

SOURCE: Adapted from Abelson et al. (1977).

TABLE 2.2   Lifetime Prevalence ("Ever Used") of Drug Use by Age Group: New York State General Population

Drugs ever used	14-19	20-24
Marihuana/hashish	40%	50%
Inhalants/solvents	2	4
Psychedelics	6	12
Cocaine	4	10
Heroin	1	3
Analgesics	4	9
Cough medicine with codeine	4	5
Methadone	1	1
Other narcotics	2	5
Prescription diet pills	2	6
Other stimulants	4	9
Methaqualone	4	7
Other barbiturates/sedative hypnotics	4	8
Minor tranquilizers	5	9
Ever used at least one of above	41	56

SOURCE: Adapted from Lipton et al., 1978a.

TABLE 2.3   Lifetime Prevalence ("Ever Used") and Recent Use of
Drugs: New York High School Survey (Grades 7-12)

Drug	Ever used	Used 10+ times in past 30 days
Marihuana	54.2%	16.6%
Hashish	25.2	2.0
Inhalants	16.0	*
Hallucinogens	8.7	*
Cocaine	10.8	*
Heroin	2.6	*
Methadone (III)	2.5	*
Cough medicine with codeine	11.0	0.5
Other narcotics	11.3	*
Stimulants	15.1	0.9
'Depressants	10.7	*
Tranquilizers	12.7	0.5
PCP	15.5	0.6

SOURCE: Adapted from Lipton et al. (1978b).
*Less than 0.5 percent.

TABLE 2.4   Lifetime Prevalence ("Ever Used") of Drug
Use Among Classes of High School Seniors:
National High School Sample

Drug	Senior class of:		
	1975	1976	1977
Marihuana	47.3%	52.8%	56.4%
Inhalants	–	10.3	11.1
Hallucinogens	16.3	15.1	13.9
Cocaine	9.0	9.7	10.8
Heroin	2.2	1.8	1.8
Other opiates	9.0	9.6	10.3
Stimulants	22.3	22.6	23.0
Sedatives	18.2	17.7	17.4
Tranquilizers	17.0	16.8	18.0
Ever used any of the above	45	48	51
Ever used any of the above other than marihuana	26	25	26

SOURCE: Adapted from Johnston et al. (1977a).

It is also apparent that drug use is related to age. Persons in their early twenties have higher prevalence rates than do those of high school age. Again, as with the younger age groups, marihuana is by far the most used drug among young adults. Stimulants also play an important role in their drug-use pattern. However, cocaine and hallucinogens emerge as much more frequently used drugs than in the younger age cohorts.

In addition to the statistics provided on the percentage of persons who have ever used a substance, one can ask the question, "How extensive is such use?" Table 2.5 provides some answers to that question. It shows the percentage of high school seniors who have used a drug ten or more times in their lifetime, a frequency I will label "heavy use." The pattern of heavy use is not that dissimilar to that noted for the "ever used" figures. The most heavily used drug is marihuana. One other drug category—stimulants—is heavily used by close to one-tenth of the students. Other drug classes heavily used by almost 5 percent of the students are sedatives, tranquilizers, and hallucinogens.

When one compares these percentages to the "ever used" data presented in Table 2.4, it is apparent that, with the exception of marihuana, in all cases a minority of "ever users" have heavily used.

Table 2.3 provides some additional data on the extensiveness of use. The most cogent figure—here referred to as heavy recent use—is found

TABLE 2.5 Percentage of High School Seniors Who Report Using Drugs Ten or More Times in Their Lifetime by Year of Graduation: National High School Sample

| | Class of: | | |
Drug	1975	1976	1977
Marihuana	29.4%	34.4%	36.6%
Inhalants	–	1.4	1.5
Hallucinogens	6.0	4.7	4.5
Cocaine	1.7	1.6	2.2
Heroin	0.4	0.2	0.3
Other opiates	2.7	2.1	2.7
Stimulants	9.8	9.0	9.4
Sedatives	6.4	5.7	6.1
Tranquilizers	4.0	3.9	4.8

SOURCE: Adapted from Johnston et al. (1977a).

in the last column of Table 2.3. It indicates the percentages of high school students who have used ten or more times in the past 30 days. It shows that such heavy recent use is extremely low. Only marihuana (17 percent) and hashish (2 percent) are used with this much frequency by the students. Fewer than 1 percent of the students have recent heavy use of any of the other drugs.

Yet another indicator of the extensiveness of drug use is the degree to which youths use more than one or two types of drugs. This phenomenon, called multiple or polydrug use, is receiving an increasing amount of attention in the literature.[4] Lipton et al. (1978a) were able to construct a Guttman scale measuring the increasing seriousness of such use, and these data are presented in Table 2.6. The data indicate that around 14 percent of male and 17 percent of female adolescents are multiple drug users. Polydrug use is higher for both sexes in the young adult group.

All of the foregoing data indicate that hard drug use is relatively widespread throughout the adolescent population. It is even more prevalent in the young adult age groups. Although many persons have only used marihuana, about one-fourth of all adolescents have at least experimented with some hard drug other than marihuana. It is equally clear, however, that the vast majority of students (and drug users) are experimental or recreational users. Later in this chapter we will attempt to see how such experimental users may differ from their peers who are "into" a heavier drug-use scene. Having established the current hard

TABLE 2.6   Lifetime Multiple Drug Use by Sex and Age Group: New York State General Population

	Male		Female	
Drug(s) used	14-19	20-24	14-19	20-24
Nonusers	57%	35%	61%	52%
Marihuana/hashish only	28	31	21	23
Legal drugs	4	10	10	16
Nonopiate illegal drugs	7	15	5	7
Nonheroin opiates	3	5	1	2
Heroin	*	4	1	1

SOURCE: Adapted from Lipton et al. (1978a).
*Less than 0.5 percent.

drug use situation, we can now turn our attention to the changes this scene has undergone in the past several years.

CHANGES IN DRUG USE PATTERNS

Three of the studies (Abelson et al., 1977; Johnston et al., 1977a, 1977b; Lipton et al., 1978b) provide prevalence data for surveys which had been conducted in previous years. Such data afford an excellent opportunity to note changes in the adolescent drug scene. Abelson et al. (see Table 2.1) present prevalence data for studies conducted in 1972, 1974, 1976, and 1977, and Johnston et al. (see Table 2.4) present data for the senior classes of 1975, 1976, and 1977. While the Lipton et al. (1978b) data, which contains a 1971 comparison point, are not presented, they generally support the data presented in Table 2.1 and Table 2.4. Some general trends are observable. There is a very notable increase in the use of marihuana. Both Lipton et al. (1978b) and Abelson et al. (1977) report a twofold increase in marihuana use among adolescents since the early 1970s. Equally notable increases can be seen for cocaine use. More moderate, but definite, increases can be found for inhalants. Use of the following drugs has remained "relatively steady with slight increases observed"—stimulants, narcotics other than heroin, tranquilizers, and sedatives. It would appear that the use of both heroin and hallucinogens is "relatively steady to slightly on the decline." Table 2.1 also shows that drug use within all categories of drugs, except heroin, is on the increase for young adults, with marihuana showing the most prominent increase.

In addition to changes in the kinds of drugs used, a number of other trends were observed in the adolescent drug scene. Cisin et al. (1977: 21) found that

> noticeable changes in the prevalence of illegal drug use began in the mid-sixties with increased marihuana use among youth and young adults, particularly males and those living in metropolitan areas and outside the South. This trend continued in the late sixties accompanied by increases of a lesser magnitude in the use of stronger drugs. During recent years drug use has become more prevalent not only within those groups in which drug use increases were initially seen, but also among groups who demonstrated relatively low use rates in the sixties. . . . Differences in drug use rates across demographic subgroups are less significant today than in former years.

Some of the demographic changes referred to by Cisin include ethnicity, sex, and place of residence. Regarding ethnicity, the New York population survey found that

> whites 24 and under are more likely to have used drugs than blacks in the same age group. *This represents a significant reversal in drug use patterns within a generation* [Emphasis mine; Lipton et al., 1978a: 34].

To underscore this fact, data for drug use by ethnicity and age is presented in Table 2.7. These data show that, except for slight differences in the use of heroin, diverted methadone, and marihuana, whites have higher prevalence rates than blacks. Such differences certainly call into question many of the conventional stereotypes concerning drug use and ethnicity.

The differences between the sexes also seem to be diminishing. Johnston et al. (1977b: 13-14) note:

TABLE 2.7   Lifetime Prevalence ("Ever Used") of Drug Use by Age and Ethnicity: New York State General Population

	White		Black	
Illegal	*14-19*	*20-24*	*14-19*	*20-24*
Cocaine	5%	10%	3%	10%
Heroin	1	2	2	3
Psychedelics	7	13	2	2
Inhalants/solvents	2	4	*	1
Marihuana/hashish	38	51	37	49
Legal				
Analgesics	5	10	1	5
Quaaludes	4	8	1	1
Barbiturates/sedatives	5	10	1	2
Minor tranquilizers	6	9	3	4
Diet pills	2	6	1	1
Other stimulants	4	10	1	1
Cough medicine with codeine	4	6	1	2
Methadone	1	1	*	4
Other narcotics	2	5	1	1
Ever used at least one of the above drugs	41	57	39	50

SOURCE: Adapted from Lipton et al. (1978a).
*Less than 0.5 percent.

If one thinks of going beyond marihuana as an important threshold point in the sequence of illicit drug use, then equal proportions of both sexes (26 percent for males vs. 25 percent for females) were willing to cross that threshold at least once during the year. The difference lies in the number of different illicit drugs taken by the male vs. female users, and the frequency with which they use them.

Yet another traditional difference in drug use rates has been found between large metropolitan and other less urbanized areas. However, even these differences are beginning to disappear. As Johnston et al., 1977b: 33 note:

> The net effect over the last two years has been some closing of the gap between the large cities and the less metropolitan areas in the proportions using any illicit drug. While the three levels of population density have not yet reached parity, they are much closer to it.

Finally, drug use among adolescents in various parts of the United States is beginning to reach a national parity. Johnston et al. (1977b) present data which shows that prevalence rates over the last three years have increased most rapidly in the South and North Central regions of the country where use was lower than in the West and Northeast. Use of the hard drugs is now separated by no more than five percentage points between the South and the Northeast, the regions with the lowest and highest prevalence rates, respectively.

SOME SPECULATIONS ABOUT THESE CHANGES

In essence, what appears to be happening is that drugs, to borrow a Nixonian phrase, are "bringing the country together." We are seeing an increase in the use of certain categories of drugs and a demographic broadening in the use of all categories throughout the country and in many segments of its population. As Cisin et al. (1977: 16) comment:

> Overall, recent trends among youth and young adults indicate that those subgroups who did not experiment with marihuana in the earlier years are now increasingly apt to try an illicit drug; previously low-use groups have tended to "catch up" with high-use groups, diminishing the significance of the differences in use rates by region, sex and population density.

What is to explain this spread of drug use? While such a question cannot be answered simply, I believe that at least some parts of the answer are to be found in the weakening of negative sanctions attached to marihuana use, changes in attitudes toward use of other drugs, the widespread availability of drugs, and, to a certain extent, the fad phenomenon associated with certain substances.

I would guess that marihuana has played an important role in leading the way for the use of other drugs. By saying this I do not mean to involve myself in the argument that marihuana *will lead* to the use of other drugs (especially the dreaded heroin!). Rather, I would argue that within the last decade we have seen the status of marihuana change from a greatly feared and heavily legally sanctioned drug to that of a substance which is now used by almost one-fifth of all those over 26 years of age and by almost half of those between the ages of 26 and 34 (Cisin et al., 1977). That such a trend is reflected in the adolescent population as well is attested to by the data on marihuana which has been presented. It would seem reasonable to me that many marihuana users, cognizant of the dramatic changes in the social definitions of marihuana use, may now be willing to consider the use of other drugs. Drugs, such as the stimulants and cocaine, may now occupy the same place marihuana did less than ten years ago. I believe that marihuana as the drug which "leads" the way for the other drugs is especially important because it is so widely used among those segments of the society (particularly the young) which constitute potential user pools for other drugs. Changes in attitudes toward marihuana may be a harbinger of changes in attitudes toward other drugs as well.

That there are already changes in attitudes toward drug use, at least among adolescents, is supported by some data contained in the studies we have cited. Johnston et al. (1977b) show that the proportion of students who attach great risk to the occasional use of psychoactive substances is steadily declining. Only 9.5 percent of the senior class of 1977 feels that use of marihuana once or twice is harmful—a decline of almost 6 percent since 1975. Roughly only one-third of the students feel that the use of any of the other drug classes—with the exception of heroin—is harmful. Yet even for these substances there has been a decline of 3-7 percent since 1975 of students seeing such use as of "great risk." Thus, it would seem that almost two-thirds of the adolescent population is not afraid of the potential ill effects of drugs.

But would they take these drugs? Johnston et al. (1977a) present data which shows that, while the vast majority of students report they do not plan to use any drugs (except for the 27 percent who probably will use marihuana in the future), many nevertheless will use drugs. The percentages range from 1.1 for heroin to 6.6 for stimulants. And for almost all drug classes there has been a slight increase since 1975 in the probability that the students would use drugs.

If the students did decide to use drugs, could they obtain them? According to Johnston et al. (1977a), almost nine out of ten students felt they could obtain marihuana. Over half felt they could get tranquilizers, amphetamines, or barbiturates. Close to a third reported that hallucinogens, cocaine, and opiates were available to them. And 18 percent of the students felt that they could obtain heroin. (That is, ten times the number of students who have ever used heroin felt that it was available to them.)[5]

The final element in our exploration for answers is the faddish nature of drugs. Some drugs spread quickly throughout the society. Two such drugs are PCP ("Angel Dust") and cocaine. The use of Angel Dust has risen in recent years from 3 percent to 6 percent, and among young adults from 10 percent to almost 14 percent. Another drug which has enjoyed a spurt in popularity is cocaine. Why the use of such drugs, especially one which has such pronounced effects as PCP, should expand so rapidly is little understood and provides fertile ground for future research.[6]

It is interesting to note that the government can have a profound effect on the kinds of drugs which are used on the streets. Gay (1971) describes the impact which the antimarihuana campaign labeled "Operation Intercept" had on the drug-use patterns in the San Francisco Bay Area. He says, "The drive against the counter-culture's drug of choice [marihuana] coincided with increased abuse of alcohol, barbiturates, amphetamines or heroin" (Gay, 1971: 54).

In summary, some of the elements of an answer to the question, "Why the spread in drug use?" have been presented. I believe these data support the explanation that there has been a decrease in concern about the effects of experimental drug use and an increase in the willingness to use them. There is also widespread availability of drugs, some of which become fad drugs.

EXPLANATIONS FOR ADOLESCENT DRUG USE

Whatever the drug-use trends, the question still remains, "Why do adolescents use drugs?" A number of explanations have been offered.

These explanations are based primarily on the adolescent's milieu—his or her family, school, peer groups—and the kinds of situations engendered in interactions within this milieu. We shall now take a brief look at these theories.

THE ROLE OF THE FAMILY

The family plays an important role in drug-use theories in two different ways. In one theoretical tradition, the family is viewed as a potential source of stress for the adolescent who may turn to drugs to cope with this stress. (Conversely, a nurturing and loving family may act as a deterrent to a youth's use of hard drugs.) In another theoretical tradition, the family may act as a model for the youth to emulate. "If the parents use drugs, so might the children" goes the reasoning of this theoretical school.

There is empirical support for both viewpoints. A number of researchers have explored the relationship between the adolescent and the family and have found that youths who are alienated or estranged from their families appear to use more drugs more often. Graham (1975: 104) found, "One of the most important differences between drug users and nonusers was the degree of separation from their parents they felt. Drug users felt rejected at home, that their parents did not trust them or genuinely care about them and that there was little to talk about in common with their parents." A number of other researchers (Streit and Oliver, 1972; Pendergast, 1974; Green, 1978; Streit et al., 1974; Spevack and Pihl, 1976; Graeven, 1977) document the correlation of drug use with hostility toward and estrangement from the family.

Coupled with this estrangement from the family, researchers have also found that drug users' families exercise little or no control over the children's activities. Pendergast (1974), for instance, found that the adolescent marihuana user sees the mother as exercising little control and of not strongly disapproving of his or her marihuana use. Streit et al. (1974) report similar findings.

It has also been found that families which are not intact seem to produce drug users. Researchers have related broken homes to polydrug use (Wechsler and Thum, 1973), heroin use (Craig and Brown, 1975), and hard drugs (Rollins and Holden, 1972).

Summarizing the relationship between drug use and adolescence, Graeven and Schaef (1978: 754) state:

Based on previous findings on family life and drug use, it is possible to create a family typology which consists of those factors considered necessary to provide an optimum environment for childhood growth and development. This type of family would not be broken by divorce, separation, or death, and would contain a high degree of emotional cohesion, a high degree of supportive interaction, positive adolescent evaluation of the parent, high behavioral integration and low amounts of conflict and external control. . . . Families lacking in these areas would be more likely to produce an adolescent who becomes involved in heroin use.

Another way in which the family helps to shape the adolescent's drug use is through providing role models for drug use. Presumably, if adolescents see their parents or siblings using psychotropic substances or at least *think* their parents use such drugs (see Kandel, 1974), these adolescents are more likely to use drugs. A number of empirical studies have been done which support this relationship (Tennant, 1976; Anhalt and Klein, 1976; Lawrence and Vellerman, 1970; Smart and Fejer, 1972; and Cisin et al., 1977). Smart and Fejer found that if the parents used psychotropics medically, their children were also more likely to use psychotropics. "For example, 67 percent of female students who had used tranquilizers reported that one or both their parents also used tranquilizers" (Smart and Fejer, 1972: 159). In addition to finding a relationship between mothers' and children's drug use, Cisin et al. (1977: 11) found that siblings may play an important modeling role.

An analysis of sibling pairs indicated that among teens with young-adult siblings still living in the parental home, teenage drug use was considerably more likely where the older brother or sister had used drugs. Furthermore, youth with older siblings are more prone to illicit drug use than those who are the eldest or only child, a finding which suggests the possibility that children may be introduced to drug use by older brothers or sisters, whether by chance or intention.

In summary, then, we find that the family assumes an important role in helping to create an atmosphere in which drug use may or may not occur. Family interaction may generate stress or anxiety which the adolescent ameliorates through the use of drugs. Whether the adolescent turns to drugs as a coping mechanism may also be due to whether the parents or siblings use drugs to deal with their own anxiety.

DRUG USE AS REACTION TO STRESS

The family may be only one source of anxiety to youths undergoing the rigors of adolescence. Equally potent stress producers include the demands of school, the process of moving from the status of child to that of adult, the anxiety of awakening sexuality, and other profound changes encountered in adolescence. A number of researchers have noted that drug users seem ill equipped to cope with life's problems (De Angelis, 1975; Duncan, 1977; Rollins and Holden, 1972; Anhalt and Klein, 1976; Pittel and Hofer, 1972). As Burke (1971: 61) has noted:

> I am suggesting that the feeling of complete helplessness or inability to confront the problems of life on a realistic basis may well be the characteristic which most distinguishes our patients and the population they represent from those who do not feel the need for using drugs at all, or who use them in a noncompulsive way.

These problems seem to lead to an increasing alienation from others and an involvement with self. A few quotes illustrate this orientation:

> The characteristic bi-modal pattern seen in both the male and female profiles suggest a personality organization based on inadequate impulse control, the relative absence of internalized values, and essentially narcissistic orientation towards others [Kendall and Pittel, 1971: 65].

> Low academic performance and conduct in school, lack of participation in non-school sponsored organizations, plans other than college or more than one plan after high school and the use of cigarettes are all associated with increased use of drugs [Jasso and Wolkon, 1978: p. 324].

In summary, what many researchers seem to suggest is that certain individuals have difficulty in coping with life's problems, become increasingly alienated, and turn to drug use to help them cope with these problems.

THE ROLE OF PEERS

The "wrong friends" or drug user peer group hypothesis is probably one of the oldest explanations of drug use. It is a truism that most recreational drug use occurs in a group context. Of course, as with all of the theories presented here, there is always the problem of the direction of causality. Did the adolescent become a user because he or she associated with a drug-using group, or did he or she seek out a drug-using group because he or she wanted to become a user? Certainly, there is evidence that neophyte heroin users often sought out heroin addicts because they wanted to become part of the heroin subculture (Stephens and McBride, 1976; Hendler and Stephens, 1977). But it is also true that users begin to interact in milieus which may encourage use.

> Experimental marihuana users may become increasingly involved in social relationships with drug using peers, including some who are using other drugs and increasingly open to the possibility of trying a variety of illicit psychoactives [Wechsler and Thum, 1973: 99].

As we have said, a number of researchers have found that users interact with other users (Green, 1978; McKillip et al., 1973; Graeven, 1977; Newmeyer, 1975; Wechsler and Thum, 1973). In fact, Spevack and Pihl's findings (1976) suggest that drug users have a stronger identification with teenagers than nonusers. They seek out as friends people who feel and behave the way they do and many choose friends who have an antiadult orientation because they themselves are estranged from their families. If this is true, it supports the contention that the user may use drugs not only for whatever pharmacologic effects they may have (in reducing tension, producing an enjoyable high, and so on), but also as a means of signaling membership in a meaningful primary group.

WHY ADOLESCENTS DO NOT USE DRUGS

Throughout this chapter, we have focused on the adolescent who uses drugs. But as we can see by the statistics presented earlier, there are many adolescents who do not use drugs (and the great majority do not use any drug other than marihuana). A few studies have been conducted which look at this nonuser. These studies show that non-drug users are more likely to come from well-integrated families (Graeven and Schaef, 1978), be more involved in religion (McLuckie et al., 1975), and to express dislike for the physiological and psychological dependence which drugs may produce (Stokes, 1974). In addition, some studies indicate that non-drug users are more likely to plan to go to college (Johnston et al., 1977b; Jasso and Wolkon, 1978; Rollins and

Holden, 1972) or to remain in high school more often than their drug-using peers. As Cisin et al. (1977: 32) note:

> The most important factor determining whether or not a teenager uses drugs seems to be whether he/she is currently in school. Our survey found that young people 14 to 19 who are in school are much less likely to use drugs than those not in school. Furthermore, teenagers in school who use drugs are much less likely to be multiple drug users.

A SUGGESTED PARADIGM FOR DRUG USE

We have covered a lot of territory in this chapter and the reader may be anxious for some closure. I will attempt to provide just such a summary. In order to accomplish this goal, I would first like to list some of the major conclusions from the chapter:

(1) Marihuana use is relatively widespread.
(2) Use of drugs other than marihuana is limited to about 25 percent of the adolescent population.
(3) Heavy or regular use is found in a minority of hard drug users.
(4) Adolescent users, and particularly those who are either polydrug or heavy users, are more alienated from their families, church, school, nondrug-oriented adolescent activities, and other institutions and activities in the community, and they less often have plans to attend college.
(5) Drug users most often have peers who support such use.
(6) Drug users are often likely to have parents or siblings who also use drugs, alcohol, or cigarettes.

In reviewing these conclusions, I believe I see at least two underlying dimensions which help us to put these facts together and explain the extent of drug use in an adolescent population. Before discussing what these dimensions are, however, I would like to say a word or two about the dependent variable in this paradigm—namely, the extent of drug use. As I see it, drug use can vary along a continuum from "no use" of any kind of drug to heavy use of a variety of substances. Extent of use can thus be conceptualized along two dimensions: type of substance and frequency of use.

Types of Drugs	Frequency of Use	
	Seldom or never	Frequent
Marihuana only	a	b
Drugs other than marihuana	c	d

All adolescents can fall into one of the cells. Obviously, the persons who fall into "d" are much more likely to become dysfunctional users, while those in "a" present little or no difficulties either to themselves or society. In fact, as we have demonstrated, marihuana use may soon become just a part of growing up in America in much the same way that alcohol was used in previous generations. "B" and "c" mark intermediate points in the extent measure.[7] I will now try to put the empirical findings together in an attempt to explain extent of drug use as I have defined it here.

As I mentioned earlier, there appear to be two dimensions underlying the facts of adolescent drug use. These are presented in Table 2.8. The first of these is the adolescent's degree of integration into the society, that is how much he or she feels a part of and interacts in the institutions of the society relevant to him or her. Such institutions for the adolescent include the family, school, church, and various adolescent peer groups. Such integration can be measured by both the number of contacts the youth has with such institutions and the degree of satisfaction he or she received from such contacts. Thus, if the youth does not participate in family activities or receives little gratification from these contacts, he or she would be classified as "low" on that

TABLE 2.8   Paradigm for Predicting Extent of Drug Use

		Youths' perceptions of primary groups' attitudes toward drug use	
		Favorable	Unfavorable
Extent of Integration into Society	Low	Highest Drug Use 1	Intermediate Drug Use 2
	High	Intermediate Drug Use 3	Lowest Drug Use 4

dimension. The second dimension is the youth's perceptions of his or her primary group's attitudes toward drug use. Such primary group attitudes can range from unfavorable to favorable. If, for instance, the youth has many close friends who use drugs, he or she might reasonably perceive that their attitudes toward drug use are favorable. This paradigm then would predict that as one moves from high integration to low integration and from unfavorable to favorable primary group attitudes toward drugs, the extent of drug use will increase. Thus, the greatest extent of drug use is found for those individuals in cell "1" and the lowest for those in cell "4." The other two cells are intermediate, with those in cell "2" probably having a greater extent of drug use than those in cell "3."

Let us take a few of the facts we have learned about different types of adolescents and see if they fit into the paradigm. One type garnered from the literature are alienated teenagers who interact mostly with other drug users. I would say they clearly fit into cell "1." If their parents use drugs, this is even more reason for them to feel that their primary groups (family and friends) favor drug use. Conversely, let us take the case of the ideal all-American kid next door who comes from an intact, nurturing family (which does not even use alcohol) and who is involved in a host of extracurricular activities including a church group. This individual could easily be placed in cell "4." A related type is the fraternity member whose fraternity uses marihuana at parties. Such individuals might be placed in cell "3." The major point is that by knowing the individual's degree of integration into the society and the orientation of his or her primary groups toward drug use one can predict extent of drug use.

While the paradigm is not perfect, and while operationalization of the variables remains difficult, the paradigm nevertheless does seem to place drug use in a social context and predictions based on it do seem to be consistent with what is known about adolescent drug use.

SUMMARY

In this chapter, we have demonstrated that hard drug use can be found in a significant minority of youth and that the trend data suggest that use of both marihuana and at least some hard drugs will continue to spread. It is also true that most hard drug users are the occasional or recreational type and probably do not present great cause for alarm.

Other individuals, however, are involved more extensively in hard drug use and may constitute potential problems either for themselves or for others. It is probably this group which should constitute the targets for either prevention or treatment programs. The explanatory paradigm presented herein suggests that such efforts should be directed at more fully integrating the individual into non-drug using groups.

NOTES

1. All adolescent drug-use data in this chapter refers to psychoactive substance use other than that prescribed by a physician.

· 2. Data in this chapter generally will be presented for both adolescents and young adults. However, the principal theoretical focus is on the adolescent.

3. One criticism of high school surveys is that they do not tap the school dropout population. The general population studies do not suffer from this limitation although they may not adequately sample certain subpopulations (i.e., young minority males).

4. See, for instance, the recent publication *Polydrug Abuse,* edited by Wesson (1978).

5. Although they do not present the full set of data, Johnston et al. (1977a, 1977b) do note the proportion of students reporting easy access to all drugs other than marihuana has dropped over the past two years. The drop has been most pronounced for the hallucinogens. However, the point still remains that drugs are widely available.

6. It is my understanding that the National Institute of Drug Abuse is currently conducting just such a study for PCP. One hallmark of that study is the significant contribution of ethnographic research to the overall design.

7. It is possible that persons have used drugs other than marihuana and never have used marihuana. This pattern, particularly for adolescents, seems rare.

REFERENCES

ABELSON, H., P. FISHBURNE, and I. CISIN (1977) National Survey on Drug Abuse: 1977. Vol. 1. Washington, DC: National Institute of Drug Abuse.

ANHALT, H. and M. KLEIN (1976) "Drug abuse in jr. high school populations." American Journal of Drug and Alcohol Abuse 3, 4: 589-603.

BURKE, E. (1971) "Drug usage and reported effects in a select adolescent population." Journal of Psychedelic Drugs 3, 2: 55-62.

CISIN, I., J. MILLER, and A. HARRELL (1977) Highlights from the National Survey on Drug Abuse: 1977. Washington, DC: National Institute of Drug Abuse.

CRAIG, S. and B. BROWN (1975) "Comparison of youthful heroin users and non-users from one urban community." International Journal of the Addictions 10, 1: 53-64.

De ANGELIS, D. (1975) "Theoretical and clinical approaches to the treatment of drug addiction: with special considerations for the adolescent abuser." Journal of Psychedelic Drugs 7, 2: 187-202.

DUNCAN, D. (1977) "Life stress as a precursor to adolescent drug dependence." International Journal of the Addictions 12, 8: 1047-1056.

GAY, G. R., J. J. WINKLER, and J. A. NEWMEYER (1971) "Emerging trends of heroin abuse in the San Francisco Bay area." Journal of Psychedelic Drugs 4, 1: 53-64.

GRAEVEN, D. (1977) "Experimental heroin users: an epidemiologic and psychosocial approach." American Journal of Drug and Alcohol Abuse 4, 3: 365-376.

GRAEVEN, D. and R. SCHAEF (1978) "Family life and levels of involvement in an adolescent heroin epidemic." International Journal of the Addictions 13, 5: 747-771.

GRAHAM, D. (1975) "Values and attitudes of high school drug users." Journal of Drug Education 5, 2: 97-108.

GREEN, J. (1978) "Overview of adolescent drug use," in G. Beschner and A. Friedman (eds.) Youth Drug Abuse. New York: Academic.

HENDLER, H. and R. STEPHENS (1977) "The addict odyssey: from experimentation to addiction." International Journal of the Addictions 12, 1: 25-42.

JASSO, N. and G. WOLKON (1978) "Drug use, attitudes and behaviors of youth in an urban free clinic." International Journal of the Addictions 13, 2: 317-326.

JOHNSTON, L., J. BACHMAN, and P. O'MALLEY (1977a) Drug Use Among American High School Students 1975-77. Washington, DC: National Institute of Drug Abuse.

——— (1977b) Highlights from Drug Use Among American High School Students 1975-77. Washington, DC: National Institute of Drug Abuse.

KANDEL, D. (1974) "Interpersonal influences on adolescent illegal drug use," pp. 207-240 in E. Josephson and E. Carroll (eds.) Drug Use Epidemiological and Sociological Approaches. New York: John Wiley.

KENDALL, R. and S. PITTEL (1971) "Three portraits of the young drug user: comparison of MMPI group profiles." Journal of Psychedelic Drugs 3, 2: 63-66.

LAWRENCE, T. and J. VELLERMAN (1970) "Drugs/teens—alcohol/parents." Science Digest 68 (October): 47-56.

LIPTON, D., R. C. STEPHENS, G. S. UPPAL, E. KAESTNER, B. D. JOHNSON, J. SCHMEIDLER, J. A. SHEMTOB, P. J. BERGMAN, S. C. DIAMOND, C. R. SPIELMAN (1978a) Drug Use in New York State. New York: State of New York Division of Substance Abuse Services.

LIPTON, D. (1978b) Substance Use Among New York State Public and Parochial School Students in Grades 7-12. New York: State of New York Division of Substance Abuse Services.

McKILLIP, J., J. E. JOHNSON, T. P. PETZEL (1973) "Patterns and correlates of drug use among urban high school students." Journal of Drug Education 3, 1: 1-12.

McLUCKIE, B. F., M. ZAHN, and R. A. WILSON (1975) "Religion correlates of teenage drug use." Journal of Drug Issues 5, 2: 129-139.

NEWMEYER, J. (1975) "The quiescent heroin scene: incidence and prevalence in the San Francisco Bay area." Journal of Psychedelic Drugs 7, 4: 389-397.

PENDERGAST, T. (1974) "Family characteristics associated with marijuana use among adolescents." International Journal of the Addictions 9, 6: 827-839.

PITTEL, S. and R. HOFER (1972) "The transition to amphetamine abuse." Journal of Psychedelic Drugs 5, 2: 105-112.

ROLLINS, J. and R. HOLDEN (1972) "Adolescent drug use and the alienation syndrome." Journal of Drug Education 2, 3: 249-262.

SMART, R. and D. FEJER (1972) "Drug use among adolescents and their parents: closing the generation gap in mood modification." Journal of Abnormal Psychology 79: 153-160.

SPEVACK, M. and R. PIHL (1976) "Non-medical drug use by high school students: a 3-year survey study." International Journal of the Addictions 11, 5: 755-792.

STEIN, K. B., W. F. SOSKIN, and S. J. KORCHIN (1975) "Drug use among disaffected high school youth." Journal of Drug Education 5, 3: 193-204.

STEPHENS, R. and D. McBRIDE (1976) "Becoming a street addict." Human Organization 35 (Spring): 87-93.

STOKES, J. (1974) "Drug use among undergraduate psychology students at an urban university." Drug Forum 3, 4: 355-362.

STREIT, F., D. HALSTED, and P. PASCALE (1974) "Differences among youthful users and non-users of drugs based on their perceptions of parental behavior." International Journal of the Addictions 9, 5: 749-755.

STEIT, F. and H. OLIVER (1972) "The child's perception of his family and its relationship to drug use." Drug Forum 1, 3: 283-289.

TENNANT, F. (1976) "Dependency traits among parents of drug abusers." Journal of Drug Education 6, 1: 83-88.

WECHSLER, H. and D. THUM (1973) "Drug use among teenagers: patterns of present and anticipated use." International Journal of the Addictions 8, 6: 909-920.

WESSON, D. [ed.] (1978) Polydrug Abuse. New York: Academic.

WOLKON, G. H., N. K. JASSO, S. GALLAGHER, and P. COHN (1974) "The hang-loose ethic and drug use revisited." International Journal of the Addictions 9, 6: 909-918.

3

MARIHUANA AND YOUTH
A Generation Gone to Pot

BRUCE D. JOHNSON
GOPAL S. UPPAL

Marihuana use has been one of the remarkable social changes of the 1970s. Persons born after 1945 have turned on to and have become regular users of marihuana in large numbers. This drug has become institutionalized into the youth culture and, given current trends, will become even more pervasive and regularly used by youth and young adults in the 1980s.

In contrast, older generations, those born prior to 1940, have generally not used marihuana. They feel that America's youth now exhibit poor morals and behaviors. Marihuana and other drugs are a visible symbol of the purported increase in lawlessness, unconventionality, and irresponsible behavior by youth. These beliefs were particularly pre-

AUTHORS' NOTE: The opinions and points of view expressed herein do not necessarily represent policies of this agency.

valent among the older generation during the Vietnam era (1966-1974), but appear to have subsided somewhat in the last half of the seventies. HEW Secretary Joseph Califano, in releasing the Seventh Annual *Marijuana and Health* report (April 1979), however, called the sharp increases in marihuana use among youth "alarming," and stated, "It is sheer folly for millions of young Americans to indulge in a drug while so little is known about its long-term consequences."

As the social history of marihuana use among American youth emerges below, several subthemes will be developed. First, marihuana use has increased relatively continuously throughout the 1970s. While the future trend in lifetime use (ever used) may not increase substantially, higher potency marihuana (e.g., from Colombia) and more frequent consumption episodes are becoming increasingly common. Current marihuana use now equals or surpasses alcohol consumption among secondary school students in some parts of the country. Second, marihuana has become institutionalized within the youth culture and is related to many spheres of youthful behavior. Third, biological and pharmacological findings about marihuana and its active ingredient, tetrahydrocannabinol (THC), indicate a potential for harm to individual health; these findings are disputed by some experts. On the other hand, psychosocial and cross-cultural research reports little, if any, harm due to marihuana consumption. Fourth the politics of marihuana are shifting as the younger generations of pot smokers move into adulthood. Marihuana decriminalization has occurred in eleven states. As America enters a new decade, it is likely that the political debate regarding marihuana use may shift from whether the drug should be decriminalized to whether it should be legalized.

TRENDS IN MARIHUANA USE, 1965-1978

All available evidence points to a marked and consistent increase in marihuana use among the U.S. population since the late 1960s when the drug first became popular. Use was initially confined to a small minority categorized by some researchers as having "counter culture" characteristics. To marihuana users, the drug symbolized opposition to "establishment" values, and smoking a joint in private or in public gatherings was a manifestation of a new way of life.

Few public officials predicted in the early 1970s that marihuana use would increase to the point where a majority of persons in some age groups would use it. Indeed, the report of the National Commission on Marihuana and Drug Abuse (1972: 131, 134), concluded from a national survey in 1971 that

> there was a recurring awareness of the possibility that marihuana use may be a fad which, if not institutionalized, may recede substantially in time. Present data suggest that this is the case. . . . We recommend to the public and its policy makers a social control policy seeking to discourage marihuana use, while concentrating primarily on the prevention of heavy and very heavy use.

The data available to the Commission in 1972, however, indicated that marihuana was well institutionalized and pointed to continued increases in use (Johnson, 1973b). Survey data collected since 1971 on a national, state, or local level show that heavy use continues to increase. This section of the chapter describes and documents one of the most profound social changes to occur among youth in America during the 1970s—"smoking pot."

National household surveys, conducted periodically since 1971, provide data on patterns of marihuana use among youth and young adults. The first two studies, conducted in 1971 and 1972 (Abelson et al., 1972, 1973), were sponsored by the National Commission on Marihuana and Drug Abuse. Subsequent surveys in 1975, 1976, and 1977 were sponsored by the National Institute on Drug Abuse (Abelson and Atkinson, 1975; Abelson and Fishburne, 1976; Abelson et al., 1977).

The trends in lifetime marihuana use are presented in Figure 3.1 for various age groups and show an increase in marihuana use over the six years between 1971 and 1977. Lifetime marihuana use is at least 20 percent higher among those 14-34 in 1977 than their counterparts in 1971. In contrast, little increase in lifetime use is recorded for the very young (12-13) or among those over 35. The majority of older teenagers and young adults (18-25) have now tried marihuana and over a quarter have used it in the past month during 1977.

Lifetime and current use of marihuana is highly contingent upon age. Table 3.1 presents data on lifetime use and recency of use. The rightmost columns present the proportions of lifetime users who are "current" (in the past month) and "previous" users (those who used more than a year ago). Current use among lifetime users is greatest in the teenage years (to age 21), peaking among those 16-17 and declining steadily among older age groups. On the other hand, the proportion of

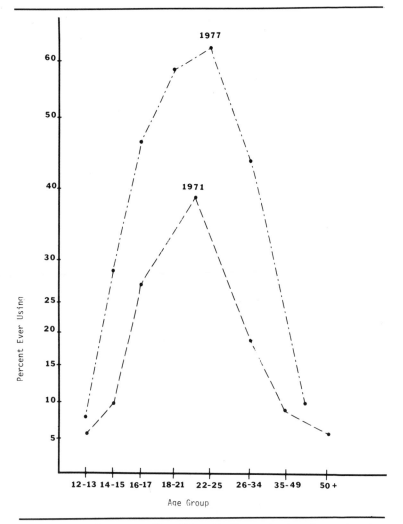

FIGURE 3.1   Percentage Ever Using Marihuana by Age Group for
National Household Surveys Conducted in 1971 and
1977

TABLE 3.1 Recency of Marihuana Use by Age Group, 1977 (National Household Survey)

Age Group	Lifetime use	Recency of use			Among lifetime users, percentage	
		Past month	Past year, not past month	Not in past year	Using in past month (current)	Not using in past year (previous)
Youth						
12–13	8	4	2	3	50	37
14–15	29	15	7	6	52	21
16–17	47	29	8	10	62	21
Adults						
18–21	59	31	10	17	53	29
22–25	62	24	12	26	39	42
26–34	44	12	9	23	27	52
35+	7	1	1	5	14	71

SOURCE: Abelson et al. (1977).

"previous" users among lifetime users is low (about 25 percent) during the teenage years but increases sharply after age 21, suggesting that marihuana users tend to use it less regularly or to cease use as they begin to assume normal adult roles in their twenties. This hypothesis is consistent with findings reported in studies of young adults and college and high school students after departure from schooling (O'Donnell et al., 1976; Brown et al., 1974; Henley and Adams, 1973).

One longitudinal study (Johnston, 1974; Bachman et al., 1978) does not support this hypothesis of reduced marihuana consumption being related to maturation. The initial study group consisted of 2000 males entering high school in 1966. The group was then restudied during the senior year of high school (1969), one year after graduation (1970), and five years after graduation (1974).

The data on marihuana use (Table 3.2) clearly show a substantial increase in daily and other frequent use of marihuana as the cohort progressed from adolescence to young adulthood. This particular cohort (high school class of 1969; birth cohort of 1951), however, was at the forefront of massive increases in marihuana use (O'Donnell et al., 1976). This increase in marihuana use may therefore reflect a generational trend. As they reach their late 20s, use may yet decline, although further evidence is needed.

Other trend data from surveys of specific portions of the youthful population suggest that use has continued to increase in recent years.

TABLE 3.2   Trends in Marihuana Use Among a Nationally Representative Longitudinal Sample of High School Males

	Senior year	One year after graduation	Five years after graduation
	1969	1970	1974
Ever used	20	35	62
Used in past year	20	33	52
Daily or weekly use sometime in past year	6	9	21
Daily use sometime in past year	1	2	9

SOURCE: Johnston, 1974.

TABLE 3.3   Marihuana Use Among U.S. High School Seniors (1975-
1978) and Among New York State High School Juniors
and Seniors (1978)

	U.S. High School Seniors[a]				New York State High School Juniors and Seniors[b]
	1975	1976	1977	1978	
Ever used	47.3	52.8	56.4	59.2	70.1
Used in past 12 months	40.0	44.5	47.6	50.2	60.1[c]
Used in past months	27.1	32.2	35.4	37.1	50.0
Used 20 or more times in past month	6.0	8.2	9.1	10.7	16.0

a. Johnston et al. (1977). The 1978 data were obtained via personal communication.
b. New York State Division of Substance Abuse Services, 1978.
c. Used after September 1977 (about 6 months prior to the survey).

Beginning in 1975, annual surveys of the nation's high school seniors have been conducted by Johnston et al. (1977, 1978); their results are summarized in Table 3.3.

These data show that the average annual increase in lifetime use, use during the past year, and use in the past month has been 3 to 5 percent; near daily use has increased roughly 1.5 percent per year. A further indication of marihuana's impressive popularity is the finding of the 1978 survey; the proportion of high school seniors using marihuana 20 or more times during the past month (11 percent) exceeds the proportion using alcohol at this same frequency (6 percent).

MARIHUANA IN THE 1980s

The previous section clearly documents the increasing trend in marihuana use during the decade of the 1970s. What do these trends imply for the future? The clear prognosis is for substantial increases in the immediate future, although saturation and stabilization at relatively high levels of use may also be hypothesized (Jessor, 1979). These two contrasting possibilities may be illustrated by analyzing trend data from surveys of drug use in San Mateo, California, in New York state, and among the national sample of high school seniors.

Between 1968 and 1977, high school students in San Mateo County have been surveyed annually about their substance use (Blackford, 1977). Data for three levels of marihuana use are shown in Table 3.4 for males in the 9th and 12th grades. Throughout this decade, 9th graders had use levels approximately 10-15 percent lower than seniors; the present discussion will focus on the seniors.

As early as 1968 when drug use was just becoming evident across the country, nearly half of the San Mateo male seniors had tried marihuana and a quarter used it about monthly. Moreover, a major increase occurred between 1970 and 1971 (lifetime use went from 51 to 59 percent; about weekly use—50+ times in past year—went from 22 to 32 percent). Subsequent to 1971, however, the levels of marihuana use have fluctuated very little (5 percent or less) at each level of use. Thus, among San Mateo seniors, marihuana use appears to have stabilized at relatively high levels after reaching such levels in 1971—a degree of stability not found in most other surveys.

A comparison of the San Mateo studies with Johnston et al.'s surveys of the nation's high school seniors suggests that rates of marihuana use among the national sample are moving toward the San Mateo levels. Johnston et al. found, for example, that 40 percent of the nation's seniors in 1975 had used marihuana in the preceding twelve

TABLE 3.4 Marihuana Use Among Male High School Students in San Mateo County, 1968-1976.

Year	Used marihuana in past year		Ten or more uses in past year		Fifty or more uses in past year	
	9th	12th	9th	12th	9th	12th
1968	27	45	14	26	NA	NA
1969	35	50	20	34	NA	NA
1970	34	51	20	34	11	22
1971	44	59	26	43	17	32
1972	44	61	27	45	16	32
1973	51	61	32	45	20	32
1974	49	62	30	47	20	34
1975	49	64	30	45	20	31
1976	48	61	27	42	17	30
1977	48	64	27	48	16	34

SOURCE: Blackford, 1977.

months, compared to 64 percent of the San Mateo senior males in the same year. By 1977, however, the rate among the nation's seniors had increased to 48 percent while the San Mateo figure remained at 64 percent. Given the annual rates of marihuana use from the Johnston et al. survey, what is the future trend likely to be? The 1969 data, obtained from Johnston's 1969 national sample as well as the 1975, 1976, 1977, and the 1978 marihuana use levels among seniors, were entered into a linear regression analysis. The actual data points indicate that continued increases are likely to occur (Figure 3.2).

These trends show that if Johnston's seniors continue to increase marihuana use at the rates established between 1969 and 1978, 61 percent of the nation's high school seniors will have used marihuana during the preceding 12 months by 1981. This level of use, meanwhile, was reached among San Mateo male seniors a decade earlier. As marihuana use among San Mateo seniors stabilized after 1971, therefore, it may be hypothesized that the same "ceiling" effect may occur among the nation's seniors in the early 1980s. This, however, is an optimistic projection because evidence from broader surveys in New York state— which will be directly compared with national surveys of the youth population—implies that increases in near-daily marihuana use may continue well into the 1980s.

Three major statewide surveys have been conducted in New York state among representative samples of high school students (Kandel et al., 1976; New York State Office of Drug Abuse Services, 1974-1975; New York State Division of Substance Abuse Services, 1978a). The levels of marihuana use in New York state have traditionally been about 1¼ to 2 times higher than national figures for youths of the same age (Abelson et al., 1977).

Levels of marihuana use among the nation's youth (14-17) equal those among the New York state high school students about two or three years later. Thus, in many respects, the findings of the New York state surveys, and impressions of use in this state, may provide major insights about marihuana and other drug use in the early 1980s across the nation.

The report from the New York State Division of Substance Abuse Services (1978a) presents data for high school juniors and seniors that can be compared to data from Johnston's high school seniors in 1978 (see Table 3.3). Of the New York state upperclassmen, 70 percent had

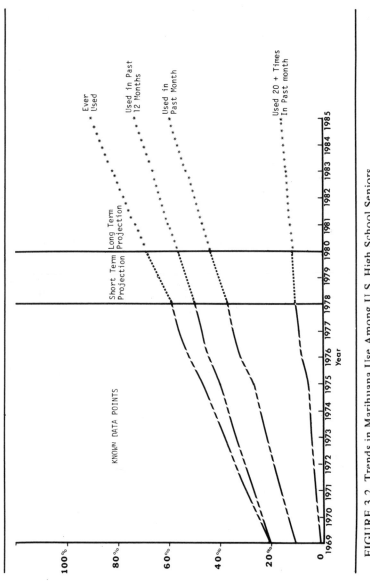

FIGURE 3.2 Trends in Marihuana Use Among U.S. High School Seniors

tried marihuana versus 59 percent of the nation's seniors; 50 percent (New York) versus 37 percent (nation) had used marihuana in the month prior to the survey; and 16 percent (New York) versus 11 percent (nation) had used marihuana 20 or more times in the past month.

Moreover, marihuana use in the past month is somewhat higher (50 percent) among 1978 New York state juniors and seniors than the roughly comparable figure (45 percent—10 or more times in past year) among San Mateo male seniors between 1972 and 1977 (Table 3.4). Thus, stabilization of marihuana use at levels equivalent to San Mateo has not occurred in New York State; further increases appear more likely than stabilization given the trend data there (New York State Division of Substance Abuse Services, 1978a).

In Figure 3.2, long-term projections of marihuana use for 1981-1985 among the nation's high school seniors have been made assuming that the same rates of increase for 1969-1978 continue throughout the first half of the 1980s. At some point, however, the lifetime use figure will have to encounter ceiling effects. But the possibility is not remote that over 90 percent of the high school seniors may have tried marihuana by the end of the 1980s. If this occurs, marihuana would be following the pattern of alcohol in which over 95 percent of the high school population has tried it (Johnston et al. 1977). On the other hand, a lower ceiling may also be possible, but little current evidence suggests at what level such stabilization will occur. Nor is it clear whether and at what level marihuana use in the past year and month, or on a daily basis, may stabilize. Therefore, the long-term prognosis is for continuing increases in use and regular use, with possible stabilization at levels considerably higher than at present.

Thus, marihuana has become and will become even more deeply embedded in the American youth culture. Akers's (1977) observations would have elicited sharp disbelief in the 1960s, but they describe the marihuana scene in New York and many other parts of the country adequately at the start of the 1980s: "Marijuana is smoked in an offhand, casual way. . . . Before, during, or after sports events, dates, public gatherings, parties, music festivals, class, or work will do; there is no special place, time, or occasion for marijuana smoking. The acceptable places and occasions are as varied as those for drinking alcohol."

To which, with some exceptions, could be added "or cigarettes." The 5 to 15 percent of the youthful population who are daily or near-daily marihuana smokers are likely to consume a joint between classes at school or during a coffee or lunch break at work in a pattern somewhat similar to cigarette smoking. This activity, however, is unlikely on school premises or while working. Nevertheless, for public health officials concerned about the physiological consequences of regular marihuana smoking (see below), a concern for the remainder of the twentieth century is that a sizable minority of the youthful and the maturing postwar cohorts may consume marihuana on a daily basis.

Johnston et al.'s 1977-1978 surveys show that the proportion of seniors using marihuana in the past month (37 percent) now almost equals the proportion using cigarettes (38 percent) in the past month. The data also show, however, that 29 percent were daily cigarette smokers and 10 percent smoked one or more packs of cigarettes per day; 5 percent smoked marihuana 40 or more times in the past month. Thus, a larger proportion of the nation's high school seniors now smoke marihuana on a more than daily basis (40 or more times in the past month) than use alcohol (3 percent) with the same frequency, but the extensive daily use of cigarettes is still higher. Nevertheless, levels of daily cigarette and alcohol consumption have remained virtually unchanged between 1975 and 1978, while near-daily marihuana use among high school seniors has increased by 1.5 percent per year (see Table 3.3 and Figure 3.2).

If trends in the daily and near-daily use of marihuana in the mid-1970s are projected for the nation's seniors or for New York state students, the proportion of daily users might approximate that of daily cigarette users toward the end of the 1980s. Whether the number of joints consumed per day may begin to equal the daily number of cigarettes is unknown and perhaps unlikely. Unfortunately, no national or large-scale state survey has yet published results on the number of joints smoked, (although Johnston et al.'s questionnaire collects these data) and the equivalency of tar content of cigarettes and marihuana has not been well established.

Some statistical and observational evidence also documents the extent to which marihuana has been institutionalized into the youth culture. The New York State Division of Substance Abuse Services (1979) survey inquired about substance use during school hours. Students were asked whether they had been "stoned" or "very high" on marihuana *while in class* during the previous six months. More than a quarter of 7-12th grade students had been stoned at least once during this period and 10 percent had been stoned twenty or more times while in class. This means that a third of lifetime users and half of those using marihuana in the past six months had been stoned one or more times while in class. Analysis of the data also revealed that the more recent and regular the marihuana use, the greater the likelihood of being high in class. Such evidence indicates that routine marihuana use has become as deeply embedded in the culture of high school students as routine alcohol use, premarital sex, and minor delinquency (Jessor and Jessor, 1977; Jessor, 1979).

Marihuana can be easily smelled and persons may be observed publicly smoking in a wide variety of settings. Teachers and administrators at many high schools or junior high schools in urban and suburban neighborhoods frequently find one or more small groups of students, especially at lunch hour, smoking marihuana outside the school building or just off school property. Inside the school, marihuana fumes are frequently encountered in bathrooms, staircases, or in other isolated areas. Health teachers and drug program instructors now find that students defend marihuana use and are unwilling to accept suggestions that marihuana may be harmful. Nonusers seldom say anything; but users are particularly willing to share their opinions about and admit to regular marihuana use (though possibly not to other forms of drug use).

The situation is somewhat different in the work force. Young workers can frequently be encountered sharing a joint in their car, at a nearby park, or in a street location during the lunch hour. In spring 1979, the Staten Island Ferry prohibited smoking in part because marihuana smoking was so common (Staten Island Advance, 1979).[1] So far, however, marihuana fumes are less frequently encountered in stairwells of offices where young adults work.

Almost as pervasive as marihuana use is its widespread distribution and sale (Leukefeld and Clayton, 1979). The latter is a major phenomenon of the 1970s that has not yet been well studied. It is apparent, however, that a vast majority of the thousands of tons of marihuana smoked is illegally imported into the United States. From the point of import, it is illegally sold and distributed in progressively smaller quantities to millions of consumers at a relatively low price per ultimate retail unit (e.g., the price per joint from a street dealer unknown to the consumer in New York City is generally a dollar or less). Moreover, low-quality marihuana commands about the same price (approximately $30 a "lid" or ounce) in 1979 as it did in the late 1960s (Carey, 1968;

Goode, 1970), although the Consumer Price Index has doubled since then. New supplies from Jamaica and Colombia also provide more potent marihuana (THC content is 5-10 percent versus less than 2 percent for Mexican marihuana)—but at prices of $50-$100 per ounce (New York Times, 1978).

The main accomplishment of the marihuana distribution system, due in part to its illegality, has been the development of a sophisticated marketing network. Most of the weekly or more regular marihuana smokers occasionally or frequently sell marihuana (Johnson, 1973a) to their friends; they also serve as role models to neophyte marihuana users and recruit and initiate nonusers. Many sales occur within relatively cohesive friendship cliques and to trustworthy acquaintances. Such marihuana sales provide a relatively safe (i.e., low probability of arrest) source of cash income plus free drugs for many youths in school or without employment. Thus, existing friendship networks and economic inducements enable the seller to provide marihuana to the typical user with little risk and effort.

Closely associated with the high levels of marihuana use and the efficient marihuana distribution system is the use and distribution of other illicit drugs. Research findings are remarkably consistent, showing that marihuana is generally the first illicit drug used (alcohol and cigarettes tend to precede marihuana), and is used on a more regular basis than other drugs. Weekly marihuana users are also very likely to try and to be irregular users of hallucinogens, cocaine, opiates, sedatives, stimulants, tranquilizers, and new fad drugs (PCP is a recent example, with nitrous oxide and butyl nitrite now popular). Strikingly, an argument widely used in the 1960s that marihuana leads to heroin (Johnson, 1973a) has become irrelevant and is seldom heard as marihuana use spirals upward while heroin addiction declines (New York State Division of Substance Abuse Services, 1978b; Rittenhouse, 1977). Nevertheless, regular marihuana use continues to be highly associated with the use of nonopiate substances.

Finally, public attitudes toward marihuana users have eased during the 1970s as eleven states have decriminalized marihuana possession or small sales.[2] Public opinion polls suggest that support for marihuana legalization has increased among youth populations. (This topic will be discussed in the "politics of marijuana" section below.) Thus, marihuana use has become institutionalized and pervasive, "transcending racial, cultural, social, and economic lines and involving millions of people using hundreds of substances" (Smith, 1979).

Much of the existing evidence suggests that marihuana use will become even more widespread in the 1980s. In all probability, a larger proportion of the youth and adult populations will be using marihuana; a substantially larger proportion of youth will use it on a daily and near-daily basis; and more potent marihuana will be smoked. While the proportion of marihuana users in youthful populations may increase, the numbers may increase less rapidly because of declining birth rates among cohorts of 12-17 year olds. (New York State Division of Substance Abuse Services, 1978c).

SCIENTISTS AND MARIHUANA

Scientific findings on marihuana use and its effects have burgeoned during the late 1960s and the 1970s. More has probably been learned about marihuana in the past fifteen years than in all previous centuries. At the turn of the 1980s, the results from psychosocial and cross-cultural research are much clearer than research findings on the pharmacology, biology, and physiology of marihuana use. Fortunately, numerous and excellent reviews of this literature exist (Petersen, 1977; Marijuana and Health, 1972, 1973, 1974, 1975; Kandel, 1978; Jessor, 1979; Josephson, 1980) obviating the need for an extensive review here.

An important feature of scientific findings about marihuana is that conclusions from psychosocial and cross-cultural research appear to diverge from those of pharmacological, biological, and physiological research.

The psychosocial research, based mainly upon large scale cross-sectional and longitudinal surveys of drug use, have intensively studied the three major arguments lodged against marihuana prior to the 1970s. The arguments charged that marihuana use leads to: (1) crime and deviance, (2) the use of heroin and other hard drugs, and (3) laziness, poor performance, or inability to function (the "amotivational syndrome").

Existing evidence from longitudinal surveys (Kandel, 1978; Jessor and Jessor, 1977; Smith and Fogg, 1978; Johnston et al., 1978) demonstrates that delinquency and criminality tend to precede nonopiate drug use. The association between marihuana use and criminality is due mainly to the fact that persons with unconventional attributes become involved in both delinquency and drug use—although the vast majority of smokers are not involved in crime. Likewise, the association between marihuana use and poor school performance, career indecision, school dropout, and poor grades reflects "a behavioral syndrome of nonconformity related to a common set of social and psychological factors that represent proneness to deviance or problem behavior" (Jessor, 1979). Thus, the existing evidence clearly shows that marihuana does not cause deviance, criminality, and other problem behaviors but usually follows them.

Research investigating the linkages between marihuana use and the use of heroin and other hard drugs, however, shows a more complex set of findings. A widely circulated pamphlet by the Federal Bureau of Narcotics (1965) in the 1960s claimed that "the smoking of the marijuana cigarette is a dangerous first step on the road which usually leads to enslavement by heroin." Johnson (1973a) carefully examined this marihuana-heroin relationship among New York metropolitan-area college students and found that an important relationship occurred only under a rare set of conditions; only those users of marihuana with heroin-using friends and who sold hard drugs were likely to try heroin. Regular marihuana users not involved in buying or selling cannabis, or without heroin-using intimates, had very low or nonexistent levels of heroin use.

Marihuana use has been clearly demonstrated to be critically important to the use of other drugs. Kandel (1975, 1978) reports that initiation to various legal and illegal drugs follows a sequence of stages. Alcohol and cigarette use tend to precede and predispose to marihuana use, but marihuana use is almost a prerequisite for the nonmedical use of other substances. Despite a plethora of data, including major longitudinal data sets, however, few researchers have attempted to delineate the causal order (if any) variables such as: the use of drugs other than marihuana, drugs used in the peer group, and drug buying and selling, which Johnson (1973a; see also Single and Kandel, 1978) found to be critical. As Clausen (1978) clearly points out in his critique of Kandel's (1978) important book, research in the 1980s will need to focus on the social and psychological reasons for regular (weekly and daily) marihuana use, the cessation of regular use, and the consequences of such regular use (use of other drugs, drug dealing, crime, delinquency, and so on). Nevertheless, important strides in understanding the etiology of marihuana use have been made in the 1970s and improved efforts will undoubtedly continue in the 1980s.

Likewise, cross-cultural research (Rubin and Comitas, 1975) has generally found little evidnce of significant health impairment from levels of marihuana consumption that would be considered "chronic" in the United States. Findings from Jamaica, Costa Rica, and Greece find little evidence of harm that can be directly attributed to cannabis consumption. While cannabis smokers in these cultures may be less healthy than the nonsmokers, differences in social class, limited access to medical care, heavy cigarette or tobacco smoking, poor nutrition, deprived childhood, or alcohol consumption appear to contribute much more to poor health than the consumption of large amounts of cannabis on a daily basis. Rubin and Comitas (1975) report that Jamaican ganja smokers believe that their work performance is actually enhanced by such consumption.

Studies from biology and physiology, frequently based upon animal studies in which high doses of THC are used, suggest that cannabis may have potential for harming the health of daily marihuana users. Controversy about the implications of such findings continues to be widespread. Nahas et al. (1976, 1979; Nahas, 1979b) have been leading proponents of the view that marihuana and THC may be deleterious to health, while Grinspoon (1977) generally disagrees and presents results or replications that fail to support the original claims made. The federal *Marihuana and Health Reports* (1972, 1973, 1974, 1975) summarize this literature effectively and generally indicate that no convincing evidence of harm from marihuana has yet been documented. Nevertheless, the popular press tends to overreport the negative findings about marihuana and ignores more careful statements (Shepard and Goode, 1977; Josephson, 1980). Some of the controversial claims about the potential effects of marihuana include concern that marihuana smoke may damage the lungs like cigarettes, that THC may negatively affect the male and female reproductive system and the functioning of the brain cells, and that THC remains in the body for up to 30 days and has effects that have not yet been measured (Nahas, 1979a, 1979b).

Nevertheless, biological researchers recognize that their work needs to be replicated, tested, and studied among humans as well as animals and that long-term longitudinal studies of marihuana smoking are needed. Nahas (1979a) claims that it took 60 or more years to establish the negative impact of tobacco smoking on health and at least a decade or two will be needed to provide equally compelling information about the health consequences of marihuana smoking.

The conclusions of sociocultural and some biological scientists are therefore diverging considerably at the end of the 1970s. The sociocultural scientists find little or no measurable harm caused by marihuana (which cannot be more reasonably attributed to other factors), while several biological scientists are finding evidence (yet to be verified) that regular marihuana use may cause harm to the health of daily smokers in the future. On both fronts, research will continue into the 1980s and may provide major new insights about the antecedents and consequences of marihuana use, especially of regular, daily, and chronic use.

THE POLITICS OF MARIHUANA

Although a generational split in attitudes toward marihuana use persists at the turn of the 1980s, the importance of marihuana use as a political issue appears to have shifted from the late 1960s and early 1970s. The first nationally representative study of marihuana use and attitudes was conducted in September 1971 for the National Commission on Marihuana and Drug Abuse (1972; Abelson et al., 1972). The attitudinal data provide clear documentation that a generational gap existed then. The adults surveyed in 1971, especially those 35 and older, described marihuana users as bored with life, not caring about the world, having many personal problems, and as being lazy. Likewise, adults believed that marihuana may lead to stronger drugs such as heroin and that users may commit crimes under its influence, or lose their desire to work. In addition, older adults denied that marihuana users could lead a normal life, gain increased enjoyment from music and art, or experience other positive benefits. Young adults (18-25), on the other hand, were more likely to deny negative beliefs and were more likely to agree with positive statements about marihuana. Thus, the middle-age and older generation in 1971 held a distinctly negative image of marihuana users.

Comparable attitudinal data in the late 1970s are not as rich, but generally show that antimarihuana beliefs have remained relatively stable among the generations born prior to 1940, but have declined among the generations born after 1945. The older adults appear to be mellowing somewhat in attitudes toward stricter drug legislation. The proportion of adults 26 and older favoring "stricter laws for marihuana" declined from 77 to 65 percent between 1971 and 1977, while the proportion favoring a decriminalization policy increased from 36 to 46 percent between 1974 and 1977 (Abelson et al., 1977).

This shift in attitudes is partially due to the maturation of the large cohort who were teenagers or college students during the Vietnam era (1966-1974). This cohort is now in their late twenties and early thirties;

current teenagers and young adults appear even more likely to have tried and to be regular users of marihuana. Thus, as the 1980s begin, over half (with larger proportions in certain states) of the nation's population of age 16-30 have tried marihuana and an important minority are almost daily users. In addition, marihuana use has become institutionalized and accepted by this population as a normal activity— as normal as under-age alcohol consumption was to their parents as teenagers. Further, youthful cohorts comprise a disproportionate share of the U.S. population.

Persons born between 1945 and 1950, for example, constitute 9 percent of the U.S. population. These postwar babies were at the forefront of the drug-using, hippie generation and the Vietnam era. Abelson et al. (1972; Figure 3.1) show that these persons, age 21-26 in 1971, included those with the highest levels of marihuana use. While the marihuana use of this cohort (age 27-32 in 1977) appears to have diminished slightly and younger cohorts now have higher levels of marihuana use, the widespread acceptance of marihuana among these postwar babies now reaching adulthood will provide marihuana users with political protection against harsher laws. This cohort and subsequent ones form an important potential constituency that may support future liberalization of marihuana laws. Many young adults from this generation are being elected to state legislatures and many more serve on legislative staffs; older legislators frequently have marihuana-using children of this age—as do their constituents.

In addition to a growing marihuana constituency, marihuana users have a well-organized pressure group, The National Organization for the Reform of Marihuana Laws (NORML), to represent their interests. Nationally distributed magazines (*High Times, High Life,* and others) which stress information on drugs and their use also provide the marihuana constituency with a communications network.

NORML (1979c) continues to monitor the legal situation of marihuana users in each of the 50 states, and lobbies directly for liberalization of laws relating to the drug's use. NORML's position received major legitimization when the National Commission on Marihuana and Drug Abuse (1972) recommended that marihuana possession and small sales be decriminalized. Although the federal government has not followed these recommendations, eleven states have partially followed the Commission's recommendations. Several major organizations (American Bar Association, American Medical Association, National Education Association) and newspapers (New York *Times,* Washington *Post,*

Boston *Globe*, Los Angeles *Times*) have endorsed decriminalization (NORML, 1978).

There is no antimarihuana equivalent to NORML; thus, no continuing or contending forces are in dispute as on the abortion issue (National Organization for Women versus Right to Life). Rather, the antimarihuana forces are generally a coalition of biologically oriented academics, drug treatment personnel, police and law enforcement spokespersons, and legislators representing conservative constituencies. Moreover, even the antimarihuana groups frequently concede that arrest or imprisonment for marihuana possession may be too severe a punishment for the perceived moral wrong committed or the possible harm caused by marihuana smoking.

Although the legislative process has seldom been studied (National Governors Conference, 1977; Select Committee, 1977; Danaceau, 1974; New York Times, 1977; Josephson, 1980), three major arguments are frequently invoked in legislative decisions to decriminalize marihuana. First, a sizable proportion of youth from all parts of society are using marihuana (the data in Table 3.1 show that over a quarter of the youths in the nation do so on a current basis). Second, large numbers of persons, both youths and young adults, are arrested on marihuana possession charges. The costs of court time for processing such cases are so large that possession arrests decrease time to handle more serious crimes. Third, legislators are aware that many of their constituents have marihuana-using children and are afraid that these children may be arrested and gain a criminal record for much of their lives. Danaceau (1974) has commented that "too many of the wrong kids were being arrested." District attorneys, law associations, and influential judges frequently support marihuana decriminalization (or remain neutral on the issue) because of the "clogged courts" argument. Legislators hear from their own children, their constituents, and increasingly from young activist supporters and staff (many of whom may smoke marihuana) that a criminal record for marihuana possession is more harmful than the drug consumed.

Significantly, with the exception of a few relatively pro-marihuana legislators, most do not believe that marihuana is harmless and generally reject user arguments about the benefits of marihuana. Thus, marihuana decriminalization has passed in several states because legislators voted for the lesser of two evils (i.e., the potential harm of criminal records and costly court processing is worse than health problems caused by the consumption of marihuana).

The evidence of scientific research, while relatively well understood by some government administrators, has generally had little impact upon political controversies about marihuana legislation (Josephson, 1980). Journalists and legislators (Eastland, 1974) generally select those scientists, facts, and government administrators that fit their ideological predispositions toward marihuana and are relatively unaware of much scientific research or of many eminent scientists (Shepard and Goode, 1977). Those opposing legal changes tend to emphasize the possible biological, physiological, and medical hazards associated with marihuana consumption, while proponents of marihuana liberalization emphasize facts about the widespread use with little apparent harm found in the social science literature. Much more common, however, is that few scientists are invited to testify at legislative hearings about marihuana policy.

The decriminalization policy now in effect in eleven states has reduced the number of marihuana arrests and associated court costs (National Governors Conference, 1977). Surveys of use patterns generally indicate that marihuana decriminalization had no or little measurable impact upon levels of marihuana use. When increases in use occurred, isolating whether the change was due to decriminalization or to long-term increases in use across the nation or a particular state is difficult (National Governors Conference, 1977).

The San Mateo data (Table 3.4) show virtually no change, and perhaps a decrease, after decriminalization occurred in January 1976; use levels increased in 1977 but equivalent levels of use had occurred prior to 1976. Yet a statewide survey showed an almost 8 percent increase in lifetime and current use between 1975 and 1976, but the California State (1977) report indicates that other factors may have been important also. The best data for testing the impact of marihuana decriminalization have been collected by Johnston for high school seniors. His analysis has yet to be performed and published but he can compare changes of usage in decriminalized states with states where the law remains unchanged. Further analysis of decriminalization is likely to occur. Other states may follow the original eleven in the early 1980s. At the federal level, DuPont (1979), the former director of the National Institute on Drug Abuse, favors marihuana decriminalization as does President Carter (1977), although both currently appear to be less enthusiastic about this policy in 1979 than in 1977. Bills to decriminalize marihuana have consistently died in congressional committees.

For almost a decade, several serious academics and writers (Kaplan,

1970; Brecher and Consumers Union, 1972; Grinspoon, 1977; Jessor, 1979) and government officials (DuPont, 1979), as well as NORML have considered marihuana legalization. The Board of Directors of NORML (1979b) for the first time adopted an official policy:

> Legalization of marijuana generally refers to a system for the sale or distribution of marijuana which is authorized by law. . . . Studies should be undertaken to consider alternative regulatory models which would both minimize the potential for abuse and not encourage use. Specifically, NORML supports the eventual legalization of marijuana and favors appointment of a Commission to conduct such a review.

Support for legalization, however, has generally contained a suggestion that alternative regulatory models be developed and carefully considered. No clear proposal of a possible model has been provided. DuPont (1979) has analyzed many issues about legalization, and clearly presents the problems which will confront almost any regulatory scheme.

Legalization of marihuana use, especially an officially approved distribution system, seems highly unlikely in the 1980s for several reasons. First, the major political concerns leading to marihuana decriminalization involved "clogged" courts and arrest records for otherwise conventional youths; these concerns will not be involved in regulatory discussions. Second, older generations, although somewhat less hostile toward marihuana, will continue to oppose legislation that may symbolically approve marihuana use. Third, the patterns of marihuana use and attitudes toward it among the postwar cohorts, who will be in their thirties during the 1980s, may be critical. The data in Table 3.1 show that over half of the lifetime users over 25 have not used marihuana in the past year; thus the "hippie" generation appears to be giving up marihuana. Whether, and to what extent, cohorts reaching adulthood will continue use during the 1980s is currently unclear. Fourth, national data suggest that a sizable proportion of the marihuana users have ambivalent attitudes toward marihuana; while over half of the 18-25 year olds in 1977 used marihuana and many of these had used prior to age 18, many would deny legal marihuana to persons under 18 (Abelson et al., 1977). For these and many other reasons, a regulatory model in which the government would license private companies or develop a monopoly to distribute marihuana to consumers seems extremely unlikely in the 1980s.

Three minor adjustments in marihuana's legal status may be somewhat more likely. First, several states and the federal government may begin to recognize marihuana's potential in medical treatment. Four states now permit medical professionals to provide marihuana to cancer chemotherapy and glaucoma victims (NORML, 1979d); other states may follow and more medical diseases may be included. Second, although a referendum to permit the cultivation of marihuana for personal use lost in California in 1972, such a referendum or bill might now pass in one or more of the states where marihuana has been decriminalized. Third, in states having a positive experience with marihuana decriminalization, future legislation may eliminate or lower the fine for marihuana possession, or increase the amounts of marihuana that can be possessed or transferred without penal sanction. Such legal changes would follow the basic recommendations of the National Commission (1972). Hence, possession and cultivation for personal use and transfer of small amounts would no longer be a crime or violation and thus be "legal." Yet the marihuana smoker would have no legal means other than cultivation for obtaining a supply. The government would not authorize, regulate, or sell marihuana and would continue to intercept illicit supplies and punish those possessing or selling large amounts.

The legal status of marihuana will continue to be ambiguous during the 1980s—as it has been in the 1970s. The proportion of youth using marihuana in the past month and on a daily basis will probably continue to increase—possibly rivaling or surpassing alcohol and cigarette consumption; a leveling in use may be a possibility. The older generation will continue to be concerned about the moral and symbolic aspects of marihuana laws and oppose legal change. More state legislatures and possibly the federal government may decriminalize possession and transfer of small amounts of marihuana, but legalization or regulation of use as well as harsher penalties or recriminalization appear remote. Thus, the ambivalent legal status of marihuana legislation and the ambiguous situation which marihuana smokers face is a fundamental reality in America at the beginning of the 1980s.

NOTES

1. This conclusion was in part arrived at through personal observation.
2. The eleven states were Oregon, Alaska, Maine, Colorado, California, Ohio, Minnesota, Mississippi, North Carolina, New York, and Nebraska.

REFERENCES

ABELSON, H., R. COHEN, and D. SCHRAYER (1972) "A nationwide study of beliefs, information and experience," in National Commission on Marihuana and Drug Abuse, Marihuana: A Signal of Misunderstanding. Vol. II. Washington, DC: Government Printing Office.

ABELSON, H., R. COHEN, D. SCHRAYER, and M. RAPPEPORT (1973) "Drug experience, attitudes and related behavior among adolescents and adults," in National Commission on Marihuana and Drug Abuse, Drug Use in America: Problem in Perspective. Vol. I. Washington, DC: Government Printing Office.

ABELSON, H. and R. ATKINSON (1975) Public Experience with Psychoactive Substances: A Nationwide Study Among Adults and Youth. Princeton, NJ: Response Analysis Corporation.

ABELSON, H. I., and P. M. FISHBURNE (1976) Nonmedical Use of Psychoactive Substances. Princeton, NJ: Response Analysis Corporation.

––– and I. H. CISIN (1977) National Survey on Drug Abuse: 1977. Princeton, NJ: Response Analysis Corporation.

AKERS, R. L. (1977) Deviant Behavior: A Social Learning Approach. Belmont, CA: Wadsworth.

BACHMAN, J. G., P. M. O'MALLEY, and H. JOHNSTON (1978) Adolescence to Adulthood, Youth in Transition. Vol. VI. Ann Arbor: University of Michigan Press.

BLACKFORD, L. S. (1977) Student Drug Use Surveys San Mateo County, California 1978-1977. San Mateo: County Department of Public Health and Welfare.

BRECHER, E. and Consumers Union (1972) Licit and Illicit Drugs. Boston: Little, Brown.

BROWN, J. S., D. GLASER, E. WAXER, and G. GEIS (1974) "Turning off: cessation of marijuana use after college." Social Problems 21: 527-538.

California State Office of Narcotics and Drug Abuse (1977) A First Report of the Impact of California's New Marijuana Law. Sacramento: Author.

CALIFANO, J. V. (1979) "Youth pot use called 'alarming.' " ADAMHA News 10 (May 18).

CAREY, J. I. (1968) The College Drug Scene. Englewoods Cliff, NJ: Prentice-Hall.

CARTER, J. [President] (1977) Message to Congress. August 2.

CLAUSEN, J. A. (1978) "Longitudinal studies of drug use in the high school: substantive theoretical issues," in D. B. Kandel (ed.) Longitudinal Research on Drug Use: Empirical Issues and Methodological Issues. New York: John Wiley.

DANACEAU, P. (1974) Pot Luck in Texas: Changing a Marijuana Law. Washington, DC: Drug Abuse Council.

DuPONT, R. L. (1979) "Marihuana: decriminalization and legalization," in G. M. Beshner and A. S. Friedman, Youth Drug Abuse: Problems, Issues and Treatment. Lexington, MA: D.C. Heath.

EASTLAND, J. (1974) Marihuana-Hashish Epidemic and Its Impact on United States Security. Hearings Before the Subcommittee to Investigate the Administration of the Internal Security Act and Other Internal Security Laws of the

Committee of the Judiciary, U.S. Senate. Washington, DC: Government Printing Office.

Federal Bureau of Narcotics (1965) Living Death: The Truth About Drug Addiction. Washington, DC: Government Printing Office.

GOODE, E. (1970) The Marijuana Smokers. New York: Basic Books.

GRINSPOON, L. (1977) Marihuana Reconsidered. Cambridge, MA: Harvard University Press.

HENLEY, J. R. and L. D. ADAMS (1973) "Marijuana use in Post-collegiate cohorts: correlates of use, prevalence patterns, and factors associated with cessation. Social Problems 20: 514-520.

JESSOR, R. (1979) "Marihuana: a review of recent psychosocial research," In R. I. DuPont et al. (eds.). Handbook on Drug Abuse. National Institute on Drug Abuse. Washington, DC: Government Printing Office.

– – – and S. L. JESSOR (1977) Problem Behavior and Psychosocial Development: A Longitudinal Study of Youth. New York: Academic.

JOHNSON, B. D. (1973a) Marijuana Users and Drug Subcultures. New York: John Wiley.

– – – (1973b) "Sense and nonsense in the 'scientific' study of drugs: an anti-commission report." Society 10, 4: 53-58.

JOHNSTON, L. D. (1974) "Drug use during and after high school: results of a national longitudinal study." American Journal of Public Health 64 (Supplement): 29-37.

– – – J. G. BACHMAN, and P. M. O'MALLEY (1977) Drug Use Among American High School Students 1975-1977. National Institute on Drug Abuse. Washington, DC: Government Printing Office.

JOHNSTON, L. D., P. M. O'MALLEY, and L. K. EVELAND (1978) "Drugs and delinquency: a search for causal connections," in D. B. Kandel (ed.) Longitudinal Research on Drug Use: Empirical Findings and Methodological Issues. New York: John Wiley.

JOSEPHSON, E. (1980) "Marihuana policy and research: a study in ambiguity," in E. Josephson and O. Ochs (eds.) Drug Policy and Social Research New York: John Wiley.

KANDEL, D. B. (1975) "Stages in adolescent involvement in drug use." Science 190: 912-914.

KANDEL, D. B. [ed.] (1978) Longitudinal Research on Drug Use: Empirical Findings and Methodological Issues. New York: John Wiley.

– – – E. SINGLE, and R. KESSLER (1976) "The epidemiology of drug use among New York state high school students: distribution, trends, and change in rates of use." American Journal of Public Health 66: 43-53.

KAPLAN, J. (1970) Marijuana–The New Prohibition. Cleveland: World.

LEUKEFELD, G. G. and R. R. CLAYTON (1979) "Drug abuse and delinquency: a study of youths in treatment," pp. 213-227 in G. Beshner and A. S. Friedman, Youth Drug Abuse Lexington, MA: D.C. Heath.

Marihuana and Health (1972) Second Annual Report to Congress from the Secretary of Health, Education, and Welfare. Washington, DC: Government Printing Office.

——— (1973) Third Annual Report to Congress from the Secretary of Health, Education, and Welfare. Washington, DC: Government Printing Office.

——— (1974) Fourth Annual Report to Congress from the Secretary of Health, Education, and Welfare. Washington, DC: Government Printing Office.

——— (1975) Fifth Annual Report to Congress from the Secretary of Health, Education, and Welfare. Washington, DC: Government Printing Office.

NAHAS, G. (1979a) "A biological indictment of marijuana use." U.S. Journal (March).

——— (1979b) Keep Off The Grass. Elmsford, NY: Pergamon.

——— W.D.M. PATON, and J. E. IDANPAAN-HEIKKILA [eds.] (1976) Marihuana: Chemistry, Biochemistry, and Cellular Effects. New York: Springer-Verlag.

NAHAS, G., W.D.M. PATON, and M. BRAUDE (1979) Marijuana: Biological Effects. Elmsford, NY: Pergamon.

National Commission on Marihuana and Drug Abuse (1972) Marihuana: A Signal of Misunderstanding. Washington, DC: Government Printing Office.

National Governors Conference, Center for Policy Research and Analysis (1977) Marijuana: A Study of State Policies and Penalities. Washington, DC: LEAA National Institute of Law Enforcement and Criminal Justice.

National Organization for the Reform of Marijuana Laws [NORML] (1978) The Marijuana Issue. Washington, DC: Author.

——— (1979a) News Digest. Washington, DC: Author.

——— (1979b) Official Policy. Washington, DC: Author.

——— (1979c) In the Courts, NORML Legal Activities. Washington, DC: Author.

——— (1979d) Marijuana and Health, A NORML Special Report. Washington, DC: Author.

New York State Division of Substance Abuse Services (1978a) Substance Use Among New York State Public and Parochial School Students in Grades 7-12. Albany: Author.

——— (1978b) Fact Sheet 1978. Albany: Author.

——— (1978c) Statewide Comprehensive Five-Year Plan, 1979-1984. Albany: Author.

——— (1979) Drug Users in New York State Secondary Schools: Polydrug Use, In-School Use, Truancy, and Participation in Prevention Programs. Albany: Author.

New York State Office of Drug Abuse Services (1974-1975) A Survey of Substance Use Among Junior and Senior High School Students in New York State. Albany: Author.

New York Times (1978) "A more potent marijuana is stirring fresh debates." (December 28).

O'DONNELL, J. A., H. L. VOSS, R. R. CLAYTON, G. T. SLATIN, and R. ROOM (1976) Young Men and Drugs: A Nationwide Survey. NIDA Research Monograph 5. Washington, DC: Government Printing Office.

PETERSEN, R. C. [ed.] (1977) Marihuana Research Findings: 1976. NIDA Research Monograph 14. Washington, DC: Government Printing Office.

RITTENHOUSE, J. D. (1977) The Epidemiology of Heroin and Other Narcotics. NIDA Research Monograph 16. Washington, DC: Government Printing Office.

RUBIN, V. and L. COMITAS (1975) Ganja in Jamaica. Amsterdam: Mouton.

SHEPARD, R. G. and E. GOODE (1977) "Scientists in the popular press." New Scientist 24 (November): 482-484.

SINGLE, E. and D. B. KANDEL (1978) "The role of buying and selling in illicit drug use," in A. S. Trebach, Drugs, Crime and Politics. New York: Praeger.

SMITH, J. P. (1979) "U.S. drug problem—from bad to worse." The Journal (April 1).

SMITH, G. M. and C. P. FOGG (1978) "Psychological predictors of early use, late use, and nonuse among teenage students," in D. B. Kandel (ed.) Longitudinal Research on Drug Use: Empirical Findings and Methodological Issues. New York: John Wiley.

Staten Island Advance (1979) Articles on Smoking Ban on Staten Island Ferry. (June 7, 9, and 12).

4

PSYCHOSOCIAL RESEARCH ON TEENAGE DRINKING
Past and Future

G. NICHOLAS BRAUCHT

INTRODUCTION

During the decade of the 1970s, an unprecedented number of national surveys of American teenagers were conducted, affording extensive knowledge about the distribution and extent of teenage drinking. In addition to this wealth of epidemiological data, the 1970s witnessed a veritable explosion of psychosocial research on teenagers' use of alcohol and other drugs. A number of recent reviews and conceptual/theoretical analyses of this empirical literature have appeared. Several of these have focused exclusively on adolescent drinking (e.g., Barnes, 1977; Blane and Hewitt, 1976; Demone and Wechsler, 1976; O'Connor, 1977; Stacey and Davies, 1970; Walker et al., 1978; Zucker, 1979). Other

AUTHOR'S NOTE: The preparation of this chapter was in part supported by Research Scientist Development Award KO2-AA-00018 and Grant Number AA 01428 from the National Institute on Alcohol Abuse and Alcoholism. The author is indebted to Karen J. Jamieson for her assistance throughout.

reviews have dealt with both teenage drinking and teenage use of illicit drugs (e.g., Braucht et al., 1973; Green, 1979; Kandel, 1978). Finally, other recent articles dealing primarily with illicit drug use have provided highly relevant theoretical/conceptual or methodological contributions (e.g., Gorsuch and Butler, 1976; Sadava, 1975; Jessor, 1979).

In the context of these existing reviews and in light of the limited space available here, the present chapter will not attempt to provide an exhaustive review of the research on teenage drinking. Instead, the aim will be to highlight our current level of knowledge regarding the epidemiology and psychosocial correlates of teenage alcohol use, with an emphasis on the more recent findings. The review is organized by the following headings: (1) epidemiology; (2) environmental correlates; (3) personality correlates; and (4) relationships of drinking to illicit drug use and other problem behaviors. Following these sections, a final section will be devoted to identifying future research needs in terms of emerging methodological, conceptual, and theoretical issues.

EPIDEMIOLOGY OF TEENAGE ALCOHOL USE

· During the decade of the 1970s, estimates of the prevalence of alcohol use in the junior and senior high school aged population of the United States were provided by a number of national household and school surveys. There were five household surveys of the general population aged 12-17, conducted in 1971, 1972, 1973, 1974, 1976, and 1977 (Josephson et al., 1972; Josephson, 1974a, 1974b; Abelson and Atkinson, 1975; Abelson and Fishburne, 1976; and Abelson et al., 1977). The nationwide school-based surveys included the 1974 survey of drinking behavior, attitudes, and correlates among students in grades 7 through 12 (Rachal et al., 1975, 1976) and the series of national surveys of high school seniors carried out in 1975, 1976, and 1977 (Johnston et al., 1977a, 1977b). The review of epidemiological findings below will rely heavily on analyses of data from these surveys.

PREVALENCE OF TEENAGE DRINKING

In comparison to other drugs, the most recent household survey of youth aged 12-17 (Abelson et al., 1977) and the most recent survey of high school seniors (Johnston et al., 1977a) both showed that the lifetime, annual, and 30-day prevalence rates for alcohol use were higher than those rates for *any* other drug, including tobacco. By all of these yardsticks, alcohol has thus been shown to be the most widely used drug among teenagers.

The national household surveys of the teenage population conducted during the 1970s consistently found that slightly over half of all adolescents aged 12-17 reported having used alcohol at some time in their lives. In the 1971, 1972, and 1973 surveys, adolescents interviewed in their homes responded to an anonymous questionnaire (which they sealed in an envelope themselves) which asked a number of drug-use questions, including whether they had ever used alcohol outside of the family setting. In the 1974, 1976, and 1977 surveys, the adolescents were interviewed and asked if they had ever used alcohol (in or out of the family setting). The lifetime prevalence percentages from these six household surveys were: 51 percent in 1971; 50 percent in 1972; 51 percent in 1974; 54 percent in 1976; and 53 percent in 1977. In each of the last three of these national household surveys, slightly less than one-half of the 12-17 year olds reported that they had used alcohol during the past year and about one-third reported some use during the past month (Abelson et al., 1977).

There have also been several recent nationwide surveys of adolescent alcohol use which have been based upon representative samples of junior and senior high school students (Rachal et al., 1975, 1976) or high school seniors (Johnston et al., 1977a, 1977b), rather than representative samples of households. Instead of the face-to-face interview or interview/questionnaire methods of data collection used in the household surveys, these school-based surveys gathered data by means of questionnaires administered to classes or other large groups in the sampled schools. The annual survey of the nation's high school seniors, carried out in 1974, 1976, and 1977 by Johnston et al. (1977a, 1977b) consistently showed that more than nine out of ten high school seniors had tried alcohol and approximately 85 percent had used alcohol during the year preceding the survey. About 70 percent had used it in the previous month, about half reported recent weekly use, and about 6 percent had used alcohol on a daily or nearly daily basis (20 or more occasions) during the previous month.

The 1974 national study of junior and senior high school students' drinking practices, attitudes, and correlates was based on a probability sample of all students in grades 7 through 12 in the 48 contiguous states and the District of Columbia (Rachal et al., 1975, 1976). The data from this survey are particularly rich in detail, including measures of frequency of drinking, quantities drunk, negative consequences of drinking, indices of problem drinking, measures of other drug use, general deviant behavior, and a variety of psychosocial measures (Donovan and Jessor, 1978a).

In terms of frequency of drinking, Rachal et al. found that approximately 23 percent of their total group of 13,021 adolescents reported drinking at least once per week, 32 percent at least once per month but less than once per week, 17 percent less than once per month but more than once per year, 9 percent less than once per year, and 19 percent reported no drinking of beer, wine, or liquor. In terms of quantity drunk, Rachal et al. found that 26 percent of their sample reported drinking one or fewer drinks per drinking occasion, 31 percent reported two to four drinks per occasion, and 24 percent reported drinking five or more drinks per occasion.

Using a combined quantity-frequency index of drinking behavior, Rachal et al. found that about 11 percent of the adolescents drank at least once per week and consumed five or more drinks on the average occasion; an additional 14 percent drank at least once per week and consumed two to four drinks per occasion, *or* drank three to four times per month and five or more drinks per occasion. Harford and Mills (1978) have compared the frequency and quantity data from the adolescents in this survey who reported drinking at least once per month with comparable data from a household survey of Boston adults which was also done in 1974. They found that while the frequency of drinking increases gradually with age well into the adult years, the mean number of drinks consumed per occasion rises to a high of nearly six drinks (males) and over four drinks (females) by age 16-17 and declines thereafter.

PROBLEM DRINKING

Rachal et al., like the Jessors and their colleagues, based their measure of problem drinking on the joint consideration of two factors: (1) the frequency of drunkenness in the past year, and (2) the number of life areas (friends, school, dates, police, driving) in which there were drinking-related negative consequences. Rachal et al. classified subjects who reported drunkenness four or more times in the past year or two or more areas of negative consequences (or both) as problem drinkers. Of their 13,122 subjects, 27.8 percent were so classified as problem drinkers, as compared with 45.0 percent nonproblem drinkers, 9.2 percent minimal drinkers, and 18.6 percent abstainers.

Donovan and Jessor's (1978a) analysis of these data indicated that the use of more stringent criteria for problem drinking of having been drunk at least six times in the past year *or* having experienced negative consequences two or more times in the past year in at least three of the five areas resulted in about 19 percent of the 13,122 adolescents being classified as problem drinkers. Alternatively, a second definition invoked by Donovan and Jessor was based on the frequency of drunkenness alone. Using the criterion of being drunk at least twice a month during the past year, they found that approximately 9.4 percent of the total sample would be classified as problem drinkers. A third definition developed by Donovan and Jessor was based on the negative consequences criterion alone: having experienced drinking-related negative consequences at least twice in any one of the five areas, with at least one such experience in an additional area. By this definition, the problem drinker prevalence rate was 8.9 percent across the total sample.

AGE DIFFERENCES

As implied in the above discussion, the junior high and high school years are ones in which great changes in drinking practices take place. The most recent data available on nationwide samples indicate that, while only about one in six 12-13 year olds reported using alcohol in the past month, about one in two 16-17 year olds had done so (Abelson et al., 1977), and about seven of every ten high school seniors had used alcohol in the past month (Johnston et al., 1977a, 1977b). Rachal et al.'s data (1975) also show that the percentage of students who use alcohol increases dramatically with advancing age, as does the percentage who drink frequently and in large quantities (Harford and Mills, 1978). Perhaps most significantly, the rates of drunkenness and problem drinking among male drinkers in 12th grade have been found to be about seven times the rate among male seventh-grade drinkers, with the corresponding ratio among females being about five to one (Donovan and Jessor, 1978a; Rachal et al., 1975, 1976; Third Special Report to the U.S. Congress on Alcohol and Health, 1978).

SEX DIFFERENCES

Several recent reviews (Blane and Hewitt, 1976; Blum and Richards, 1979; Demone and Wechsler, 1976; Third Special Report to the U.S.

Congress on Alcohol and Health, 1978) and surveys based on local or convenient samples (Wechsler and Thum, 1973; Blackford, 1977; Engs, 1977; Wechsler and McFadden, 1976) have suggested that the historical gap between males and females reported in many earlier studies (e.g., Forsland and Gustafson, 1970; Maddox and McCall, 1964; Straus and Bacon, 1953; Cahalan et al., 1969) is narrowing or has even disappeared.

Data from the recent nationwide household and school-based surveys are all consistent with this argument insofar as minimal or infrequent drinking is concerned—lifetime prevalence and light drinking is only slightly more prevalent among male adolescents. However, it is clear from the recent major surveys that heavier, more frequent, and problem-level drinking practices are much more prevalent among adolescent males than females (Abelson et al., 1977; Johnston et al., 1977a; Donovan and Jessor, 1978a; Wilsnack and Wilsnack, 1978). For example, this pattern of near sexual equality at lower levels of drinking behavior but increasing differences at higher and higher levels is clearly shown in Johnston et al.'s (1977a) survey of high school seniors. By the time of the senior year in high school, the lifetime prevalence figures are nearly equivalent: 94 percent for males and 91 percent for females. However, 78 percent of the male seniors had used alcohol in the month preceding the survey as compared with 65 percent of the female seniors; 29 percent of the male seniors had used alcohol more than 40 times during the year as compared to only 14 percent of the female seniors (Johnston et al., 1977a). Similarly, 15 percent of all males in the nationwide survey of seventh through twelfth graders (Rachal et al., 1975) were classed as heavy drinkers (drinking at least once per week, five or more drinks per occasion) as compared to only 6 percent of the females.

All three alternative definitions of problem drinking which Donovan and Jessor (1978a) applied to Rachal's data resulted in ratios of approximately three male drinkers for every two female problem drinkers in their total sample of seventh through twelfth graders. Although quite a different criterion for problem drinking was used, Globetti (1972) has also found more high school males than females to be problem drinkers. Finally, analyses of Rachal et al.'s data by grade in school revealed that while approximately equal percentages of both male and female seventh graders (5 percent and 4 percent) were classed as problem drinkers, approximately twice as many twelfth-grade boys as girls (40 percent versus 21 percent) were classed as problem drinkers (Donovan and Jessor, 1978a; Third Special Report to the U.S. Congress on Alcohol and Health, 1978).

OTHER DIFFERENCES

In addition to the age and sex differences outlined above, teenage drinking varies according to several other demographic variables. When one considers the whole teenage group, there is substantial agreement that the South has the lowest lifetime prevalence rate and also the fewest heavy drinkers while the Northeast and North Central regions' rates are highest (Abelson et al., 1977; Rachal et al., 1976). Although regional differences in alcohol use were not reported in the most recent survey of young men (O'Donnel et al., 1976), this finding is similar to Cahalan et al.'s (1969) older national study of young adult men. In addition, current drinking rates are positively correlated with level of urbanicity, both among the inclusive group of 12-17 year olds (Abelson et al., 1977) and among high school seniors (Johnston et al., 1977a).

Among high school seniors, the prevalence of weekly use of alcohol is slightly lower among those who are planning on four years of college than among those who are not college-bound (19 percent versus 24 percent). This slight differential increases with increasing levels of drinking, so that daily drinking is only half as prevalent among the college-bound as it is among those not planning on college (4 percent versus 8 percent; Johnston et al., 1977a).

Rachal et al.'s (1975) data also show that there are some noteworthy ethnic group differences in teenage drinking. In the total sample of seventh to twelfth graders, whites had the lowest percentage of abstainers and blacks had the highest; about twice as many whites as blacks were heavy drinkers. In Donovan and Jessor's (1978a) analyses of these data, problem-drinking rates (by their primary definition) were far lower for blacks than for whites, Spanish Americans, or American Indians; these ethnic group differences were particularly striking among males. Ethnic group differences have also been reported by others (Riester and Zucker, 1968; Brunswick and Tarica, 1974) but disputed by some others (Cahalan et al., 1969; Globetti and McReynolds, 1964).

TRENDS IN PREVALENCE OF DRINKING

The interpretation of some of the cross-sectional differences noted above are complicated by the fact that teenage drinking appears to have increased slightly over the past decade. Although this recent trend is not nearly as marked as the longer-term increases suggested by some (e.g., Blane and Hewitt, 1976; Engs, 1977; Third Special Report to the U.S. Congress, 1978), there are several indications that more and more adolescents are having their first drink and starting to drink regularly at younger ages as time goes on (Abelson et al., 1977; Kandel et al., 1976; Blackford, 1977). For example, Blackford's (1977) summary of the series of annual school surveys in San Mateo, California, shows that in 1969, 11 percent of the seventh-grade boys reported using alcohol in the past six months as compared to 23 percent in 1977. This trend of earlier onset has been particularly noted among teenage girls in both national (Johnston et al., 1977a) and local surveys (Demone and Wechsler, 1976).

CAUTIONS AND SUMMARY

Because of such past trends, as well as potential present and future ones, the reader is cautioned against interpreting cross-sectional survey results in a longitudinal sense. It should be clearly recognized that (for example) a difference between the problem-drinking rates of seventh graders and twelfth graders in any given survey may reflect generational effects, maturational effects, or both. There are also a number of other difficulties which may arise in interpreting the results of surveys such as those reviewed here. An outstanding example of one kind of problem may be found in the data presented by Abelson et al. (1977).

Abelson et al. (1977: 97) summarized their data on current drinking for the years 1972-1977 in these terms, "Making comparisons across time, current drinking among youth rose from 24 percent in 1972 to 34 percent in 1974 and has remained remarkably stable since then (1976—32.4 percent; 1977—31.2 percent)." Referring to Abelson and

TABLE 4.1 Current Drinking Among White and Nonwhite Youth
Aged 12-17: 1972-1977

	1972	1974	1976	1977
White	24%	37%	34%	33%
Nonwhite	19	21	23	23
All youth: age 12–17	24	34	32.4	31.2

SOURCE: From Abelson et al. (1977: 110, Table 77).

Fishburne (1976), Green (1979) interpreted the 1972-1976 data in the first two rows of Table 4.1 as follows: "The disparity between drinking rates in whites and non-whites was shown to be related to a much steeper rise in the use of alcohol by white youth in recent years (Abelson and Fishburne, 1976). Between 1972 and 1975/76 current drinkers increased by nearly 50 percent in white youth but by less than 25 percent in non-white."

Apparently overlooked by the authors of these survey findings, however, was a crucially important difference in the way "current drinking" was defined in 1972 as compared with the way it was defined in 1974, 1976, and 1977. In their glossary of key terms, Abelson et al. (1977: 8) state the meaning of "current drinker" as follows: "1977, 1976, 1974: Drank in past month. 1972: Drank in past seven days." In this light Abelson et al.'s statement that current drinking among youth rose from 1972 to 1974 is certainly a careless one which could easily lead others into erroneous interpretations.

It can also be seen how Green's overlooking of this critical definitional change, or her misplaced reliance on the summary conclusion of the survey's primary authors (Abelson and Fishburne, 1976) also lead her into serious misinterpretations of these data. Leaving aside the 1972 figures in Table 4.1, the 1974-1977 figures (or the 1974-1976 data which Green was examining) show that, if anything, the rate of current drinking among whites *declined* very slightly while the rate among nonwhites *increased* very slightly—a trend directly opposite to that identified by Green (1979). This example merely illustrates the need for extreme care in comparing the results of one survey with another and shows how illusory apparent trends may be upon close examination. Because these kinds of data and their interpretation often have major policy implications (for programs of research, prevention, treatment, and legislation, for example), it should be clear that the greatest possible specificity and care in analysis and interpretation is required.

With these caveats, the above review of the epidemiological evidence *does* show that alcohol is the most widely used drug among teenagers and that its use in this age group is markedly patterned by age. There are also some notable differences in distribution and extent of drinking by sex (particularly at the heavier drinking levels), ethnicity, region of the country, urbanicity, and between those teenagers who plan on four years of college versus those who do not. With this epidemiological perspective, we now turn to a review of psychosocial correlates of teenage drinking.

PERSONALITY CORRELATES OF TEENAGE DRINKING

In a review of older research (Braucht et al., 1973), a summary of the personality correlates of adolescent problem drinkers prominently featured the characteristics of aggressiveness, impulsiveness, low self-esteem, high anxiety, depression, and a general lack of success in the attainment of life goals. Because most of the work which Braucht et al. (1973) reviewed was based on college-aged youth, it is worthwhile to examine more recent evidence for these kinds of characteristics from younger samples.

Some of this more recent research has seemed to corroborate the presence of psychopathology-like characteristics among teenage drinkers. For example, Wechsler and Thum (1973) have found more personal problems among their sample of heavier drinkers. In a very different sample of black youth in Harlem Brunswick and Tarica (1974) also found that both personal worries and symptoms of anxiety characterized drinkers of both sexes. In yet a third setting, markedly different from both of those above, Globetti (1972) found that problem drinkers were alienated from important social groups such as their families and churches. In general, however, the bulk of the more recent research on junior/senior high school aged youth suggests that personality variables with more psychopathological connotations do not play significant roles in the development of teenage drinking behaviors. For example, Kandel and her colleagues (1978) have failed to find significant relationships between hard liquor use onset and these kinds of variables (including indices of depression, normlessness, self-image, and personality growth). Similarly, Jessor and Jessor (1977: 98) found that frequency of drunkenness was not significantly related to their measures of alienation, self-esteem, or internal-external control locus. These psychopathologically oriented variables aside, recent research on junior and senior high school samples has shown that certain kinds of personality variables are consistently but not strongly related to drinking. In the brief review which follows, these personality characteristics will be identified and the strength of their relationship to drinking behavior will be assessed relative to other classes of influence.

In their analyses of individual, environmental, and behavioral factors associated with adolescent initiation into progressive states of drug use, Kandel and her colleagues (1976, 1978) studied a panel of 1936 New York state secondary school students who were all nonusers of hard liquor at the beginning of their longitudinal study. Six months later, 30 percent of them had started to use hard liquor. Kandel et al. found that initiation into use of hard liquor was not significantly associated with individual differences in intrapsychic states, attitudes, values, or beliefs, with the exception that the specific belief that liquor is harmful was negatively related at a statistically significant but low level ($r = -.12$) to entry into hard liquor use. In contrast, individual differences in prior behaviors, including minor delinquency, cutting classes, participation in political activities, and the use of beer, wine, and tobacco were more important predictors of starting to drink. By itself, a cluster of these behavioral characteristics accounted for over ten times the proportion of variance accounted for by the beliefs/values cluster alone. Parental and peer influence were also more powerful as predictors, accounting for four times and seven times more variance, respectively, as personality values and beliefs (Kandel et al., 1978: 90). In this study, however, none of these four clusters of variables accounted for much variance in the criterion of initiation into hard liquor use; the strongest single cluster (the behavioral cluster) accounted for only 15.6 percent of the variance and a linear combination of all four clusters accounted for only 20.7 percent.

This general pattern of low associations between personality factors and drinking behavior in adolescence is also illustrated in' a carefully done recent study of Canadian high school males reported by Schlegel et al. (1977). These authors examined the utility of a model of drinking behavior in differing situational contexts. Their model assumed actual drinking behavior to be a function of the intention to drink, where the intention to drink was hypothesized to be a function of individuals' attitudes toward drinking and their normative beliefs that others expect them to engage in drinking. Schlegel et al. were able to demonstrate that reported *intentions* to drink were indeed associated with the hypothesized attitudes and beliefs at impressive levels. Attitudes and beliefs typically accounted for over 50 percent of the variance in the intention to drink criterion, regardless of the type of alcohol (beer, wine, or liquor) or type of situation (at home, at a party, or at a pub). However, the measure of intention to drink was related at a very low level with a later self-report of actual drinking. Averaged across the nine correlations (three alcohol types by three situations), their measure of actual drinking behavior shared only 11 percent of its variance with their measure of intention to drink. Reasoning that a number of extraneous factors might have prevented subjects under 18 years old (88 percent of their subjects) from actually drinking even if they intended to do so, Schlegel et al. also calculated the mean correlation for those 18 or over (N = 15). In this case 22 percent of the variance in the measure of intention to drink and the subsequent self-report drinking measure was shared.

This example shows that individual differences in adolescents' attitudes and beliefs bear only a weak linear relationship to their drinking behavior, however strongly they might be related to other cognitive variables (i.e., intentions). In fact, even the low-magnitude relationship between intention and behavior found by Schlegel et al. must be viewed with considerable caution, as it is not implausible that any systematic individual differences in reporting biases which were influencing their subjects' reports of intentions, attitudes, and beliefs may have similarly influenced their self-reports of drinking behavior. Any such biases (e.g., social desirability) would result in spuriously inflated correlations between intentions to drink and drinking behavior. In such a case, drinking behavior data from an independent source(s) might relate even less strongly to intention. Despite sanguine assessments of the validity of self-report data in this kind of research (e.g., Smart, 1975), the possibility of spuriously high relationships cannot be ruled out in any empirical research which depends exclusively on individuals' self-reports (as is essentially all of the research in this review).

In their four-year longitudinal study of the development of problem behavior in youth, Jessor and Jessor (1975) examined personality, perceived environmental, and behavioral variables as they related to the development of drinking behavior. They analyzed their data on drinking onset in two ways: (1) predicting the timing of the onset of drinking from data collected at the beginning of their four-year study; and (2) comparing groups of adolescents who made the transition from abstainer to drinker status at various times on measures collected at the end of the study. In both sorts of analyses, five groups of junior/senior high school students were compared: (1) those who had already become drinkers by the first year of their study; (2) those who made the transition from abstainer to drinker status in the second year; (3) those who made the transition in the third year; (4) those who made the transition in the final year; and (5) those who remained abstainers throughout the study.

Several of their personality measures collected at year one were significantly predictive of the timing of onset. Those who made the earlier transitions to drinker status generally placed lower value on achievement, placed higher value on independence relative to achievement, had lower expectations of achievement, were more tolerant of deviance, had lower religiosity scores, and endorsed fewer negative functions (reasons) for not drinking.

Using the same five types of onset groups but examining personality measures collected in year four, Jessor and Jessor found that all of the above personality variables were significantly related to time of onset. In addition, the five groups were shown to differ on two additional personality measures: value on independence and alienation (both were generally higher for those making the earlier transitions). In general, the relationships between groups differing in time of onset and the year-four personality measures (postdictive or concurrent correlate relationships) were stronger than relationships involving year-one measure (predictive relationships). It should be noted, however, that the means of the five transition groups did not "order" perfectly on these eight personality measures. On both the year-one and year-four data, only three of the eight variables did so while five did not.

In later analyses of these data, Jessor and Jessor (1977) showed that several of the personality variables were correlated with the number of times the adolescents reported being drunk during the past year (year-four data). For both sexes, being drunk more often was significantly related to lower value on academic achievement, higher tolerance for deviance, more positive relative to negative functions (reasons) for drinking, and more positive relative to negative functions for drug use.

In their tests of year-four personality differences between drinkers and *problem* drinkers, however, the Jessors (1977: Chapter 5) found that the two groups differed for both males and females on only the tolerance of deviance measure (problem drinkers were more tolerant), the positive-negative drinking functions measure, and a similar positive-negative functions disjunctions measure regarding sexual behavior, another of their problem behaviors. The later report (1977) also showed that only 14.4 percent of the variance in problem drinker status (a dichotomous variable) was accounted for by a multiple linear combination of the measures in their personality system (averaged across year-three and year-four data), excluding the positive-negative functions disjunctions.

Thus, the Jessors's program of research has shown that teenage abstainers differ from drinkers on a number of personality variables. The pattern of these variables is clearly suggestive of a syndrome reflecting personal unconventionality or nonconformity. They have also shown that the drinkers' pattern of personality characteristics represents a later developmental level than the abstainers' pattern—more so for those who became drinkers earlier than later. They cautiously interpreted these findings as being consonant with the conclusion of Stacey and Davies's earlier review (1970: 210), "Consumption of alcohol at a very early age . . . may . . . indicate mere precocity in development." In view of the care with which these data were collected and analyzed (e.g., the multivariate analyses were replicated across sexes, across sex by grade cohorts, and so on), and the fact that similar results were found for other problem behaviors, their findings must be viewed as rather well established ones, at least within the limits of their sample, the period in which their study took place, and other constraints of their approach (see Jessor and Jessor, 1977: 232-235).

In their analyses of adolescent problem drinking in a national sample study, Donovan and Jessor (1978a) found statistically significant differences between problem and nonproblem drinkers on all eight of their personality measures. These differences, all in the expected direction, were statistically significant among both males and females and across all three of their problem drinker definitions (the sole exception: a nonsignificant difference on independence value for both males and females by their third alternative definition of problem drinking). However, only about 10 percent of the variance in the problem-drinking criterion was accounted for by a linear combination of four personality variables (10.6 percent for males and 10.1 percent for females). This set of personality measures accounted for a greater percentage of the variance in the criterion of number of times drunk in the past year (13.9 percent for males and 15.1 percent for females), but an even lower percentage of the variance in the criterion of drinking-related consequences (6.6 percent for males and 6.3 percent for females). Thus, although Donovan and Jessor's large sample sizes enabled tests involving all of their personality factors to attain statistical significance, their personality measures accounted for a small portion of the variance in their key problem-drinking measures—typically less than half as much as their environmental measures. Balanced against this, however, is the fact that either tolerance for deviance or expectations for academic achievement was a significant variable (third to be entered in their stepwise regression) in predicting times drunk among male ethnic subsamples. These variables played an even stronger role among female subsamples in general, and among black and Asian American females in particular. In view of their large national sample, Donovan and Jessor's findings must be viewed as extremely credible evidence that a number of relatively enduring individual difference (personality) variables are associated at a rather low level with problem drinking among the junior/senior high school population of this country, and that they are somehow differentially salient in various sex-ethnic subpopulations.

ENVIRONMENTAL CORRELATES OF TEENAGE DRINKING

Most investigators regard the acquisition of drinking behavior as a developmental phenomenon which starts in the home for the majority of youths and then progresses to a more peer-controlled context. However, as Zucker (1976) observed, there have been few efforts to conceptually outline the pathways by which parental influence systematically produces differences in children's drinking patterns. Zucker's heuristic model delineates a six-level process of indirect and direct parental and family influences. The first level includes traditional socioeconomic and sociocultural influences which are considered to be transmitted via the behavior, ideology, and values of the parents. The second and third levels focus on the parents as an interacting dyad and as separate individuals, respectively. The fourth level considers peer effects while the fifth level is concerned with the child's personality. Finally, the child's actual drinking behavior comprises the sixth level of Zucker's model. Within this framework, Zucker and associates (Zucker and Barron, 1973; Zucker and De Voe, 1975) have examined the influences of familial environment in general and parental characteristics and behavior on adolescent drinking behavior. Zucker and Barron (1973) examined the familial environment of adolescent males. Compared to other parents, both mothers and fathers of heavier-drinking and problem-drinking boys were found to be heavier drinkers themselves, were more antisocial, and utilized social isolation and deprivation as disciplinary techniques. Father's worries about his own drinking were negatively related to his son's problem drinking whereas mother's worries were positively related. These results, however, were based on data collected from the parents and stand in contrast to the adolescent's reports. Although the parent reports indicate mother-father similarity in treatment of the adolescent, the heavier-drinking boys see their mothers as less often present but neutral figures. They see their fathers in a highly negative perspective, as being emotionally distant and unrewarding and uncaring about their son's achievements.

The pattern of parent-child relationships and drinking behavior of adolescent females has also been investigated (Zucker and DeVoe, 1975). The girls' heavier drinking was related to several maternal characteristics and behavior patterns. Mothers of heavier-drinking girls were heavier drinkers themselves, were characterized as having an aggressive sociability personality style, and utilized social isolation and little praise or affection to shape behavior. Fathers' physical absence and drinking problems were related to daughters' heavier drinking. Thus, heavier drinking among girls is related to a family pattern of psychological or physical parental absence. The only difference between families of heavier-drinking versus problem-drinking girls is that problem-drinking girls see their fathers as using more effective punishment. Thus, these studies found the family environments of problem drinkers to be marked by harsher and more negative, tension-filled interactions and lacking parental involvement.

Zucker (1979) suggests that the above findings and those of Jessor et al. (1968) all point to major disturbances in three areas of families of adolescent problem drinkers: (1) parental deviance in personal behavior and heavier drinking; (2) parental disinterest and lack of involvement; and (3) lack of positive parent-child interaction, affection, and nurturance. Zucker considers these kinds of familial environmental conditions to have an indirect influence on later adolescent drinking behavior, persuasively arguing that evidence from other research (e.g., Alexander and Campbell, 1967; Kandel, 1973) suggests that later drinking is more directly influenced by peer behavior.

Prendergast and Schaefer (1974) investigated the importance and interrelations of three mechanisms through which parental influence might be exerted on adolescent drinking. They described these mechanisms as: (1) parents as models; (2) parents as educators; and (3) parents as sources of general support for adolescent problems. In a sample of middle-class high school students, Prendergast and Schaefer found there was a slight tendency for more frequent drinking by mothers or fathers to be correlated with more frequent adolescent drinking. These findings, however, were not statistically significant and variables which measured the parent-child relationship were better predictors of frequency of drinking or drunkenness. After controlling for parents' drinking behavior, lax maternal control and perceived rejection and psychological tension in the relationship with the father accounted for 46 percent of the variance in frequency of adolescent drinking. Lax maternal control and perceived paternal rejection also accounted for 34 percent of the variance of frequency of drunkenness. There was no indication that parents' attitudes toward drugs were significantly related to adolescent drinking or drunkenness. Thus, Prendergast and Schaefer found disturbances in two of the three areas of family disturbance suggested by Zucker (1979).

Kandel and her colleagues (1976, 1978) focused on what Zucker defined as third- and fourth-level variables. A guiding assumption in the research by Kandel et al. has been that acquisition of behaviors is in large part determined by the matrix of social relationships in which individuals are embedded and that it is crucial to consider the influence of various aspects of this matrix simultaneously. Kandel et al. (1978) analyzed the relative influence of parents and peers and the extent which these two sources of influence overlap with respect to initiation into use of hard liquor. They found that parents influence initiation into hard liquor use primarily by acting as role models. Both fathers' and mothers' use of hard liquor were more strongly related than either parental attitudes regarding the harmful consequences of hard liquor use or their emphasis on rules against legal drug use. The importance of parental modeling is underscored by their data showing that 81 percent of families in which both parents drank produced children who drank while, conversely, 72 percent of the families in which the parents abstained had children who were abstainers. Moreover, while Smart and Fejer (1972) had found a positive relationship between teenagers' perceptions of parental use of alcohol and psychoactive drugs, Kandel et al., reported that it was the parents' use of distilled spirits specifically that was imitated rather than general propensity to take drugs. Parenthetically, some similar results reported by Forslund and Gustafson (1970) suggest that specificity of imitation of drinking behavior includes consideration of parent sex. Forslund and Gustafson found that mothers' drinking was correlated with that of both sons and daughters while fathers' drinking was correlated only with daughters' drinking.

Kandel et al. also found that the behaviors of peers were important in predicting use of hard liquor. The most important variable in predicting onset of hard liquor use was the degree of adolescent involvement in peer activities such as getting together with friends, dating, attending parties, or driving around. Perceptions of how many friends used hard liquor, an independent datum regarding friends' actual hard liquor use, and best-friend attitudes about the harmfulness of hard liquor were more powerful predictors than perceptions of friends' use of other legal drugs. Kandel suggested that the relative predictive powers of the various indicators of peer behaviors indicate that drug use in the peer group as a whole may be a more important source of influence than use by a single friend. Kandel et al. concluded that parental and peer influences on adolescent initiation into hard liquor use exert themselves in similar ways. Both exert modeling effects and a cognitive restraining effect. Additionally, they concluded that involvement in peer activities has a significant nonspecific effect associated with beginning use of hard liquor. In their analysis of the relative influence of peers and parents, Kandel et al. found that peer influences accounted for nearly twice as much variance as parental influences in the hard liquor onset criterion.

In further analyses of the onset of drinking, Margulies et al. (1977) found that peers' use of alcohol and illicit drugs and paternal drinking predicted onset in girls but not boys. They reported that parent and peer influences had three times more influence on females than males for onset of drinking. In contrast, while neither parental nor peer influences were too important for males, attitudes, involvement in politics, and delinquency were two to four times more important for males than females. In an analysis which included both sexes, the influence of peers was increasingly more powerful at older ages, while parental influence remained at essentially equivalent levels throughout the high school years.

In an earlier study, Alexander and Campbell (1967) provided more detailed data on the interactions between attempted parental restraint of alcohol use and peer modeling. They found that when parents disapproved of adolescent drinking and no peers drank, only 12 percent of the youths used alcohol extensively. Despite parental disapproval, 66 percent drank when two or more peers drank. In contrast, 43 percent drank when parental attitude was neutral and no friends drank whereas 89 percent drank when parental attitude was neutral and more than two friends drank. Forslund and Gustafson (1970) also found that parental pressures had little effect in discouraging drinking when peer pressure was high.

In examining predictions of the onset of drinking from antecedent perceived environmental variables in their four-year longitudinal study, Jessor and Jessor (1975) found that timing of onset was significantly related to parental support (a distal measure not specific to drinking), to parental and friends' approval of drinking, and to friends' models for drinking. Those who remained abstainers throughout the study perceived themselves to be in an environment that provided the least approval and opportunity for drinking—lowest parents' and friends' approval of and lowest friends' models for drinking—in contrast to those who made the earliest transition and scored highest on these variables. Friends' models for drinking was the only year-one variable that showed a perfect rank ordering for the five time-of-onset groups.

The Jessors's analyses of data collected in year four revealed that all the variables that had been significant in predicting timing on onset in year one maintained significance. As was true in their analysis of personality variables, the year-four results were generally stronger than year-one results; in year four, an additional variable—parents-friends compatibility—also reached significance in discriminating between the groups (generally lower for groups which had made earlier transition to drinking status).

In further analyses of their high school data, Jessor and Jessor (1977) found that several perceived environmental variables were related to problem drinking. Less compatibility between parents' and friends' expectations, greater friends' than parents' influence, less parental disapproval, and greater perceived prevalence of models for problem behavior among friends and peers were related to problem-drinker status. A multiple linear combination of these perceived environment variables accounted for 22.1 percent and 20.5 percent of the variance in problem-drinking status for males and females, respectively (averaged over year-three and year-four relationships; see Jessor and Jessor, 1977: 135).

Perceived environment variables were also consistently significant as discriminators between problem and non-problem drinkers in Donovan and Jessor's national sample study (1978a). The differences between these two groups were significant for males and females and across all three definitions of problem drinkers for all environmental measures except for the family models for drinking variable. Similar to the findings reported above, Donovan and Jessor reported that problem drinkers perceived less compatibility between their friends' and parents' expectations, attributed relatively more influence to their friends rather than parents, and perceived more positive models and approval of drinking than did non-problem drinkers. Among females, a set of five perceived environment variables accounted for a greater percentage of variance in predicting problem drinking status (20 percent), number of times drunk (31.8 percent), and total number of negative consequences of drinking (11.5 percent) than a set of personality variables (10.1 percent, 15.1 percent, and 6.3 percent, respectively). Among males, the corresponding percentages for the set of environmental variables were 21.7 percent, 30.9 percent, and 14.5 percent, as compared to 10.6 percent, 13.9 percent, and 6.6 percent for the set of personality variables. Additionally, when the two sets of predictors were combined, the stepwise multiple regressions revealed that the environmental measures had greater predictive power than the personality measures. In the regression predicting problem-drinker status, friends' models for marihuana use and friends' models for drinking entered the equation before any of the three personality system measures. Donovan and Jessor suggested that the greater strength of the environmental variables was probably due to the fact that the personality variables were more distal and referred to fairly generalized attitudes, values, and expectations while the environmental variables were more proximal and were concerned with variables directly implicating adolescent drinking. Personality system variables, however, appeared to play a stronger role in predicting number of times drunk in female ethnic subsamples.

Jessor and associates (Jessor and Jessor, 1975, 1977; Donovan and Jessor, 1978a) interpreted their findings as consistent with a general developmental trend away from conventionality over the teenage years (irrespective of alcohol use or other problem behaviors). This pattern (also apparent in their analysis of personality variables) was manifested in the perceived environment system by developmental changes toward less parent-friend compatibility and greater friends' relative to parents' influence. These findings suggest that young problem drinkers have loosened the ties with parents and are oriented more toward their peers than non-problem drinkers. Donovan and Jessor (1978a) concluded that problem drinkers perceive greater approval, models, and pressure for drinking than the non-problem drinkers, thus experiencing more social support and probably more opportunity for drinking.

Within a canonical correlation analysis strategy, Huba et al. (1979) recently examined the relationships between the use of five classes of drugs and (five) social interaction dimensions among a large sample of seventh to ninth graders in Los Angeles. They found a canonical variate defined by frequent use of beer, wine, and liquor to be related to a canonical social interaction variate defined by knowing many adults who drink, frequently getting together with friends, driving around with friends, having friends who were not liked by one's parents, having friends who drink, and having many friends who function as suppliers of alcohol. In contrast, their first canonical drug-use variate (on which there were high loadings for the use of marihuana and hashish) was related to a canonical social interaction variate on which high loadings were found for knowing many marihuana-using adults and peers, attending many parties, having many friends who use beer or wine, and being supplied with cigarettes, beer, wine, and marihuana by friends.

Huba et al. (1979: 273, 265) interpreted their findings as evidence for "drug-specific interactional nets formed by adolescent substance users" such that "users of various classes of substances associated with other individuals who use the same substances." Their interpretations, however, must be tempered by at least one important caveat. Huba et al. analyzed their data in a sophisticated way, but interpreted their results without regard for the degree of correlation across classes of substances. Put another way, they neglected to consider an unknown degree of overlap among their subjects: i.e., What proportion of their subjects reported using more than one class of substances? As a recent analysis has shown (Donovan and Jessor, 1978b), the degree of such overlap is of a very high magnitude indeed: Of the adolescents in their nationwide sample who were users of marihuana or hashish, 97.4 percent were also current drinkers and 40 percent of the drinkers were users of marihuana or hashish. In view of this problem, and also in view of their particular use of canonical analysis (which was explicitly designed to maximally distinguish the use and correlates of independent classes of substances from each other), their interpretations were not warranted. In particular, the implication that there are a number of distinct, drug-specific social interactional networks formed by distinct, nonoverlapping groups of young teenage users and their associates (i.e., that there is no single drug-use subculture among users at this age) was simply not addressed by their analysis.

Smart et al. (1978) investigated the relationship between a variety of social-environment variables and alcohol use, frequency of drinking, average alcohol consumption, drinking highs, and frequency of drunkenness for a sample of over 1400 Canadian high school students. Variables contributing most to a linear equation predicting frequency of drinking were extent of alcohol use, drinking in cars, drinking milieu, mothers' drinking, and age. These five variables accounted for 27.1

percent of the variance in drinking frequency. Extent of alcohol use, drinking in cars, drinking milieu, sex, and type of alcoholic beverage accounted for 34.7 percent of the variance in alcohol consumption. A similar set of variables—extent of alcohol use, drinking in cars, drinking milieu, and parents' knowledge of alcohol use—explained 30.1 percent of the variance in drinking highs. Finally, extent of alcohol use, drinking in cars, and parents' knowledge accounted for 29 percent of the variance in frequency of drunkenness.

While the percentage of variance accounted for across the five dependent measures of drinking behavior was greater than other studies have reported for social-environment variables, consideration of the particular variables utilized may explain this discrepancy. Extent of alcohol use, drinking in cars, and drinking milieu were responsible for most of the variance accounted for in four of the five dependent measures. These variables are clearly (merely) correlates of drinking behavior and certainly do not have any predictive power for identifying environmental variables which appear to influence progression from casual to problem drinking. Variables which are more useful in these respects, such as mothers' and fathers' drinking, were related only to Smart et al.'s dichotomous measure of alcohol use. Parenthetically, the relative importance of parental modeling effects can be understood within the more extensive conceptualization and empirical investigations of Jessor, Kandel, Zucker, and their colleagues. In sum, the results found by Smart et al. serve to underscore the importance of using a theoretical framework to guide the selection of variables in any empirical study.

RELATIONSHIPS OF DRINKING TO ILLICIT DRUG USE AND OTHER PROBLEM BEHAVIORS

At every level of experience with alcohol, drinking among teenagers has been found to be related to their use of illicit drugs. In their four-year longitudinal study of junior/senior high school students, Jessor and Jessor (1975) found that the precocity with which the abstainer-drinker transition was made was directly related to subsequent marihuana use (as well as sexual intercourse and problem drinking). For all three of these behaviors, the percentage of students who reported the behavior (at the end of the study) was highest among students who made the transition earliest. Among students who made the transition to drinking at successively later times, fewer and fewer students reported the three other behaviors; the percentage was lowest among the students who had remained nondrinkers through the end of their study. A number of others have also found sizable relationships between the use of illicit drugs and whether, how often, or how much teenagers drink (Block and Goodman, 1978; Braucht, 1974; Donovan and Jessor, 1978a; Jessor et al., 1973; Johnston, 1973; Kandel, 1975, 1978; Kandel and Faust, 1975; Kandel et al., 1976, 1978; Margulies et al., 1977; National Commission on Marijuana and Drug Abuse, 1972; Prendergast and Schaefer, 1974; Single et al., 1974; Tennant et al., 1975; Wechsler, 1976; Wechsler and Thum, 1973; Whitehead and Cabral, 1975; Zucker and Barron, 1973; Zucker and De Voe, 1975).

In view of this abundant evidence that alcohol and drug use are associated behaviors, a considerable amount of recent attention has also been given to the *order* in which teenagers first experience alcohol vis-à-vis their initial experience with other drugs. Based on their analyses of New York state high school students, Kandel and her colleagues (Kandel, 1975, 1978; Kandel et al., 1978; Single et al., 1974) have suggested that there are at least four progressive stages of drug use: (1) use of beer and/or wine is a necessary first step; followed by (2) cigarettes or hard liquor; (3) marihuana; and (4) other illicit drugs.

More recently, Donovan and Jessor's (1978b) analysis of nationwide data from a 1974 survey has shown that illicit drug use was almost nonexistent among seventh to twelfth graders who were not drinkers; better than 97 percent of those who used illicit drugs in their massive sample were also current drinkers. With regard to marihuana use, for example, they found that only 1 percent of their abstainers, 6 percent of their minimal drinkers, 28 percent of their current non-problem drinkers, and 77 percent of the problem drinkers had used marihuana. Thus, they found problem drinkers to be almost 3 times as likely as current drinkers, 12 times as likely as minimal drinkers, and about 75 times as likely as abstainers to be users of marihuana. In other analyses involving problem drinking, marihuana use, and illicit drugs other than marihuana, Donovan and Jessor (1978b) persuasively suggest that not only is the use of alcohol a prerequisite to marihuana use (as Kandel and her colleagues have shown), but also that *problem* drinking may be a prerequisite to the use of other illicit drugs such as psychedelics, amphetamines, barbiturates, cocaine, and heroin. As they recognize, because their analyses were based on cross-sectional data, a conclusive test of this hypothesis will require longitudinal data.

A number of recent investigators have also found significant relationships between antisocial or delinquent behavior and teenage drinking, particularly at the heavier levels of drinking (Braucht, 1974; Demone, 1973; Donovan and Jessor, 1978a; Globetti, 1972; Jessor and Jessor, 1977; Johnston, 1973; Stacey and Davies, 1970; Wechsler and Thum, 1973; Zucker and Barron, 1973; and Zucker and De Voe, 1975). In addition to being related to delinquent/antisocial behavior, illicit drug use, and sexual behavior, teenage drinking has also been found to be related to (poor) school performance (e.g., Braucht, 1974; Donovan and Jessor, 1978a; Jessor and Jessor, 1975), to problem behavior in the classroom (Braucht, 1974), to number of classes cut (Kandel et al., 1978), and to be more prevalent among dropouts (Mandell et al., 1962).

In their recent article, Huba et al. (1979) reached conclusions contrary to all those reviewed in this section. Referring to the work of the Jessor and Jessor (1977) and Kandel (1975), Huba et al. (1979) reported data which they considered germane to the related issues of whether teenage drinking is associated with "global social deviance" and thus, whether teenage drinking (and/or other drug use) may appropriately be studied from a multidimensional deviance theory perspective. For example, Huba et al. reported that the average absolute bivariate correlate between their 13 substance-use variables and friends' use and supply characteristics was .257, compared to .162 with adult models variables and only .086 with generalized interaction indicators. They thereupon concluded that these last-mentioned generalized interaction indicators (which they considered to be indicative of "global social deviance or nonconventionality," "atypical social interactions," and "maladaptive, antiachievement social patterns") shared little variance with drug use and thus did not provide any evidence for deviance-oriented viewpoints (1979: 274).

Unfortunately, almost none of the particular 22 variables which Huba et al. chose as generalized indicators of global deviance, unconventionality, or social problem behavior bears any relationship at all to these constructs. For example, it is not clear how the frequency (high *or* low) of calling friends to discuss homework, listening to records with friends, reading for pleasure, getting together with friends outside of school, or telling parents about friends (and vice versa) is related to unconventional, nonconforming, and/or deviant behavior. In this regard, it is worth noting that Huba et al. provided no rationale for their blanket criterion of a high *absolute* correlation (of these and other similar variables with drug use) as indicative of unconventionality and/or deviance. In light of this lack of face (or other) validity, the reasoning which Huba et al. presented regarding these issues is considerably less than compelling. It is also worth noting that in their attempt to isolate differential (drug-specific) social interaction patterns, Huba et al. noted (1979: Note 4) that they could not reject the possibility of a single, progressive continuum of drug use among adolescents.

With the exception of the study by Huba et al. (1979) and the additional exception that teenage problem drinking has not been found to be significantly related to activist or protest behaviors, the studies reviewed above have shown teenage problem drinking to be related to an array of behavioral correlates which is fully consistent with those which Jessor's recent review (1979) found to be related to marihuana use. There seems to be a general syndrome of unconventional, nonconforming, social *problem* behaviors among a select group of teenagers in which problem drinking, marihuana and other illicit drug use, precocious sexual behavior, delinquent behavior, and other antisocial behavior patterns are component parts.

PRESENT KNOWLEDGE AND FUTURE RESEARCH NEEDS

During the last decade there has been an increasing quantity of increasingly high-quality research on teenage drinking and drug use. More and more studies of teenage drinking are now appearing which feature some or all of the following desirable characteristics (of course, not all of these are necessarily desirable for a given research task): (1) theory-based, theory-testing research; (2) multivariate assessment of individual, environmental, and behavioral constructs; (3) large-scale, carefully drawn samples—some national in scope; (4) longitudinal research designs appropriate for testing developmental theory; and (5) the use of sophisticated multivariate data analysis procedures.

This review has shown that this kind of quality research has yielded a rich harvest of knowledge; we now know a good deal about teenage drinking and its correlates. In broad brush outline, we know that drinking is widespread among teenagers and poses an immediate problem for 10 percent to 20 percent of them. During the teenage years, there are differential probabilities of problem drinking within different age, sex, and ethnic groups.

We also know that drinking and problem drinking is associated with a number of parental, peer group, and other perceived environmental influences. A number of personality characteristics which are (also) consistent with a trend away from conformity are also related at somewhat lower levels. Finally, there are now converging lines of evidence which suggest that problem drinking is a significant part of a syndrome of progressive involvement in unconventional, nonconforming social problem behaviors among a select subgroup of teenagers.

However, we still do not have an understanding of some very important basic and applied questions. For example, we do not know if there are *different* pathways from abstinence to drinking to problem drinking status (and so on) as has been hypothesized by Gorsuch and Butler (1976) in the specific domain of substance use and by Block (1971) regarding adolescent development in general. Another related unanswered question is of major applied interest: Are different kinds of adolescents *in situ* (who may have arrived at a given level of drinking via different pathways) differentially receptive to various kinds of influences (either naturally occurring ones or planned interventions) toward or away from greater involvement with alcohol and other socially deviant behaviors?

In attempting to achieve satisfying answers to questions such as the two above, it appears that the prosecution of research with four specific characteristics would be particularly fruitful. First, it should be evident that the assumption of a frankly field-theoretical, interactional, or transactional perspective would be desirable, if not essential (see Ekehammar, 1974; Endler and Magnusson, 1976; and Olweus, 1977, for conceptual analyses of these perspectives). Both the Jessor and Jessor (1977) and Zucker (1979) have persuasively advocated the adoption of an interactional framework embracing representations of (developmental) time, individual differences, environmental features, and behaviors as a requirement for understanding the development of teenage drinking.

Second, in designing empirical research within this kind of theoretical framework, an important consideration is choosing a basic unit of analysis. In this regard, there is an increasing number of provocative and persuasive arguments in the modern theoretical literature suggesting that one cannot meaningfully separate (conceptually or analytically) the person from the environment in the interaction process and that therefore one's basic unit of analysis should be the (person-environment) unit (Alker, 1977; Nuttin, 1977; Pervin, 1977). In order to address questions such as the two posed above, this unit of analysis would ideally be a molar one suited to the task of reflecting the course(s) of development of *whole* persons *in situ* (see Braucht, 1974, and Donovan and Jessor, 1978b).

Third, there are also some compelling arguments which suggest that attempts to decompose this basic (person-environment) unit of analysis into separate additive linear components of variance are neither fruitful nor enlightening in understanding how individual differences and situations interact in evoking behavior (Olweus, 1977; Overton, 1973). Furthermore, it would also be well to recognize here that the fundamental postulate of the conception which is being suggested is that it is the *dialectic* between the individual and the environment which defines the meaning and force which they jointly have for behavior. There is a formal identity between the potential analytic problem inherent in this conception and the seemingly paradoxical problem originally posed by Meehl (1950) 30 years ago.

An example of this kind of analytic problem in concrete terms may be useful in illuminating the importance of this point. Assume that one is interested in understanding how individual differences in adolescents' capacities to achieve academic success and the variable of environmental press or demand for academic achievement interact in their relationship to drinking. Table 2 presents a set of hypothetical data on these variables for four cases of adolescents *in situ*. In examining Table 4.2, readers should satisfy themselves that neither the individual variable alone nor the environmental variable alone, nor a linear combination of the two bears any relationship to the drinking variable. Despite this, the *pattern* of these two predictor variables together enables a complete accounting of the variance in drinking events. Cases one and four in Table 4.2 could be viewed as "ecological matches" between the individuals' capacities for academic achievement (high and low) and environmental demand for academic performance (high and low). In both cases, the associated drinking events are of a low magnitude (e.g., moderate drinking). In contrast, Case two represents an adolescent with low academic ability relative to his or her situation in which there is a high level of demand for him or her to excel. Case three represents the obverse: an individual with high ability relative to an environment where there is little value or demand for achievement. Both Cases two and three could be viewed as ecological mismatches: Case two being fraught with the potential for failure, feelings of frustration, and so on; and Case three being pregnant with possibilities for ideleness, boredom, and the like. In both cases, the associated drinking events are high magnitude ones (e.g., problem-drinking events).

Horst (1954) and, in a more general way, Horn (1963) have shown that the kind of quasi-paradox represented in the data of Table 4.2 is really no paradox at all, but that its solution does require a nonlinear mode of scoring or analysis. Horn's (1963) formal analysis of this problem also reminds us that nonlinear formulations contain at least as much information as linear ones and potentially much more. Unless one can achieve a *direct* measurement of the interaction between persons and their environments, a goal which Cattell rather wistfully referred to nearly 40 years ago as the "queen of measurement" (1944: 299), these facts imply both a challenge and a promise of reward. A test of the full potential of transactional conceptions of adolescent drinking will *require* nonlinear analyses. If this challenge can be met, the implied promise is that configural, typological, or other nonlinear modes of analysis may enable us to account for a substantially greater portion of the variance in adolescent drinking than is the case within the more restrictive linear formulations now predominant in the field.

This hypothetical (but theoretically extremely plausible) example also forcefully illustrates the necessity for truly representative sampling designs (Brunswik, 1956; Pervin, 1977) reflecting the range of naturally occurring variation in both environmental and individual variables *and* their joint occurrences. With regard to this fourth point, assume that the four cases in Table 4.2 were truly representative of (individual-

TABLE 4.2   Hypothetical Data on Four Drinking Events to be Predicted from Individual and Environmental Data

	Predictor variables		Criterion variable
	Individual capacity/ability for academic achievement	Environmental press/demand for academic performance	Level of drinking
Case one	2	2	1
Case two	1	2	2
Case three	2	1	2
Case four	1	1	1

environmental) variation in nature, but that sampling from only one kind of environment in Table 4.2—say that characterized by high demand for academic achievement—was done in a given empirical study. In this event, only Cases one and two would be observed. From these (environmentally nonrepresentative) data, it is clear that one would be very likely to conclude that individual ability is positively (and perfectly) related to level of drinking. Note that: (1) the relationship observed here would be observed whether the nonrepresentative sampling of environments had been done by accident or design (the latter commonly referred to as "with the situation, stimulus, etc. 'held constant' "); and (2) the observed positive bivariate relationship is the exact *opposite* of the inverse relationship which would be identified if the other kind of environment—that characterized by low demand for academic achievement—were the only one sampled. Conversely, it should also be clear from inspection of Table 4.2 that nonrepresentative sampling of the other sort—in which individual differences were (in effect) "held constant"—would result in equally fragmentary and contradictory apparent relationships between environmental press for academic achievement and drinking. With truly representative sampling and a nonlinear transactional analysis, however, out of this welter of seemingly contradictory observed relationships emerges a single simple and elegant transactional one: Where there is a match between individual ability and environmental demand, non-problem drinking occurs; where there are mismatches, problem drinking occurs.

In sum, this brief discussion has hopefully suggested one particularly promising kind of empirical inquiry. In its basic form, this kind of research: (1) would be based on a frankly transactional conceptualization; (2) would take as its basic unit of analysis some kind of molar [person-environment] unit; (3) would explore relationships between these units and other transactional events (e.g., drinking events) within some kind of typological, configural, or other mode of data analysis optimally suited to analyzing nonlinear relationships; and (4) would fully recognize the signal necessity of achieving truly representative designs in empirical work.

Rather than making suggestions about *what* substantive questions or issues should be investigated, this brief discussion has primarily been meant to suggest *how* substantive questions might be approached. This focus has been taken because, without a shift in the *way* research problems are viewed and analyzed, it now appears that we may have reached a point at which gains in our knowledge will be derived with increasing difficulty and in increasingly smaller increments. The major challenge for the future thus appears to lie in developing conceptualizations, theories, and analytic models which do justice to the complexity of adolescent behavior.

REFERENCES

ABELSON, H. I and R. B. ATKINSON (1975) Public Experience with Psychoactive Substances: A Nationwide Study Among Adults and Youth. Princeton, NJ: Response Analysis Corporation.

ABELSON, H. I and P. M. FISHBURNE (1976) Nonmedical Use of Psychoactive Substances. Princeton, NJ: Response Analysis Corporation.

––– and I. H. CISIN (1977) National Survey on Drug Abuse: 1977. Princeton, NJ: Response Analysis Corporation.

ALEXANDER, C. N. and E. R. CAMPBELL (1967) "Peer influences on adolescent drinking." Quarterly Journal of Studies on Alcohol 28: 444-453.

ALKER, H. A. (1977) "Beyond ANOVA psychology in the study of person-situation interactions," pp. 243-260 in D. Magnusson and N. S. Endler (eds.) Personality at the Crossroads. Hillsdale, NJ: Erlbaum.

BARNES, G. (1977) "The development of adolescent drinking behavior: an evaluative review of the impact of the socialization process within the family." Adolescence 12, 48: 571-591.

BLACKFORD, L. (1977) "Summary report—surveys of student drug use, San Mateo, California." San Mateo: San Mateo County Department of Public Health and Welfare.

BLANE, H. T. and L. E. HEWITT (1976) "Alcohol and youth: an analysis of the literature 1960-1975." Prepared for National Institute on Alcohol Abuse and Alcoholism, Contract (ADM) 281-75-0026.

BLOCK, J. (1971) Lives Through Time. Berkeley, CA: Bancroft Books.

BLOCK, J. R. and N. GOODMAN (1978) "Illicit drug use and consumption of alcohol, tobacco, and over-the-counter medicine among adolescents." International Journal of the Addictions 13: 933-946.

BLUM, R. and L. RICHARDS (1979) "Youthful drug use," pp. 257-269 in R. L. DuPont et al., Handbook on Drug Abuse. Washington, DC: National Institute on Drug Abuse.

BRAUCHT, G. N. (1974) "A psychosocial typology of adolescent alcohol and drug users," in Drinking: A Multilevel Problem. Proceedings, Third Annual Alcoholism Conference. National Institute on Alcohol Abuse and Alcoholism. Washington, DC: Government Printing Office.

BRAUCHT, G. N., D. BRAKARSH, D. FOLLINGSTAD, and K. L. BERRY (1973) "Deviant drug use in adolescence: a review of psychosocial correlates." Psychological Bulletin 79: 92-106.

BRUNSWICK, A. F. and C. TARICA (1974) "Drinking and health of urban Black adolescents." Addictive Diseases: An International Journal 1: 21-42.

BRUNSWIK, E. (1956) Perception and the Representative Design of Psychological Experiments. Berkeley: University of California Press.

CAHALAN, D., I. H. CISIN, and H. M. CROSSLEY (1969) American Drinking Practices: A National Study of Drinking Behavior and Attitudes. New Brunswick, NJ: Rutgers Center of Alcohol Studies.

CATTELL, R. B. (1944) "Psychological measurement: normative, ipsative, interactive." Psychological Review 51: 292-303.

DEMONE, H. W. (1973) "The nonuse and abuse of alcohol by the male adolescent," in M. E. Chafetz (ed.) Proceedings of the Second Annual Conference of the National Institute on Alcohol Abuse and Alcoholism. Washington, DC: Department of Health, Education, and Welfare.

DEMONE, H. W. and H. WECHSLER (1976) "Changing drinking patterns of adolescents since the 1960's" in M. Greenblatt and M. A. Schuckit (eds.) Alcoholism Problems in Women and Children. New York: Grune and Stratton.

DONOVAN, J. E. and R. JESSOR (1978a) "Adolescent problem drinking: psychosocial correlates in a national sample study." Journal of Studies on Alcohol 39: 1506-1524.

——— (1978b) "Drinking, problem drinking, and illicit drug use among American adolescents: a psychosocial study of a nationwide sample." Final Report to the National Institute on Alcohol Abuse and Alcoholism, Contract No. ADM 281-75-0026.

EKEHAMMAR, B. (1974) "Interactionism in personality from a historical perspective." Psychological Bulletin 81: 1026-1048.

ENDLER, N. S. and D. MAGNUSSON (1976) "Toward an interactional psychology of personality." Psychological Bulletin 83: 956-974.

ENGS, R. C. (1977) "Drinking patterns and drinking problems of college students." Journal of Studies on Alcohol 38: 2144-2156.

FORSLUND, M. A. and T. J. GUSTAFSON (1970) "Influence of peers and parents and sex differences in drinking by high school students." Quarterly Journal of Studies on Alcohol 31: 868-875.

GLOBETTI, G. (1972) "Problem and no problem drinking among high school students in abstinence communities." International Journal of the Addictions 7: 511-523.

——— and M. McREYNOLDS (1964) "A comparative study of the white and the Negro high school students' use of alcohol in two Mississippi communities." Preliminary Report 4, State College. Mississippi State University: Social Science Research Center.

GORSUCH, R. L. and M. C. BUTLER (1976) "Initial drug abuse: a review of predisposing social psychological factors." Psychological Bulletin 83: 120-137.

GREEN, J. (1979) "Overview of adolescent drug use," in G. M. Beschner and A. S. Friedman, Youth and Drugs: Problems, Issues and Treatment. Lexington, MA: D. C. Heath.

HARFORD, T. C. and G. S. MILLS (1978) "Age-related trends in alcohol consumption." Journal of Studies on Alcohol 39: 207-210.

HORN, J. L. (1963) "Equations representing combinations of components in scoring psychological variables." Acta Psychologica 21: 184-217.

HORST, P. (1954) "Pattern analysis and configural scoring." Journal of Clinical Psychology 10: 3-11.

HUBA, G. J., J. A. WINGARD, and P. M. BENTLER (1979) "Beginning adolescent drug use and peer and adult interaction patterns." Journal of Consulting and Clinical Psychology 47: 265-276.

JESSOR, R. (1979) "Marijuana: a review of recent psychosocial research," in R. L. DuPont et al., Handbook on Drug Abuse. Washington, DC: Government Printing Office.

———, T. D. GRAVES, R. C. HANSON, and S. L. JESSOR (1968) Society, Personality, and Deviant Behavior: A Study of a Tri-Ethnic Community. New York: Holt, Rinehart & Winston.

JESSOR, R. and S. L. JESSOR (1977). Problem Behavior and Psychosocial Development: A Longitudinal Study of Youth. New York: Academic.

——— (1975) "Adolescent development and the onset of drinking." Journal of Studies on Alcohol 36, 1: 27-51.

——— and J. W. FINNEY, Jr. (1973) "A social psychology of marijuana use: longitudinal studies of high school and college youth." Journal of Personality and Social Psychology 26: 1-15.

JOHNSTON, L. D. (1973) Drugs and American youth. Ann Arbor: Institute for Social Research, University of Michigan.

———, J. G. BACHMAN, and P. M. O'MALLEY (1977a) Drug Use Among American High School Students 1975-1977 National Institute on Drug Abuse, DHEW Publication (ADM-78-619). Washington, DC: Government Printing Office.

——— (1977b) Highlights from Drug Use Among American High School Students 1975-1977. National Institute of Drug Abuse, DHEW Publication (ADM) 78-621. Washington, DC: Government Printing Office.

JOSEPHSON, E. (1974a) "Adolescent marijuana use, 1971-1972: findings from two national surveys." Addictive Diseases 1: 55-72.

——— (1974b) "Trends in adolescent marijuana use," in E. Josephson and E. E. Carroll (eds.) Drug Use: Epidemiological and Sociological Approaches. New York: John Wiley.

———, P. W. HABERMAN, A. Zanes, and J. ELINSON (1972) "Adolescent marijuana use: report on a national survey," in S. Einstein and S. Allen (eds.) Proceedings of the First International Conference on Student Drug Surveys. Farmingdale, NY: Baywood.

KANDEL, D. B. (1978) "Convergences in prospective longitudinal surveys of drug use in normal populations," in D. B. Kandel (ed.) Longitudinal research on drug use: empirical findings and methodological issues. New York: John Wiley.

——— (1975) "Stages in adolescent involvement in drug use." Science 190: 912-914.

——— (1973) "Adolescent marijuana use: the role of parents and peers." Science 181: 1067-1070.

——— and R. FAUST (1975) "Sequence and stages in patterns of adolescent drug use." Archives of General Psychiatry 32: 923-932.

KANDEL, D. B., R. C. KESSLER, and R. Z. MARGULIES (1978) "Antecedents of adolescent initiation into stages of drug use: a developmental analysis," in D. B. Kandel (ed.) Longitudinal Research on Drug Use: Empirical Findings and Methodological Issues. New York: John Wiley.

KANDEL, D. B., D. TREIMAN, R. FAUST, and E. SINGLE (1976) "Adolescent involvement in legal and illegal drug use: a multiple classification analysis." Social Forces 32: 375-382.

MADDOX, G. L. and B. C. McCALL (1964) Drinking Among Teenagers. New Brunswick, NJ: Rutgers Center of Alcohol Studies.

MANDELL, W., A. COOPER, R. M. SILBERSTEIN, J. NOVICK, and E. KOLO-SKI (1962) Youthful Drinking, New York State 1962. Staten Island, NY: Wakoff Research Center, Staten Island Mental Health Society.

MARGULIES, R. Z., R. C. KESSLER and D. B. KANDEL (1977) "A longitudinal study of onset of drinking among high school students." Journal of Studies on Alcohol 38: 897-912.

MEEHL, P. E. (1950) "Configural scoring." Journal of Consulting Psychology 24: 165-171.

National Commission on Marijuana and Drug Abuse (1972) Marijuana: A Signal of Misunderstanding. Washington, DC: Government Printing Office.

NUTTIN, J. R. (1977) "A conceptual frame of personality-world interaction: a relational theory," pp. 201-206 in D. Magnusson and N. S. Endler (eds.) Personality at the Crossroads. Hillsdale, NJ: Erlbaum.

O'CONNOR, J. (1977) "Normal and problem drinking among children." Journal of Child Psychology and Psychiatry 18: 279-284.

O'DONNEL, J. A., H. L. VOSS, R. R. CLAYTON, G. T. SLATIN, and R.G.W. ROOM (1976) Young Men and Drugs—a Nationwide Survey. NIDA Research Monograph 5. Washington, DC: Government Printing Office.

OLWEUS, D. (1977) "A critical analysis of the 'modern' interactionist position," pp. 221-234 in D. Magnusson and N. S. Endler (eds.) Personality at the Crossroads. Hillsdale, NJ: Erlbaum.

OVERTON, W. F. (1973) "On the assumptive base of the nature-nurture controversy: additive versus interactive conceptions." Human Development 16: 74-89.

PERVIN, L. A. (1977) "The representative design of person-situation research," pp. 371-384 in D. Magnusson and N. S. Endler (eds.) Personality at the crossroads. Hillsdale, NJ: Erlbaum.

PRENDERGAST, T. J. and E. S. SCHAEFER (1974) "Correlates of drinking and drunkenness among high school students." Quarterly Journal on the Studies of Alcohol 35: 232-242.

RACHAL, J. V., R. L. HUBBARD, J. R. WILLIAMS, and B. S. TUCHFIELD (1976) "Drinking levels and problem drinking among junior and senior high school students." Journal of Studies on Alcohol 37: 1751-1761.

RACHAL, J. V., J. R. WILLIAMS, M. L. BREHM, B. CAVANAUGH, R. P. MOORE, and W. L. ECKERMAN (1975) A National Study of Adolescent Drinking Behavior, Attitudes, and Correlates. Report PB-246-002. Springfield, VA: National Technical Information Service.

RIESTER, A. E. and R. A. ZUCKER (1968) "Adolescent social-structure and drinking behavior." Personnel and Guidance Journal 47: 304-312.

SADAVA, S. W. (1975) "Research approaches in illicit drug use: a critical review." Genetic Psychology Monographs 91: 3-59.

SCHLEGEL, R. P., C. A. DRAWFORD, and M. D. SANBORN (1977) "Correspondence and mediational properties of the Fishbein Model: an application to adolescent alcohol use." Journal of Experimental Social Psychology 13: 421-430.

SINGLE, E., D. KANDEL, and R. FAUST (1974) "Patterns of multiple drug use in high school." Journal of Health and Social Behavior 15: 344-357.

SMART, R. C. (1975) "Recent studies of the validity and reliability of self-reported drug use 1970-1974." Canadian Journal of Criminology and Corrections 17: 326-333.

——— and D. FEJER (1972) "Drug use among adolescents and their parents: closing the generation gap in mood modification." Journal of Abnormal Psychology 79: 153-160.

SMART, R. G., G. GRAY, and C. BENNETT (1978) "Predictors of drinking and signs of heavy drinking among high school students." International Journal of the Addictions 13: 1079-1094.

STACEY, B. and J. DAVIES (1970) "Drinking behavior in childhood and adolescence." British Journal of Addiction 65: 203-212.

STRAUS, R. and S. D. BACON (1953) Drinking in College. New Haven, CT: Yale University Press.

TENNANT, F. S., R. DETELS, and V. CLARK (1975) "Some childhood antecedents of drug and alcohol abuse." American Journal of Epidemiology 102: 377-385.

Third Special Report to the U.S. Congress on Alcohol and Health (1978) Washington, DC: Government Printing Office.

WALKER, B. A., M. D. JASINSKA, and E. F. CARNES (1978) "Adolescent alcohol abuse: a review of the literature." Journal of Alcohol and Drug Education 23: 51-65.

WECHSLER, H. (1976) "Alcohol intoxication and drug use among teenagers." Journal of Studies on Alcohol 37: 1672-1677.

——— and M. McFADDEN (1976) "Sex differences in adolescent alcohol and drug use." Journal of Studies on Alcohol 37: 1291-1301.

———, WECHSLER, H. and D. THUM (1973) "Teenage drinking, drug use and social correlates." Quarterly Journal on the Studies of Alcoholism 34: 1220-1227.

WHITEHEAD, P. C. and R. M. CABRAL (1975) "Scaling the sequence of drug using behaviors: a test of the stepping-stone hypothesis." Drug Forum 5: 45-54.

WILSNACK, R. W. and S. C. WILSNACK (1978) "Sex roles and drinking among adolescent girls." Journal of Studies on Alcohol 39: 1855-1874.

ZUCKER, R. A. (1979) "Developmental aspects of drinking through the young adult years," in H. T. Blane and M. E. Chafetz (eds.) Youth, Alcohol and Social Policy. New York: Plenum.

——— (1976) "Parental influences on the drinking patterns of their children," pp. 211-238 in M. Greenblatt and M. A. Schuckit (eds.) Alcoholism Problems in Women and Children. New York: Grune and Stratton.

——— and F. H. BARRON (1973) "Parental behaviors associated with problem drinking and antisocial behavior among adolescent males," pp. 276-296 in Proceedings of the First Annual Conference of the National Institute of

Alcohol Abuse and Alcoholism, June 1971. Washington, DC: Government Printing Office.

ZUCKER, R. A. and C. I. De VOE (1975) "Life history characteristics associated with problem drinking and antisocial behavior in antisocial girls, a comparison with male findings," In R. D. Wirt et al. (eds.) Life History Research in Psychopathology. Vol. 4. Minneapolis: University of Minnesota Press.

PART II

RECURRENT ISSUES

5

TEENAGE SMOKING BEHAVIOR

DOROTHY E. GREEN

BACKGROUND

Tobacco was first introduced into Europe in 1558. Shortly thereafter, concern was expressed over the effects which uses of this leaf had on human health (U.S. Department of Health, Education, and Welfare, 1979). This concern steadily increased over the years as tobacco consumption increased. However, it was not until the twentieth century that systematic scientific studies of the problem were conducted. These studies were, in large part, prompted by dramatic changes in cigarette consumption during this century, when use of cigarettes after World War I grew sharply, particularly among men, and the use of chewing tobacco and other forms of tobacco usage declined to a very low level. Another large increase in cigarette consumption was observed during World War II. During this period, there was an increased consumption of cigarettes by American troops, and large numbers of women also adopted the habit. It was a time of change and experimentation. These changes in cigarette consumption influenced disease patterns and prompted the initiation of prospective studies of cigarette smokers. These studies have shown, without any doubt, that cigarette smoking is a cause of some diseases (e.g., lung cancer in men) and is associated with many other diseases (e.g., heart disease, chronic bronchitis, and other lung disorders). As a result of these studies, an indictment of cigarette smoking has led to efforts on the part of health professionals, educators, and concerned citizens to stop the acceleration of cigarette consumption and thereby decrease the incidence of death and disease related to smoking.

These efforts have taken two directions. First, adult smokers have been encouraged to give up the habit and have been offered self-help techniques and also opportunities to receive help in cessation clinics. Second, young people have been encouraged to refrain from taking up cigarette smoking, not only for their healths' sake, but also to prevent them from being faced with the difficulties of breaking the habit later on. This chapter focuses on the prevention of smoking in young people, with some of its attendant problems, trends in teenage smoking, characteristics, attitudes and perceptions of teenage smokers, and how society in general affects the teenager's smoking behavior.

Prevention efforts have largely emphasized the deleterious effects of smoking on health. As early as kindergarten, many children already know that smoking is harmful to health, and by junior high school it is the rare teenager who is not aware of the danger. If the decision to take up cigarette smoking were a purely rational, intellectual one, cigarette smoking would probably disappear in a generation or two. But social and psychological reasons become more important to the adolescent than any possible, far-off threat to health. He or she can rationalize smoking in many ways, as we will see and, in any case, the danger of illness 20 to 30 years from now seems to have little influence on present behavior. It is, perhaps, understandably difficult for persons who are 16 or 18 years of age to recognize the fact that the use of cigarettes or other harmful substances can, in later years, damage or destroy their health. Knowledge alone, then, appears to be insufficient motivation for refraining from smoking.

Closely related to the health threat is the use of fear arousal. Young children may become so afraid of the harmfulness of smoking that they live in terror that the death of their cigarette-smoking mothers or fathers is imminent. But, as they mature, they are able to observe that there are many older adults around them who smoke, are healthy, and live to old age. Preadolescent children who are very sure they will never smoke a cigarette may very well change when they become teenagers. The effect of the mass media is difficult to assess. During the late 1960s, antismoking public service television spots were frequently seen. The novelty of these announcements drew a great deal of attention, and, it is thought by many, probably had a positive influence. When cigarette advertising was banned from television and radio, the antismoking commercials disappeared with them.

The sections that follow will discuss the overall effects of these prevention measures on the behavior and attitudes of adolescents.

TRENDS IN PREVALENCE OF TEENAGE SMOKING

Four national surveys of teenagers were conducted by the National Clearinghouse for Smoking and Health between 1968 and 1974. Much of the data reported in this section, and in later sections were derived from these surveys (U.S. Department of Health, Education, and Welfare, 1972, 1976b).

METHODOLOGY AND DEFINITION

Each of the surveys was carried out during the months before and after Christmas. The first survey was begun in December 1967 and completed in January 1968. This is referred to here as the 1968 survey. The second survey was conducted in December 1969 and January 1970; the third in December 1971 and January 1972; and the fourth in December 1973 and January 1974. A fifth survey, under the sponsorship of the National Institute of Education, was conducted in December 1978 and January 1979. Results of this survey have not been completely analyzed at this time.

The 1968 sample consisted of 4931 boys and girls aged 12 to 18 inclusive. Approximately 90 percent were interviewed by long-distance telephone. The other young people, who lived in homes without telephones, were interviewed face to face in their homes. The results of this survey revealed little appreciable change in the data when the findings from the nontelephone households were added to those obtained by telephone. Because of this, and because the proportion of households with telephones has steadily increased, subsequent surveys included interviews by telephone only, and, for comparison purposes, data from nontelephone households in the 1968 survey have been deleted.

The telephone samples were randomly selected by computer from a data bank that included all possible combinations of area codes (in the contiguous 48 states), telephone exchanges, and subscriber numbers, with a sufficient surplus number of selections to allow for the elimination of nonresidence telephones or residences containing no teenagers. Standardized questionnaires were administered by trained professional interviewers and took about fifteen minutes to complete. The respondents were classified by smoking status into one of five categories—those who have never smoked, experimenters, ex-smokers, current occasional smokers, and current regular smokers. We defined these categories as follows:

(1) Those in the "Never smoked" category have never smoked a cigarette, not even a few puffs.
(2) Those designated as "experimenters" have smoked at least a few puffs of a cigarette, but have not smoked as many as 100 cigarettes.
(3) The "ex-smoker" is characterized as one who has smoked at least 100 cigarettes but no longer smokes them. This category includes both ex-regular and ex-occasional smokers.
(4) "Current occasional smokers" include those who smoke less than one cigarette a week.

Those defined as "current regular smokers" smoke one or more cigarettes per week or one or more per day. Those who have never smoked and those who have experimented only were classified in a single category for purposes of analysis. The sample size in each category, age by sex by smoking habits, is small. Therefore, in analyzing the relationships between smoking behavior and other characteristics of the teenagers studied, age groups were combined in order to have a more stable base for comparisons. Thus, ages 12, 13, and 14 were combined; ages 15 and 16 were combined; and ages 17 and 18 were combined. Except where otherwise specified, current regular smokers are referred to as "smokers" and all others are combined into one category of "nonsmokers."

TRENDS IN PREVALENCE OF TEENAGE SMOKING

The years between the first national teenage survey conducted in 1968 and the latest one in 1979 have been marked by change. Furthermore, this change has been an encouraging one since, overall, there has been a decrease in the proportion of teenage boys and girls who smoke. During the first half of the period (1968-1974) prevalence of smoking among boys stayed about the same, with the proportion of smokers in the 12-18 year age group studied remaining around 16 percent. During the last half of the period (1974-1979), however, there was a decrease in the proportion of boys who smoked. This proportion dropped from 16 percent in the first period to 11 percent in the second half. Furthermore, this decrease was observed in every age group, but was most dramatic in the oldest group of boys—aged 17 and 18—where the proportion decreased from 31 percent in 1974 to 19 percent in 1979. In other words, instead of almost one in three teenage boys smoking in the years 1968—1974, only one in five smoked in 1979.

A similar but not so striking decrease was observed in the smoking behavior of 15 and 16-year-old boys, where the smoking rate dropped from about 18 percent in the first half of the period studied to less than 14 percent in 1979. Consistently, in line with the other age groups, there was a decrease in the youngest age group—12, 13, and 14. This was a very slight decrease, but cigarette smoking in this age group has always been so low that there is little room for decrease.

Changes among girls have shown a different pattern. Between 1968 and 1974, there were increases in proportion of cigarette smoking among girls in every age group; overall, the proportion of girls smoking increased from 8.4 percent in 1968 to 15.3 percent in 1974. A promising reversal of this overall trend was seen in the 1979 survey, when the proportion dropped to 12.7 percent. This decrease was not seen in every age group, however. Among the 17 and 18 year olds there was no change. It appears that the smoking rate for this age group has leveled off, since 1972, at about one smoker in every four. The biggest change was in the 15 and 16 year olds, who had shown a steady rise from 10 percent in 1968 to 20 percent in 1974. In 1979, this rate had dropped back to 12 percent. As with the boys, the prevalence of smoking in the 12, 13, and 14 year age group remained very low.

Traditionally, smoking has been much more prevalent among boys than among girls. In 1968, for example, nearly twice as many boys smoked as girls (15 percent and 8 percent, respectively). By 1979, the girls had passed the boys, with 13 percent of girls and 11 percent of boys being classified as smokers. The overall difference is accounted for by one age group, the 17 and 18 year olds, where 26 percent of the girls smoke compared with 19 percent of the boys. It is possible that the

TABLE 5.1   Teenage Cigarette Smoking (Age by Sex)

Smoking status		*Girls*							
		12–13–14		*15–16*		*17–18*		*Total*	
		N	*%*	*N*	*%*	*N*	*%*	*N*	*%*
Never smoked or experimented only	1968	919	97.9	552	84.4	462	73.0	1933	86.8
	1970	536	95.0	312	81.5	264	70.0	1112	84.0
	1972	569	95.3	312	77.0	277	66.7	1158	81.7
	1974	495	90.2	250	69.3	228	62.1	973	76.2
	1979	514	92.3	318	81.7	239	63.9	1071	81.1
Ex-smoker	1968	7	0.7	25	3.8	38	6.0	70	3.1
	1970	8	1.4	15	3.9	22	5.8	45	3.4
	1972	11	1.8	26	6.4	30	7.2	67	4.7
	1974	26	4.7	33	9.1	42	11.4	101	7.9
	1979	19	3.4	23	5.9	34	9.1	76	5.8
Current occasional smoker	1968	7	0.7	14	2.1	15	2.4	36	1.6
	1970	3	0.5	1	0.3	5	1.3	9	0.7
	1972	0	0.0	1	0.2	3	0.7	4	0.3
	1974	1	0.2	5	1.4	2	0.5	8	0.6
	1979	0	0.0	2	0.5	3	0.8	5	0.4
Current regular smoking	1968	6	0.6	63	9.6	118	18.6	187	8.4
	1970	17	3.0	55	14.4	86	22.8	158	11.9
	1972	17	2.8	66	16.3	105	25.3	188	13.3
	1974	27	4.9	73	20.2	95	25.9	195	15.3
	1979	24	4.3	46	11.8	98	26.2	168	12.7
Total	1968	939	99.9	654	99.9	633	100.0	2226	99.9
	1970	564	99.9	383	100.1	377	99.9	1324	100.0
	1972	597	99.9	405	99.9	415	99.9	1417	100.0
	1974	549	100.0	361	100.0	367	99.9	1277	100.0
	1979	557	100.0	389	99.9	374	100.0	1320	100.0

SOURCE: Chilton Teenage Telephone Surveys—1968, 1970, 1972, 1974.

TABLE 5.1 (Cont)

Smoking status		Boys							
		12–13–14		15–16		17–18		Total	
		N	%	N	%	N	%	N	%
Never smoked or experimented only	1968	876	93.1	465	75.2	344	54.7	1685	77.0
	1970	512	90.5	268	70.5	178	48.1	958	72.8
	1972	533	91.1	273	68.3	211	54.4	1017	74.1
	1974	496	90.7	253	69.5	202	55.3	951	74.5
	1979	526	92.8	284	75.3	254	68.1	1064	80.8
Ex-smoker	1968	25	2.7	34	5.5	71	11.3	130	5.9
	1970	21	3.7	35	9.2	52	14.1	108	8.2
	1972	20	3.4	50	12.5	56	14.4	126	9.2
	1974	28	5.1	45	12.4	44	12.1	117	9.2
	1979	23	4.1	38	10.1	46	12.3	101	8.1
Current occasional smoker	1968	13	1.4	14	2.3	24	3.8	51	2.3
	1970	1	0.2	3	0.8	2	0.5	6	0.5
	1972	5	0.9	6	1.5	4	1.0	15	1.1
	1974	0	0.0	0	0.0	6	1.6	6	0.5
	1979	0	0.0	4	1.1	1	0.3	5	0.4
Current regular smoker	1968	27	2.9	105	17.0	190	30.2	322	14.7
	1970	32	5.7	74	19.5	138	37.3	244	18.5
	1972	27	4.6	71	17.8	117	30.2	215	15.7
	1974	23	4.2	66	18.1	113	31.0	202	15.8
	1979	18	3.2	51	13.5	72	19.3	141	10.7
Total	1968	941	100.1	618	100.0	629	100.0	2188	99.9
	1970	566	100.1	380	100.0	370	100.0	1316	100.0
	1972	585	100.0	400	100.1	388	100.0	1373	100.1
	1974	547	100.0	364	100.0	365	100.0	1276	100.0
	1979	567	100.0	377	100.0	373	100.0	1317	100.0

SOURCE: Chilton Teenage Telephone Surveys—1968, 1970, 1972, 1974.

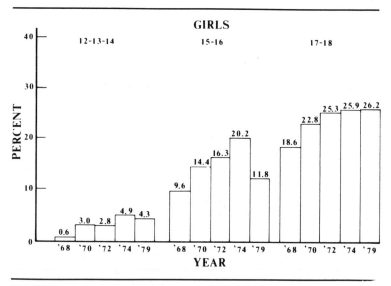

FIGURE 5.1 Percentage of Current Regular Smokers—Teenage,
           1968-1979

girls in this age group, having leveled off just as the boys did in the late
1960s and early 1970s, will begin to show a decrease in the future.
Certainly, the marked decrease in the smoking of 15-16 year olds
supports this speculation.

While there are often alarming statements made to the effect that
teenagers, particularly girls, are starting to smoke at earlier ages, the
data lend no support to these statements (see Figure 5.1). In fact, the
changes in smoking prevalence in those age 16 and below have shown a
marked decrease among both boys and girls (see Table 5.1).

CHARACTERISTICS OF TEENAGE SMOKERS
COMPARED WITH NONSMOKERS

While most adolescents experiment with cigarettes, only about one
in three has become a regular smoker by the time he or she is 18 years
old. Those who go on to become regular smokers differ from those who
experiment only or who do not even try cigarettes at all in a number of
ways—demographically, in life-style, and in the way they see the world
around them. Some of these differences are described below.

DEMOGRAPHIC CHARACTERISTICS

The composition of the household in which the teenager lives seems to play a part in determining whether a teenager smokes or not. If the adolescent lives in a home where both a mother and father are members of the household, he or she is less likely to be a smoker than if he or she lives with one parent or in a place where no parent is present (for example, where the older teenager has moved from the family home). In the 1979 survey, in households where both parents were present, 9 percent of boys were smokers, whereas in other households, 19 percent were smokers. The same relationship holds for girls, where the percentages are 11 percent and 21 percent, respectively. This was true for all age groups, and findings were consistent for all four surveys.

Whether parents smoke or not influences teenage smoking at all ages. For example, in 1979, in families where both parents are in the home and both parents smoke, 13.5 percent of the boys smoke; yet when only one parent smokes, the percentage of boys who smoke dropped to 9.1 percent; when neither parent smokes, the percentage was even lower—5.6 percent. There has been little change in this relationship between parental smoking and teenage smoking over the years of the surveys. For girls, the rates are 15.1 percent when both parents smoke, 12.7 percent when one parent smokes, and 6.5 percent when neither parent smokes.

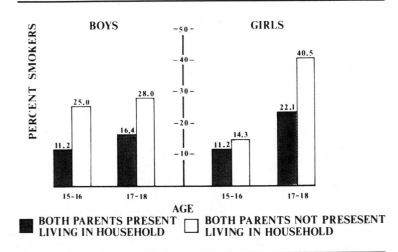

FIGURE 5.2   Smoking Behavior and Family Structure—1979

The smoking behavior of older brothers and sisters also influences teenage smoking. In fact, both boys and girls with older siblings are more likely to smoke if one or more older siblings smoke than if none of their older brothers or sisters smoke. Boys who have older siblings who smoke are almost three times as likely to smoke as are boys whose older siblings do not smoke. Boys with no older siblings who smoke are more similar to those with no older brothers or sisters. The findings for girls follow the same pattern with a smoking rate of 20.7 percent (in 1979) in homes where an older sibling smokes, a rate of 9.1 percent in homes where no older sibling smokes, and 8.2 percent where there is no older brother or sister. These relationships have remained practically unchanged through the five surveys.

Still another area of family smoking habits was explored. Were boys more likely to smoke if their fathers smoked? Were girls more likely to take up the habit if their mothers smoked? Did the sex of the older sibling who smoked make a difference? What was found was that both boys and girls were more likely to start smoking if their mother smoked than if their father did. Although this was true more often for girls than for boys, the fact remains that the smoking behavior of the so-called "weaker sex" has the greater influence. As far as older siblings are concerned, the female dominance again prevailed—in other words, if an older sister smoked, the teenagers studied were more likely to smoke than if an older brother smoked. Mothers and older sisters should, then, be aware of the importance of their role as exemplars.

Now, what about the proportions when parents and older siblings smoke? If at least one parent and one older sibling smoke, the teenager is four times as likely to smoke than if no parent or no older sibling smokes (27.9 percent and 7.2 percent for boys; 26.2 percent and 6.0 percent for girls in 1974). *Either* a parent or a sibling smoker in the home increases the teenager's likelihood of smoking, but not nearly to the extent that it does when both smoke. In these latter households, smoking is an accepted family pattern that the adolescent is very likely to adopt as he or she approaches maturity.

Another family characteristic that is related to teenage smoking is the educational level of the parents. In families where one or both parents attended college, the adolescent is much less likely to smoke than in those families where neither parent attended college. In 1974, it was found that among boys in families where at least one parent reached an educational level beyond high school, only 12.5 percent were smokers, compared with 18.6 percent in families where neither parent attended college. Smoking among girls showed the same pattern; comparable percentages for girls were 12.6 percent and 17.0 percent, respectively. The findings may be summarized as follows:

Teenagers in intact families (that is, those in which both parents were present) were less likely to smoke than were those in homes where there was not both a mother and a father. About one in four lives in a home without both parents, some because one parent is dead or the parents are divorced, and some, particularly the older teenagers, because they have left the family home and have set up their own living arrangements. They have adopted a life-style that is somewhat precocious; perhaps smoking is one characteristic of this life-style.

Another family characteristic that is related to teenage smoking is socioeconomic status, as measured by the education of the parents. Those with better-educated parents are less likely to smoke than are those with less-educated parents. This is consistent with studies of adults which find that the higher the educational level a man has attained, the more likely he is to have quit smoking, if he ever did so.

In spite of the notion that adolescents, in rebellion against their parents, reject the customs and beliefs of their elders, they do not turn away from their parents' smoking paractices. Parents who smoke are likely to have children who smoke. In fact, teenagers with two parents who use cigarettes are more than twice as likely to smoke as are those with no parent who indulges in this habit.

Teenagers emulate older brothers and sisters too. A boy or girl with an older sibling who smokes is extremely likely to be a smoker as well.

If a youngster has both a parent *and* an older sibling who smoke, his or her likelihood of becoming a smoker is amplified. In fact, he or she is four times as likely to smoke as one who has no smoking example in the immediate family. Smoking appears to be one of those customs which families as a whole either adopt or do not adopt. Just as in some families a coffee pot is always on the back of the stove, in some homes cigarettes are readily available for family members to help themselves.

SMOKING BEHAVIOR OF FRIENDS

Teenagers not only have families who smoke, but they also have friends who smoke. Almost nine out of ten smokers acknowledge that at least one of his or her four best friends smokes on a regular basis, while only one in three of the nonsmokers claims a smoker among his or her four best friends. At the other extreme, one in five nonsmokers claims that *none* of his or her four best friends has even experimented with smoking, while only one in a hundred of the smokers makes this claim.

When we discuss parents' and older siblings' smoking patterns, we can talk about their influence on teenagers since, presumably, these older family members set the stage for them. But when we talk about friends' smoking, there is no way to guess who influenced whom. Did Tom's friends exert pressure to get him to smoke? Did Tom urge his friends to smoke? Did he select friends *because* they smoked, or did they select *him* because *he* smoked? Or do they share the same kind of life-style, congenial to all in this group, that includes cigarette smoking? Tom cannot tell us; no one can. It is likely, however, that Tom and his friends share a life pattern that includes smoking.

WORKING PRACTICES

Approximately three-quarters of the boys surveyed in 1974 said that they had worked at some time during the preceding year, and one-half of the girls reported that they had worked during that time period. The proportion of workers was highest in the oldest age group studied—seventeen and eighteen year olds—(89.9 percent of the boys and 73.8 percent of the girls) had been employed. Even in the youngest group (twelve, thirteen, and fourteen year olds), however, 63.3 percent of the boys and 40.1 percent of the girls had held jobs in the preceding year.

A relationship was found between working and smoking—those who worked were more likely to be smokers than were those who were not employed. The study showed that 18.1 percent of the boys who worked also smoked while about half of that number, 9.3 percent, of the boys who did not work were smokers. For girls, 20.5 percent of the workers said they were smokers, and 9.4 percent of the nonworkers smoked.

Perhaps the nonworking minority is somewhat more protected and less likely to have achieved much independence. Those who work often participate with adults in a work situation, and therefore are more likely to experiment with smoking and other adult behaviors.

EDUCATIONAL ASPIRATIONS

One measure of a high school student's educational plans is the courses he or she is taking in high school. Thus, the respondents who were attending high school were asked whether they were in college preparatory courses or in some other courses. Boys in college preparatory courses are much less likely to smoke. The same holds true for girls, but the differences are not as large. Among high school boys in 1979, only 9.0 percent of those in college preparatory courses smoked, while 18.3 percent of those in any other courses smoked. Comparable percentages for high school girls are 12.0 percent and 20.1 percent.

USE OF ALCOHOL AND OTHER DRUGS

A 1977 study of adolescents age 12 to 17 by the National Institute of Drug Abuse compared the drug and alcohol experience of smokers with that of nonsmokers (U.S. Department of Health, Education, and Welfare, 1978). It was found that smokers were much more likely than nonsmokers to have had experience with other substances that are abused. In the case of alcohol, it was found that more than half (52.6 percent) of the youths had ever used it. Its use was much more prevalent among smokers than among nonsmokers; 80 percent of smokers had ever used alcohol compared with 45 percent of the nonsmokers. At the other end of the spectrum, very few young people, around 5 percent, had ever used prescription drugs—stimulants, sedatives, tranquilizers—for nonmedical use.

Again, however, smokers were much more likely than nonsmokers to be classified as "nonmedical psychotherapeutic pill users". The percentage of smokers so classified was 28 percent, compared with only 4 percent of nonsmokers. Among all adolescents, 28 percent had ever used marihuana and/or hashish; 68 percent of smokers and 17 percent of nonsmokers reported using either or both of these substances in their lifetimes. Finally, "stronger drugs", i.e., hallucinogens, cocaine, heroin, and other opiates, had been used by 26 percent of smokers and only 4 percent of nonsmokers.

Cigarette smoking has sometimes been described as a "gateway" behavior; that is, there has been some speculation that use of cigarettes leads to the use of other substances of abuse. It is true that cigarettes are experimented with at an earlier age than are other substances, and that those who smoke cigarettes are more likely than nonsmokers to use other substances. However, it does not necessarily follow that use of cigarettes leads to use of alcohol, marihuana, and other drugs. It is possible that these behaviors are all part of a life-style that embraces experimentation. Teenager who dare to try one "forbidden fruit" are the ones who are likely to try others. They may have the kind of temperaments that are satisfied only when they take risks.

ATTITUDES AND PERCEPTIONS OF SMOKERS COMPARED WITH NONSMOKERS

PERCEPTION OF THREAT TO HEALTH

The overwhelming majority of adolescents see cigarette smoking as a potential threat to health. When asked "Would you say smoking is harmful to health?" 96.5 percent answered "yes," 2.2 percent answered "no," and 1.4 percent said they did not know whether it is harmful or not. These proportions remained essentially the same for all surveys conducted between 1968 and 1974 when 94 percent answered "yes" to this question.

One might have hoped that the tremendous amount of information that was disseminated during that period about the hazards of smoking might have convinced additional teenagers that smoking is harmful, and thus increased the proportion of those who answered "yes" to this question. However, it was not until the 1979 survey that an increase was observed. Perhaps there will always be a small minority who deny that the scientific findings are valid, and another small minority who have never gotten the message. Compared with nonsmokers, smokers are a little more likely to say that smoking is not harmful. However, 91.6 percent of *smokers* say that they perceive smoking as harmful to health. Further proclamations, then, that smoking is harmful to health are unlikely to have any appreciable effect on the number of teenagers who smoke.

INTENTIONS FOR FUTURE BEHAVIOR

In all of the national surveys, respondents were asked the question, "What would you say is the possibility that five years from now you will be a cigarette smoker?" The response categories were "definitely yes," "probably yes," and "probably not." In 1979, almost 90 percent indicated that they would definitely or probably not be smokers five years from now. This proportion showed a marked increase from the 1968 percentage for the boys, 77 percent to 91 percent, and a smaller but encouraging increase for the girls, 82 percent to 89 percent. Less than 6 percent of nonsmokers and 50 percent of smokers indicated that they intended to smoke in the future.

In all surveys, very few nonsmokers saw themselves as being smokers five years in the future. Fewer than one in ten predicted such a possibility. On the other hand, more than half of those who were already smokers said that they would definitely or probably be smokers in the future. Perhaps some of these smokers already see themselves as "hooked" and are being realistic in expecting that they will probably not quit. Even among smokers, however, there is a positive note. Smokers were less likely in 1979 than in 1968 to predict that they would continue to smoke. The proportion who answered "definitely

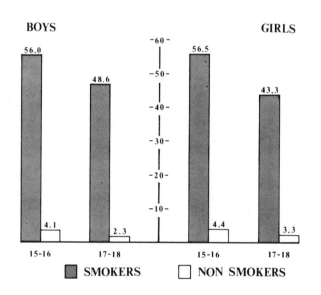

FIGURE 5.3   Possibility of Being a Cigarette Smoker Five Years from Now (Percentage Answering Definitely or Probably Yes in 1979)

yes" or "probably yes" to this question dropped from 59 percent to 49 percent for boys between 1968 and 1979, and from 58 percent to 52 percent for girls. If these predictions are accurate, we should begin to see a decrease in smoking among young adults.

DYNAMICS OF TAKING UP SMOKING

A research project (Milne and Colmen, 1973) sponsored by the National Clearinghouse for Smoking and Health, and carried out by Education and Public Affairs, Washington, D.C., was designed to better understand the forces which operate upon adolescents and influence them to initiate or to continue to experiment with cigarette smoking. Since this study is quite different from the surveys in that it is an in-depth study, and since it is the only large-scale study of its kind in the United States, it is described in some detail in this section.

Methodology

Hypothesis formulation was accomplished in three steps. First, a comprehensive review of the literature (Williams, 1971) was undertaken and a summary report was prepared. Second, this report was made available to an advisory committee made up of individuals representing research and practical experience related to adolescents and their behavior vis à vis cigarette smoking. The members of this committee supplemented the findings of the literature search with their views and ideas. Third, and finally, depth interviews, both of an individual and a group nature, were carried out with students in grades eight and twelve. These students were from schools in four types of environments: inner-city, suburbs, blue-collar neighborhoods, and rural. School locations were selected so as to provide both white and black students. Interviews were conducted by eight graduate students—four male and four female—who were trained specifically for conducting these interviews.

Groups of nine students each were interviewed by same-sex interviewers. At the end of the interview, members of the group were asked to volunteer for individual interviews the following week. In all, 216 students in grade 8 were interviewed in groups and 47 were interviewed individually. In grade 12, 142 were interviewed in groups and 48 were interviewed individually. The results of these openended interviews were analyzed and the findings summarized. From the ideas generated by the foregoing process, 205 initial attitude items were constructed, comprising statements about smoking behavior, beliefs, personal motivations, and knowledge about cigarette smoking. Each item was written as an attitude statement designed to be responded to on a five-point agree-disagree continuum—strongly agree, agree, neither agree nor disagree, disagree, or strongly disagree. These statements, insofar as was possible, were expressed in the same words the students had used when they were interviewed. In addition, 43 background and general information items were included.

Using drafts of the questionnaire, individual interviews of one-hour duration were later conducted with 264 teenagers in grades 7-12. These interviews were conducted on the assumption that (1) the items were phrased in readable language understood by young people, age 12 to 18, (2) the reading level was manageable by the youngest respondents, without being so simple as to "turn off" the older respondents, and (3) the questions were understood in a uniform manner by all. On the basis of the first set of interviews, problem items were revised and the new questionnaire tested with another set of interviews. This procedure was iterated until all items that were found to present problems were eliminated. This final questionnaire was pilot-tested, in written form, on 256 seventh and eighth graders to unearth any possible problems concerned with format, layout, or instructional materials.

The final questionnaire was administered in two stages to a national probability sample of school districts; schools within districts were then sampled, and students within schools were randomly sampled. In the first stage, 2618 questionnaires were completed in 98 schools. The data from this administration were analyzed to reduce the size of the questionnaire by eliminating noncontributing items. After applying the results of examination of responses to the questionnaire and factor analyses, the initial questionnaire was reduced to 83 items. This questionnaire, with items arranged in cyclical omnibus form to distribute like-factored items, plus 14 background items, was administered in February 1973. A total of 5110 usable questionnaires were returned. Analyses of the data were completed using the results obtained from these questionnaires.

Findings

The 83 items were subjected to factor analysis, and 8 factors were identified comprising 64 of the original items. These 8 factors, with the items contained in them, are listed below.

Score 1. Effects of Smoking on Health

(1) Adults who smoke risk getting serious lung or heart disease.
(2) People can become addicted to cigarettes just as they can to alcohol or drugs.
(3) Even though lung cancer and heart disease can be caused by other things, smoking cigarettes still makes a real difference.
(4) Cigarette smoking can harm the health of teenagers.
(5) Cigarette smoking can harm you even after smoking for only a year.
(6) Even if cigarettes don't kill you, they can cut down on what you might get out of life.
(7) I believe the health information about smoking is true.
(8) It's better not to start smoking than to have to stop.
(9) There's nothing wrong with smoking cigarettes as long as you don't smoke too many.
(10) Cigarette smoking is only a minor health problem.

Score 2. Nonsmokers' Rights

(1) Cigarette smokers don't think enough about how their smoking bothers nonsmokers.
(2) I prefer the company of boys who don't smoke.
(3) It seems that more and more nonsmokers complain about having someone smoke near them.
(4) Cigarette smoke smells bad.
(5) Cigarette smokers should be kept apart from nonsmokers in public places.
(6) I prefer the company of girls who don't smoke.
(7) If I have children, I hope they never smoke cigarettes.
(8) Cigarettes are a form of air pollution.
(9) Cigarette smoking should be forbidden inside public places.
(10) If I smoke around other people, I take away their right to breathe clean air.

Score 3. Positive Effects of Smoking

(1) People smoke cigarettes to make everyday life less boring.
(2) People smoke cigarettes to help them think more clearly.
(3) Smoking cigarettes can help you enjoy life more.
(4) Cigarette smokers are usually easygoing people.
(5) People who smoke seem to be more at ease with others.
(6) Smoking cigarettes gives you a good feeling.
(7) People smoke cigarettes to calm their nerves.
(8) Smoking cigarettes seems to make good times even better.
(9) People who smoke are usually more sociable than people who don't.

Score 4. Rationalization

(1) It's okay for teenagers to experiment with cigarettes if they quit before it becomes a habit.
(2) Cigarette smoking is harmful only if a person inhales.
(3) There is no danger in smoking cigars or pipes.
(4) Cigarettes low in tar and nicotine can't harm your health.
(5) Teenagers who smoke regularly can quit for good any time they like.

Score 5. Reasons for Starting

(1) Most girls *start* smoking cigarettes to try to become more popular.
(2) Most boys *start* smoking cigarettes because most of their friends smoke.
(3) Most girls *start* smoking cigarettes to try to attract boys.
(4) Most boys *start* smoking cigarettes to try to become more popular.
(5) Most girls *start* smoking cigarettes because most of their friends smoke.
(6) Most boys *start* smoking cigarettes to try to attract girls.
(7) If you don't smoke cigarettes, other teenagers put you down.
(8) Students who smoke cigarettes tend to be more popular.
(9) I am under pressure from my friends to smoke.

Score 6. Negative Smoker Attributes

(1) Teenagers who smoke cigarettes are more likely to be trouble-makers than those who don't.
(2) A person who smokes is more of a follower than one who doesn't smoke.
(3) Kids who smoke are show-offs.
(4) Parents who smoke set a bad example for their children.
(5) Teenagers *start* to smoke as a way of rebelling against their parents.
(6) Teenage smokers think they are grown-up, but they really aren't.
(7) People smoke cigarettes to try to escape from troubles they face.
(8) Teenage smokers think they look cool, but they don't really.

Score 7. Feeling Toward Authority

(1) I feel good knowing I can turn to my parents for advice.
(2) Punishing kids for smoking cigarettes is useless.
(3) Adults try to stop teenagers from smoking just to show their power.

(4) I often do things even when I know inside myself that they are not the right things to do.
(5) Teenagers should do what their parents tell them to do.
(6) It annoys me that my parents have so much control over things I want to do.
(7) I wish I were older than I am now.
(8) A teenager should be able to do the things he wants to do when he wants to do them.

Score 8. Destiny Control

(1) Making something of my life is important to me.
(2) I use my own set of values to decide what I will or will not do.
(3) I don't want to get hooked on anything, including cigarettes.
(4) I can control the kind of person I will become.
(5) I do not want to be just one of the crowd.

The first two factor scores might be said to describe the "costs" of cigarette smoking, or its negative attributes. Score 1 measures the knowledge that teenagers have of the effects of cigarette smoking on health, and the extent to which they accept what they have learned. As we noted earlier, 94 percent of teenagers agree that smoking is harmful to health. In response to the single statement, "There's nothing wrong with smoking cigarettes if you don't smoke too many," many agreed, which seems to indicate a denial of their overall position on harmfulness to health. Thus, this factor score measures the perception of the health threat in more depth than does the single item on harmfulness. The score on this set of statements, then, is a measure of the respondents' perceptions of the cost, in terms of health, of cigarette smoking to the smoker.

Score 2 also measures cost of smoking, but to *other people* rather than to smokers themselves. It has been named Nonsmokers' Rights, since it shows the extent to which the respondent is concerned with the effect of secondhand smoke on the people around the smoker and on the environment. If cigarette smoking did not have some positive aspects, if people did not benefit in some ways from the practice, certainly it would not have had such widespread acceptance over a fairly short period of time.

Score 3 examines how teenagers see the benefits of cigarette smoking. Almost two-thirds of the teenagers, for example, believe that people smoke to calm their nerves. Most teenagers, although they believe that smoking is harmful to health, can find reasons for ignoring this fact. They try to make up reasons for overlooking the dangers of smoking or pretend there are circumstances in which there are no dangers in smoking. While they may accept the disadvantages to individual smokers and those around them, and may feel that there are few advantages to smoking, some will still try to find reasons why smoking is all right. Score 4 is a measure of the extent to which teenagers rationalize the discrepancy between their knowledge of costs of smoking and their perceptions of its benefits. If they are smokers it becomes imperative that they reduce the cognitive dissonance created by behaving contrary to their beliefs.

The set of statements that make up Score 5 form a picture of teenage smokers as other teenagers see them. Whatever reasons teenagers actually have for starting to smoke, this score shows why you *think* teenagers start to smoke. Perhaps their opinions on why they start to smoke are affected by what they see in advertisements, which show smokers as popular, attractive to the opposite sex, and, in general, completely accepted by others in their age group. The older teenager is much less likely than the younger one to see the taking up of smoking as necessary for obtaining social acceptance.

While Score 5 describes the way teenagers see the taking up of smoking, Score 6 shows a picture of teenage smokers. This score is based on a group of statements that are very critical of teenage smokers. A high score shows agreement with the idea that smokers are show-offs, troublemakers, are trying to look grown-up, and so on. They have very little liking or respect for the smoker, even though they may be smokers themselves. Persons who have very low scores do not believe these negative statements about smokers, or else they refuse to believe them because they don't want to think they are this kind of person.

The statements that make up Score 7 deal with how teenagers feel, about parents and other people who have authority over them. Score 7 indicates how individuals feel about satisfying their own needs and at the same time meeting the demands imposed upon them by those in authority. The higher the score on this set, the more the teenager likes to turn to his or her parents for advice and support. Those with low scores want more independence, and very low scores show that the teenager is rebelling against authority.

Although most teenagers want to decide the kind of person they will become, and believe that they *can* become the kind of person they want to be, some feel this more strongly than others. A high score on

Score 8 is an expression of importance to the individual of controlling his or her own destiny as opposed to being subject to the chances of good or bad luck, or being subject to control by others. It also shows a belief in the ability to exercise this control.

These attitude factors were included in the 1974 and 1979 national surveys. However, in order to keep the length of the telephone interview to a manageable time, only 3 items in each factor were used. The items were selected in such a way that the internal consistency reliability of each score was maximized. Items selected were as follows: Score 1, items 4, 7, and 9; Score 2, items 4, 9, and 10; Score 3, items 2, 5, and 6; Score 4, items 1, 2, and 5; Score 5, items 3, 4, and 7; Score 6, items 3, 6, and 8; Score 7, items 1, 7, and 8; Score 8, items 3, 4, and 5. Each item was scored on a scale of 1 to 5, with 1 representing Strongly Disagree; 2, Mildly Disagree; 3, Neither Agree nor Disagree; 4, Mildly Agree; and 5, Strongly Agree for most items. Scoring was reversed, that is Strongly Disagree was given a score of 5 and Strongly Agree a score of 1 for the following items: item 9 in Score 1; items 7 and 8 in Score 7. Each respondent, then, was given a score from 3 to 15 on each of the 8 factor scores. The mean scores for the 1974 and 1979 surveys are shown in Table 5.2.

While it might be expected that nonsmokers would show a much higher score than smokers on acceptance of the health threat, Factor 1, there is actually only a very small difference. However, the difference is in the expected direction in both surveys, among both boys and girls. There is a much larger difference between smokers and nonsmokers on Factor 2, which measures recognition of the rights of nonsmokers, with smokers tending to deny the fact that their secondhand smoke might be offensive to others.

Just as the first two factors measure the negative consequences of smoking, the third deals with the positive effects. The smokers, of course, are more likely to indicate that there are positive effects than are nonsmokers. Differences in response to all these items in this factor are small, however.

While nearly all teenagers admit to the health hazards of smoking, many of the teenagers smoke. How can they reconcile their knowledge with their behavior? Factor 4 contains some of the statements that teenagers use to rationalize their behavior. The differences between the mean scores of smokers and those of nonsmokers are very small, but are all in the expected direction.

TABLE 5.2 Mean Scores on Attitude Factors 1974-1979

| | Boys | | | | Girls | | | |
| | 1974 | | 1979 | | 1974 | | 1979 | |
Factor	Smokers	Nonsmokers	Smokers	Nonsmokers	Smokers	Nonsmokers	Smokers	Nonsmokers
1. Health	11.74	13.21	12.26	13.46	11.94	13.17	12.63	13.47
2. Nonsmokers' rights	9.30	12.41	10.06	13.22	9.70	12.76	10.69	13.28
3. Positive aspects of smoking	8.07	6.56	17.99	6.38	7.48	6.47	7.57	6.30
4. Rationalization	9.06	7.20	8.59	8.12	8.80	8.52	8.38	8.31
5. Stereotype of smoking	7.00	9.08	7.01	9.16	6.29	8.78	6.43	8.89
6. Stereotype of smoker	8.56	11.84	8.84	12.30	8.38	11.66	8.85	12.24
7. Feeling toward authority	10.26	10.99	10.67	11.15	10.56	11.34	10.76	11.44
8. Control of future	11.95	12.91	11.92	13.15	12.17	13.17	12.26	13.42

Smokers have higher mean scores on Factor 5 which describes the common stereotype of smoking as a social behavior engaged in to be popular or attract the opposite sex. The belief that smoking is a result of peer pressure is held by many more nonsmokers than smokers, as evidenced by the fact that 35.1 percent of nonsmokers agree that "If you don't smoke, other teenagers put you down," while only 17.5 percent of smokers agree with this statement.

On Factor 6 which describes the smoker in unfavorable terms, smokers, understandably, have a smaller proportion who agree with every one of the three statements than nonsmokers. This, of course, results in higher mean scores for the nonsmokers.

Factor 7 shows little difference between smokers and nonsmokers, indicating that smokers are really not as anxious to grow up and get out from under parental authority as might be expected.

Factor 8 measures the extent to which individuals want to control their future, and how they perceive their capabilities of doing so. One of the items in this factor differentiates between smokers and non-smokers: "I don't want to get hooked on anything, including cigar-ettes." In the five years between the 1974 and 1979 surveys, little change in mean scores was observed. The greatest difference, a small one, was seen on Factor 2, Rights of the nonsmoker. This is probably the result of the recent emphasis placed on the harmful effects of sidestream smoke, and pleas for consideration of those who might be affected by it. It is somewhat surprising that there was not a larger change in the average score on this factor.

EXAMPLE SET BY SOCIETY

The culture in which teenagers grow up must, of necessity, have a profound effect on their attitudes, beliefs, and their habits. Besides their parents and older siblings, other adults set an example for teen-agers. They are influenced by adults in general, by those in the health professions, and by their teachers. The prevalence of cigarette smoking in each of these groups is discussed briefly in this section.

PREVALENCE OF SMOKING IN THE ADULT POPULATION

A survey of a national probability sample of adults conducted in 1975 (Department of Health, Education, and Welfare, 1976a) showed a marked decrease from the time of the Surgeon General's Report in

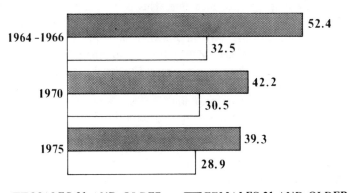

■■■ MALES 21 AND OLDER   □ FEMALES 21 AND OLDER

(PERCENTAGE IN EACH CATEGORY WHO ARE SMOKERS)

SOURCE: U.S. Department of Health, Education, and Welfare, 1976a.

FIGURE 5.4   Cigarette Smokers—A Declining Minority

1964. While a majority of adult males were smokers in 1964, less than 40 percent were smokers in 1975. This is a decline of one in four. The decrease in smoking among women was less dramatic; however, there was a decrease. Adults who smoke cigarettes are a minority, and a declining minority.

Some of the characteristics of adult smokers are revealing. Those who are married are much less likely to smoke than those who are separated or divorced. Among men, the smoking rate among blue-collar workers is much higher than that of men in white-collar occupations, but among women there is little difference. Women who are *not* employed outside the home show the lowest rate of smoking. Both men and women show a relationship between cigarette smoking and highest educational level attained, with a smaller proportion of smoking among college graduates. This relationship is more clear-cut for the men than for the women. These data are encouraging in that the teenager lives in a climate where the majority of adults do not smoke, and those who do smoke are not the adults that teenagers typically want to emulate.

SMOKING AMONG HEALTH PROFESSIONALS

People in the health professions are the authorities on matters pertaining to health. They are looked to for advice and are expected to be exemplars in preventive medicine. This is certainly the case with cigarette smoking. Physicians have taken their role as exemplars seriously and have led the way in quitting smoking. In fact, of all physicians who ever smoked, almost two out of three have quit (64 percent). In a 1975 survey of physicians, (National Clearinghouse for Smoking and Health, 1977), only 21 percent were cigarette smokers, compared with 39 percent of *all* adult males. This same survey shows that physicians feel that they have a responsibility to set a good example for their patients, and that those who do smoke rarely do so in front of patients. Dentists who, perhaps, come in contact with teenagers more often than do doctors show similar concerns. Of all dentists who ever smoked, 61 percent have quit so that, by 1975, only 23 percent were still smoking.

These two groups of health professionals are certainly setting a good example for teenagers. Most have quit smoking, and of those who continue to smoke, the large majority say that they seldom or never smoke in the presence of a patient (73 percent of physicians, 81 percent of dentists).

SMOKING AMONG TEACHERS

Aside from family influence, it has often been speculated that teachers have the greatest influence on the adolescent. If large numbers of teachers smoke, it might appear to the teenager that they endorse the habit, while, at the same time, they exhort against smoking to their students. To the teenager, what teachers do may speak more loudly than what they say.

A 1976 survey of teachers (American Cancer Society, 1976) showed that the prevalence of smoking among teachers was the same as that found among physicians—21 percent. Surprisingly, the prevalence was higher among female teachers (23 percent) than among male teachers (18 percent). The rate was the same for high school teachers as for grade school teachers. Most of the teachers who smoke cigarettes report that they smoke in school (80 percent). However, most indicate that they seldom smoke in the presence of students (70 percent). The most popular place for teachers to smoke is in the teachers' lounge.

While cigarette smoking among teachers has decreased to a very low level, there is still a small minority who continue to smoke, and an even smaller minority who smoke in front of students.

SUMMARY

Although tobacco has been used since the sixteenth century, studies of its effects on human users were not made until the twentieth century. Recent studies have shown that cigarette smoking causes some diseases and is associated with others. As a result, efforts were initiated and continue to encourage smokers to give up the habit and to convince young people to refrain from taking it up. Data provided in this chapter have assessed the overall effects of these prevention measures on the behavior and attitudes of adolescents.

Between 1968 and 1979, interesting trends in the prevalence of teenage smoking can be seen. Overall, there has been a decrease in the proportion of teenage boys and girls who smoke. Particularly in recent years, there has been a decrease in the proportion of boys smoking, observed in every age group. The recent decrease in smoking among girls was not seen in every age group, with no change being observed among the 17 and 18 year olds. Contrary to tradition, by 1979 a larger proportion of girls, 13 percent, than boys, 11 percent, were classified as smokers. Further, available data lend no support to the popular fear that teenagers are starting to smoke at earlier ages.

Although a large number of adolescents experiment with cigarettes, only about one in three has become a regular smoker by the time he or she is 18 years of age. Those who become regular smokers differ from those who do not in terms of relevant demographic characteristics, life-style, and attitudes toward the world around them. Of necessity, the culture in which a teenager grows up plays an important role in his or her willingness to become a smoker. Cigarette smoking among parents, siblings, teachers, health professionals, and other adults often sets a bad example for youth and tends to encourage their smoking behavior. Data indicates, however, that the adolescent today is growing up in a world where smoking is practiced by a minority of adults, and an even smaller minority of adults he or she is likely to see as exemplars.

REFERENCES

American Cancer Society (1976) A Study of Public School Teachers' Cigarette Smoking Attitudes and Habits. New York: Author.
GREEN, D. E. (1978a) "Changing cigarette habits in the United States:

1964-1977." Editorial in the American College of Preventive Medicine Newsletter 18, 3.

——— (1978b) "Psychological factors in smoking," in M. E. Jarvik et al. (eds.) Research on Smoking Behavior. NIDA Monograph 17. Rockville, MD: Department of Health, Education, and Welfare, Public Health Service, Alcohol, Drug Abuse, and Mental Health Administration, National Institute on Drug Abuse.

——— (1975) "Teenage cigarette smoking in the United States," in Proceedings of the 3rd World Conference on Smoking and Health. Bethesda, MD: Department of Health, Education, and Welfare, Public Health Service, National Institutes of Health.

MILNE, A. M. and J. G. COLMEN (1973) Development of a Teenager's Self-Testing Kit (Cigarette Smoking). Washington, DC: Education and Public Affairs.

National Clearinghouse for Smoking and Health (1977) "Smoking behavior and attitudes of physicians, dentists, nurses, and pharmacists, 1975. Center for Disease Control Morbidity and Mortality Weekly Report 26, 23.

U.S. Department of Health, Education, and Welfare, Public Health Service, Center for Disease Control and National Institutes of Health (1976a) Adult Use of Tobacco—1975. Washington, DC: Government Printing Office.

U.S. Department of Health, Education, and Welfare, Public Health Service, Office of Assistant Secretary for Health, Office on Smoking and Health (1979) Smoking and Health—A Report of the Surgeon General. Washington, DC: Government Printing Office.

U.S. Department of Health, Education, and Welfare, Public Health Service, National Institutes of Health (1976b) Teenage Smoking. National Patterns of Cigarette Smoking, Ages 12 Through 18, in 1972 and 1974. Washington, DC: Government Printing Office.

U.S. Department of Health, Education, and Welfare, Public Health Service, Health Services and Mental Health Administration, National Clearinghouse for Smoking and Health (1972) Teenage Smoking. National Patterns of Cigarette Smoking, Ages 12 Through 18, in 1968 and 1970. Washington, DC: Government Printing Office.

U.S. Department of Health, Education, and Welfare, Public Health Service, Alcohol, Drug Abuse, and Mental Health Administration, National Institute of Drug Abuse (1978). National Survey on Drug Abuse: 1977. Washington, DC: Government Printing Office.

WILLIAMS, T. M. (1971) Summary and Implications of Review of Literature Related to Adolescent Smoking. Washington, DC: Department of Health, Education, and Welfare, Health Services and Mental Health Administration, National Clearinghouse for Smoking and Health.

6

YOUTH, DRUGS, AND STREET CRIME

JAMES A. INCIARDI

For the better part of the twentieth century, crime and the youthful drug abuser have received extended coverage in both political and public sectors. As early as 1918, a campaign of hysteria instigated by Mrs. William K. Vanderbilt of New York society's elite "Four Hundred" combined with the efforts of the U.S. Treasury Department served to focus initial attention on America's alleged "drug-crazed" youth (King, 1972: 23-32). These endeavors resulted in a series of newspaper accounts which described an epidemic of heavy addiction within the youth culture and an army of more than a million and a half violent and dangerous addicts at large in the streets. Furthermore, such propaganda included rumors of fiendish enemy agents prowling through the school yards of urban America with candy laced with heroin, seducing innocent children and teenagers into lives of addiction and crime. The following decade, similar stories were offered to the public by Captain Richard Pearson Hobson, an avid prohibitionist and the first celebrated hero of the Spanish-American War. Through syndicated newspaper columns and national radio broadcasts, Hobson popularized the notion that addicts were "beasts" and "monsters" who spread their

disease like medieval vampires and who were responsible for much of
the nation's street crime. He noted that teenagers were well represented
in the addict population, that they were being infected by heroin
secreted in ice cream cones, and that their "disease" accounted for the
alarming increases in daytime robberies, brutal murders, and other
serious crimes of violence (Epstein, 1977: 23-34). And beginning in the
late 1930s, the crusade was then carried on by Harry J. Anslinger and
his Federal Bureau of Narcotics, who targeted marihuana as the
"assassin of youth." Using *American Magazine* as his national forum,
Anslinger initiated a series of reports in 1937 aimed at shocking the
American public and designating marihuana use as a root cause of
youthful crime and degradation (see Sloman, 1979).

The end product of these moral enterprises has been well
documented. By the 1940s, a body of literature had begun to develop
which stereotyped drug users as sex-crazed maniacs, degenerate street
criminals, and members of the "living dead." Narcotics reportedly
ravaged the human body; they destroyed morality; addicts were
sexually violent and criminally aggressive; drug users in general were
weak and ineffective members of society; addiction was contagious
since users had a mania for perpetuating the social anathema of
drug-taking; and finally, once addicted, the user entered a lifetime of
slavery to drugs. Furthermore, the erroneous conception was typically
emphasized that marihuana and cocaine, like heroin, were addicting
narcotics, and that drug use and addiction were concentrated almost
exclusively in the American youth population.[1]

The nature and extent of drug use and crime among the youth
culture during the early part of this century may never be fully
understood, for our literature in this behalf is so contaminated by
myth, propaganda, and biased research that an accurate representation
would be difficult to reconstruct. As the twentieth century grew more
mature, however, efforts to assess these phenomena became more
critical and objective. Medical facilities structured for the treatment of
addict populations placed a greater emphasis on social science research,
and independent funding for the study of drug addiction began to
surface. In time, a body of literature developed which served as a
preliminary base for understanding the nature and extent of drug-taking
and drug-seeking behaviors. However, not all phases of the drug
problem were fully assessed, and even today our images of drug use and
its relation to youth crime are, at best, incomplete. Furthermore, the
1950s, 1960s, and early 1970s seem to have emerged as individual
summits in our perceptions of youthful drug abuse, and it is intended

here to briefly examine these crucial periods with a view toward the contemporary setting and beyond.

THE FIFTIES: A DECADE OF REPRESSION

The United States entered mid-century as the most powerful nation on earth. World War II had ended the Great Depression and unleashed a prosperous postwar era; unemployment had stabilized at a uniquely low level and most Americans reveled in a new economic privilege. The period has been called "the fabulous fifties," for retrospective glances have characterized it as a golden age of simplicity and innocence—the thrilling days of bobby sox and soda fountains, of hot rods and Elvis Presley. There were no real wars, no riots, and no protests. But within much of the youth culture the decade was hardly a time of enthusiasm and contentment. For the teenager and young adult there was an enforcement of conformity, a transparency of sexual morals, and a set of cultural prescriptions and proscriptions that stressed achievement, prejudice, waste, compliance, and consensus, all of which resulted in a new youth ethic which made serious value judgments as to the nature and meaning of life.

Of the many forms of youthful rebellion, juvenile delinquency was clearly the most visible. New York *Times* education reporter Benjamin Fine predicted in the early 1950s that by the middle of the decade the number of youths being processed by the police would exceed one million. His estimates were quickly realized, and property crimes and car theft were the major juvenile offenses. The young were also committing acts of inexplicable and pointless violence—rape, beatings, and murders. Although statistically few of America's teenage groups were involved in violent crime, the few that were had seemingly terrorized entire cities (Miller and Nowak, 1977: 279-287). These were the fighting gangs of the fifties—the Roman Lords, Young Stars, Scorpions, and other gangs as portrayed in Irving Shulman's *The Amboy Dukes* and Hal Ellson's *Jailbait Street*.

Curiously, however, although street crime was heavily tied to delinquency, at least in the media, juvenile drug use seemed to be absent from the gang culture. Chein's (1964) pioneering study of narcotics use among juveniles reflected what most other informed efforts had found. Adolescent drug use was concentrated in the ghetto, and was most widespread where income and education were lowest. Drug use, however, was not intricately tied to gang activities; there were some drug users in organized juvenile gangs, yet they were less often involved in gang fighting.[2]

Although heroin use seemed to be confined to central cities and minority groups, there was some concern within the white middle-class as to what effect the new "rock and roll" music might have on the drug-using and other behaviors of the more socially privileged youth. When Alan Freed, a disc jockey for WJW in Cleveland, Ohio, introduced the term in 1951, little did he know what its future impact on American life would be. The music was what had been previously known as "rhythm and blues," a product of the black community that clearly had a racial stigma attached to it (Whitcomb, 1974: 219-241). Freed brought it from the ghetto and introduced it to white youth—and it was an immediate success. The acceptance of rock and roll was part and parcel of the new youth rebellion, and at the same time, it served to threaten every phobia of white American respectability. Social commentaries of the period claimed that it had infected white teenagers all across the country: It introduced them to their sexuality, to interracial contacts, to bizarre dance rituals, and most seriously, *to drugs*. This position was clearly articulated, for example, in the 1952 bestseller *U.S.A. Confidential:*

> Like a heathen religion, it is all tied up with tom toms and hot jive and ritualistic orgies of erotic dancing, weed-smoking and mass mania, with African jungle background. Many music shops purvey dope; assignations are made in them. White girls are recruited for colored lovers. Another cog in the giant delinquency machine is the radio disc jockey. . . . We know that many platter spinners are hopheads. Many others are Reds, left-wingers, or hecklers of social convention. . . . Through disc jocks, kids get to know colored and other hit musicians; they frequent places the radio oracles plug, which is done with design . . . to hook jives and guarantee a new generation subservient to the Mafia (Lait and Mortimer, 1952: 37-38).

Although rock and roll endured, its relationship to drug use and youth crime could never be established. And in spite of media contentions as to the relationship of drug use to middle-class delinquency, throughout the fifties youthful drug abuse appeared to remain at a relatively low level in white neighborhoods. Heroin use had grown at an alarming rate within the ghetto communities, however, especially among the youths of black America and other minority populations. For many of them, drug use had become a way of life, and street crime was typically a part of their drug-seeking activities (Chein et al., 1964; Zimmering et al., 1951; Wilner et al., 1957).

THE SIXTIES: A DECADE OF REVOLUTION

The enforced conformity, growing delinquency and youth rebellion, racism, and other problems that had festered throughout the forties and fifties seemed to merge during the following decade, resulting in one of the most revolutionary decades in recent history. It was a time characterized by civil rights movements, political assassinations, campus and antiwar protests, and ghetto riots, combined with increasing levels of crime and violence. Among the more startling occurrences of the 1960s was the unavoidable awareness of an actual emergence of youthful drug use on an apparently unprecedented scale. During the early part of the decade, the use of drugs seemed to leap from the marginal zones of society into the very center of stable middle-class community life. No longer were "drugs" limited to the ghetto or the half-worlds of the jazz scene or underground bohemias. Rather, they had become suddenly and dramatically apparent among members of the adolescent middle class and the young adult populations of both rural and urban America. By the close of the decade, commentators on the era were maintaining that ours was "the addicted society," that through drugs youth had become "seekers" of "instant enlightenment," and that "drugs and youth" would persist as a continuing fact of American social life (see Farber, 1966; Simmons and Winograd, 1966; Fort, 1969; Geller and Boas, 1969; Nowlis, 1969; and Blum et al., 1970).

In retrospect, what were then considered the logical causes of the youth drug phenomenon now seem less clear. A variety of changes in the fabric of American life were occurring during these years which undoubtedly had profound implications for youth and drugs. Notably, the revolution in the technology and handling of drugs which had begun in the 1950s was of sufficient magnitude to justify the designation of the following decade as "a new chemical age." Recently compounded psychotropic agents were enthusiastically introduced and effectively promoted, with the consequence of exposing the national consciousness to an impressive catalog of chemical temptations—sedatives, tranquilizers, stimulants, antidepressants, analgesics, and hallucinogens—which could offer fresh inspiration as well as simple and immediate relief from fear, anxiety, tension, frustration, and boredom (Inciardi, 1974a; Johnson, 1967). Concomitant with this emergence of a new chemical age, a new youth ethos had become manifest, one characterized by widely celebrated generational disaffiliation, a prejudicial dependence on the self and the peer group for value orientation, a critical view of how the world was being run, and mistrust for an "establishment" drug policy whose "facts" and "warnings" ran counter with reported peer experiences (see Suchman, 1968). This new ethos could itself be traced back, if one wished, to other alterations in American society—the population shift represented by the baby boom children then coming of age, the economic changes resulting from two decades of postwar prosperity, or the cultural and legal transformations entailed in the civil rights movement and the growing protests against American involvement in Vietnam.

Whatever the ultimate causes, American youth, or at least noticeable segments of it, had embraced drugs. The drug scene had become the arena of "happening" America, and "turning on" to drugs for relaxation and "kicks" seemed to have become commonplace. Most typically, however, the hysteria and ignorance of many politicians, parents, and opinion makers focused almost exclusively on the reported events at Woodstock and other mass gatherings, or on the more lurid segments of media coverage of drug-related crime incidents as "evidence" of a drug-crazed youth culture. Estimates of drug involvement among teenagers were often overstated, resulting in the impression that the new social order, especially in the youth culture, was indeed an addicted society.

In counterpoint, however, a backward glance at available data suggest that the incidence and prevalence of youthful drug abuse was never fully defined, nor were there meaningful analyses of the relationship between drug use and youth crime. Some studies documented the use of drugs on the college campus (see Pottieger and Inciardi, 1980), but in the main the drugs-crime issue remained unstudied—at least in terms of white America. There was some interest in the relationship between narcotics use and street crime, but in general the focus was on the *total,* rather than the *youthful,* heroin population. A number of enlightened studies were generated by the Clinical Research Center at Lexington, Kentucky (see Ball and Chambers, 1970; National Institute on Drug Abuse, 1978), but these focused almost exclusively on addicts in treatment, the majority of whom were well beyond their adolescent years.

Perhaps the few exceptions to these patterns of research endeavor were the ethnographic investigations of the drug scene which, ultimately, brought into question a major finding of the delinquency studies of the previous decade. During the late 1950s, the Chicago Area Project's study of drug use in the black ghetto resulted in Finestone's (1957) well-known "Cats, Kicks, and Color." Finestone's analysis of the black addicts belonging to Chicago's "elite society of cats" found them to be aloof and detached from traditional social interests. In dealing with typical adolescent problems, "cats" rejected the norms and values of the larger society and found security within a cultural system which searched for ecstatic experiences through drugs. Finestone's report became the basis for the Cloward and Ohlin (1960: 27) "double-failure" hypothesis. Accordingly, some adolescents were unable to find places for themselves in gang subcultures, criminal subcultures, or conventional youth subcultures. In attempting to deal with this status dilemma, many would select a "retreatist role adaptation" and use drugs as a form of escape. As such, youths who could not accommodate themselves to conventional or criminal roles would escape this "double-failure" by using drugs. And if addiction occurred, esteem and status could be had in an addict subculture where escape was complete.

Ethnographic studies during the sixties described the life of addicts on the street, and demonstrated that they were hardly members of retreatist groups. The findings of Sutter (1966), Feldman (1968), and Preble and Casey (1969), for example, challenged the then predominant clinical and sociological theories that described heroin addicts as escapists or retreatists—dependent and passive with inadequate personalities and unsuccessful in both legitimate and illegitimate domains. Rather, addicts were found to be engaged in meaningful activities and relationships on a day-to-day basis. In many communities, thousands of youths were using heroin to become a "somebody," and to enhance their positions in the neighborhood social system. These studies also pointed to the fact that heroin use was often only one part of a multiple pattern of drug-taking, and that crime was present, but varied from one type of user to another. The ethnographers, however, did not provide all the answers, and it was not until the following decade that more conclusive data on drugs and youth crime began to emerge.

THE SEVENTIES AND THE WAR ON DRUGS

On June 18, 1971, in his address to an audience of media executives in Rochester, New York, President Richard M. Nixon declared an all-out war on drugs, commenting that drug abuse had grown to epidemic proportions, that it was the nation's "public enemy number one," and that it was destroying American youth and breeding lawlessness, violence, and death. Similar statements were offered repeatedly by Nixon throughout the balance of his administration, and by other federal officials, all of whom focused on the issue of crime and drugs within the American youth culture (National Journal, 1971; U.S. News & World Report, 1972). Much of the commentary was reminiscent of the ravings from earlier decades in the century by Mrs. Vanderbilt, Captain Hobson, and Commissioner Anslinger. Furthermore, one current evaluation has suggested the drug rhetoric of the Nixon platform was designed as an organization of fear which would mask the activities of new agencies created specifically to execute presidential orders free of the normal due process constraints (Epstein, 1977). Yet whatever the texture and purposes of Nixon's "war" may or may not have been, it did have some impact on our awareness of drug-taking and drug-seeking within youthful populations.

As part of the Nixon "war on drugs," a variety of new agencies evolved, including the Special Action Office for Drug Abuse Prevention (SAODAP), created in 1971 by a presidential order to oversee and coordinate the development of a comprehensive treatment and prevention program (Domestic Council Drug Abuse Task Force, 1975).

This latter agency, SAODAP, stimulated considerable research of a social scientific nature, and its successor, the National Institute on Drug Abuse (NIDA), established permanently in the U.S. Department of Health, Education, and Welfare by 1974, further broadened the research enterprise. Since that time, the studies of drugs and youth have been impressive, and many of the long-standing questions as to the nature and extent of youthful drug abuse were finally addressed (see Beschner and Friedman, 1979).

By contrast, however, enlightened analyses of the relationships between drug use and crime remained limited. Indeed, there had been many scientific assessments of the drugs-crime nexus, asking such questions as, Does heroin addiction cause crime? Is heroin use simply an additional pattern of deviant behavior manifested by an already criminal population? Are the two phenomena related in some other manner, or at all? Yet, in the main, the conclusions, hypotheses, and theories that could be drawn from many decades of efforts in this behalf were for the most part meaningless and irrelevant if one considered the awesome biases and deficiencies in the information generated. The data gathered on criminal behavior were typically based on arrests, and those that probed beyond the limitations of official statistics focused on extremely small samples. In terms of the youthful drug-abusing population, many of these issues were almost totally ignored, and the information available had to make projections based on the activities of selected groups of older users.[3]

THE NATIONAL CRIME/DRUGS PANEL

During the early 1970s, crime rates continued to increase in the almost geometric patterns that had been established during the previous decade. Official criminal statistics indicated that there were almost one million violent crimes and more than nine million property offenses reported to law enforcement agencies in 1974, and these figures were even higher during the following year. Furthermore, the Drug Enforcement Administration (DEA) estimated that in 1975 there were between 655,000 and 751,000 heroin users in the country, while another intensive analysis projected that several million Americans had used heroin at least once during that year (Hunt, 1976). Combined with these figures were the data that documented the notion that heroin use and crime were closely related. In 1972, nine out of ten adults interviewed in a survey sponsored by the National Commission on Marihuana and Drug Abuse believed that heroin users committed crimes that they would have not otherwise committed had they been drug-free, and half of these respondents agreed with similar statements on marihuana use (Abelson et al., 1973). In addition, estimates as to the proportion of property crimes attributed to heroin addiction ranged as high as 70 percent (Research Triangle Institute, 1976: 3). Yet, in spite of these figures and concerns, during the first half of that decade less than 1 percent of all federal drug abuse research dollars had been allocated for the study of drug use as it was related to crime. There had been a number of individual research efforts which had targeted this important policy-related issue, but there had never been any overall, coordinated, research plan.

In an effort to alleviate this research gap, Research Triangle Institute (RTI) under a contract with the National Institute on Drug Abuse (NIDA), organized the Panel on Drug Use and Criminal Behavior in 1975 for the purpose of constructing state-of-the-art summaries, articulating the major questions to be asked, analyzing existing drugs-crime data, and formulating extensive research recommendations. For those who expected the Panel to suggest "answers" to the drugs-crime problem, the final report of the effort was somewhat disappointing (see Research Triangle Institute, 1976). However, what the Panel did provide was the basis for a coordinated research effort which would ultimately focus on the drugs-crime issue both at the general level and within the context of specific populations of users, including the youthful drug abuser.

Much of the data reported in the balance of this essay are an outgrowth of one of the research endeavors recommended by the Panel, and the findings described below focus on the nature and extent of drug use and criminal behavior within several contemporary youth cultures. These data were drawn from a broader NIDA-funded study which examined the self-reported patterns of drug use and crime characteristic of numerous geographically and demographically diverse population groups, and a segment of these data have already been reported elsewhere (Inciardi, forthcoming, 1980; Pottieger and Inciardi, 1980).[4] All interviewing was undertaken during 1977-1978 on a face-to-face basis with a structured, precoded instrument, and the youth cohorts reported on were drawn from a campus population in the northeastern quadrant of the United States, and from a street population in the Liberty City community of Dade County (Miami), Florida.

CRIME AND DRUGS WITHIN A CAMPUS SETTING

From a university population of some 13,000 liberal arts, business, health sciences, and engineering undergraduates, a multistage nonrandom sample was drawn which focused primarily on first- and second-year students. The resulting 514 interviews, although not fully representative of the population as a whole, nevertheless reflected many of the general characteristics of the student body. The respondents were primarily whites (96.4 percent), the median age of the sample was some 19.3 years, and the proportions of males and females were almost equal.

In terms of the drug-taking of the 514 students studied, it was readily evident that most had engaged in some form of substance abuse. Initially, and not unexpectedly, 492 respondents reported the use of alcohol at least once, and 98.6 percent of these (or 94.4 percent of the sample) indicated having used alcohol to excess on one or more occasions with the first such incident at a median age of 15.1 years.

Beyond alcohol, marihuana was the drug most typically experienced, although the use of stimulants, sedatives, hallucinogens, and narcotics was also evident. More specifically, for example, some 71.2 percent of the students surveyed reported having used marihuana at least once, with only small proportions having "ever used" amphetamines (15.4 percent) and cocaine (13.2 percent), and few having experienced the effects of sedatives and hallucinogens. Furthermore, only two students reported any prior use of heroin and none indicated any methadone use.

In terms of the students' *current use* of drugs (any use during the 90 days prior to interview), the prevalence was less dramatic. Some 78 percent were alcohol users, 55.1 percent were marihuana users, and less than 8 percent were users of one of the more dangerous types of substances. And finally, the proportions using drugs on a *regular* basis (at least once a week) were even lower—55.8 percent for alcohol, 27.4 percent for marihuana, and 1 percent or less for all other substance categories. Thus, aside from the use of marihuana and/or alcohol, drug use did not appear to be widespread within this campus population. Although 287 students were using alcohol at least once a week and 141 students were using marihuana with the same frequency, only 19 students sampled (3.7 percent) were abusing any of the amphetamines, other stimulants (including cocaine), tranquilizers, sedatives, hallucinogens, or solvents/inhalants regularly, and *none* was using any of the hard narcotics.

If these data are in any way representative of college students in general, they suggest a shift in the pattern of campus drug use that was apparent a decade ago. Estimates of the *regular use* of alcohol and marihuana during the late 1960s were 50 percent and 20 percent respectively, and from 4 percent to 8 percent for amphetamines, methamphetamines, prescription sedatives, and LSD (see Goode, 1970; Kaplan, 1970; McGlothlin et al., 1970; Chambers, 1970; Blum et al., 1970; Suchman, 1968; Johnson, 1973). By contrast, current campus drug activity seems to be slightly more widespread, yet considerably more focused. The current-regular use of drugs is restricted almost exclusively to marihuana and alcohol, with few involved with the more dangerous illicit or prescription substances. Whether this shift is the result of the drug education programs of the early 1970s, the decreased availability of the amphetamines, barbiturates, and other high abuse potential prescription drugs, or changes in the general attitudes and values of today's students is only open to speculation. Nevertheless, a change does seem apparent, and only replication in other campus settings will substantiate this finding.

In terms of criminality, some 72.2 percent (N = 371) reported having committed a crime on at least one occasion during their lives, with the first crime having occurred at a median age of 14.3 years. More importantly, however, students were questioned extensively in terms of their criminal involvement during the twelve-month period prior to interview, and a pattern seemed to emerge. A total of 23 offense categories were examined, and considered together, 24.9 percent (N = 128) of the students admitted to one or more crimes with the majority of these (99, or 19.3 percent of all students) reporting some type of theft. In addition, 4.9 percent (N = 25) reported crimes against persons (assault, rape, or robbery), 5.8 percent (N = 30) reported felonious property destruction, and 8.4 percent (N = 43) admitted to having sold drugs during the twelve-month period prior to interview.

A more focused view of crime and drug use within this sampled university population suggests that the prevalence of crime is clustered among both males and among those for whom drug use is most current and regular. For example, only 4.9 percent of *all* students reported crimes against persons. This proportion increases to 7.7 percent for *male students,* and to 11.3 percent for *regular users of marihuana.* For crimes of theft, property destruction, and drug sales, similar clusterings are also apparent. *Most important in these data is the finding that crime is most evident among persons who use drugs on a regular basis.*

In sum, if these data are at all representative of college populations in general, two implications can be suggested. First, drug use on the college campus simply means the use of alcohol and marihuana. The "current" use of these substances is characteristic of the majority, not the minority, of students, while involvement with sedatives, stimulants, hallucinogens, and narcotics is minimal at best. Second, the data indicate that crime is most prevalent among regular users of marihuana and other drugs, suggesting that these phenomena may be encompassed within a larger sociocultural matrix. This perspective received some additional support when the variable of "drug selling" was introduced. The prevalence of crimes against persons and property was highest among those students who were regular users of alcohol, marihuana, and other drugs, and who at the same time were sellers of drugs (see Pottieger and Inciardi, 1980). Thus, while alcohol and marihuana use are a significant part of campus life, crime is not. Rather, crime seems to be most apparent among that select minority who not only use drugs regularly, but sell them as well.

CRIME AND DRUGS WITHIN A STREET SETTING

While the campus population studied reflected a high prevalence of alcohol and marihuana use, with criminality focused among the drug sellers who abused marihuana and other substances on a regular basis, the patterns were somewhat different within a street community of drug users. From a population of some 800 active and institutionalized heroin and other drug users interviewed in Dade County, Florida, a subsample of 166 "youths" aged 21 and under were drawn for analysis.[5] Of these 166 respondents, 42.2 percent (N = 70) were primarily heroin users with the remaining 57.8 percent (N = 96) using a variety of other types of substances. In addition, 45.8 percent (N = 76) were white, 42.2 percent (N = 70) were black, 9 percent (N = 15) were Hispanic, and the remainder were Asian or native American. The majority were males (58.4 percent), the median age of the entire group was 19.8 years (as compared to 19.3 years for the campus population), and only 3.6 percent (N = 6) were students. Furthermore, 68.7 percent (N = 114) of these subjects were "active" drug users in that they were at large in the street community at the time of interview, 24.1 percent (N = 40) were incarcerated, and 7.2 percent (N = 12) were in treatment for drug-abuse problems.

The 70 heroin users had long histories of substance abuse, typically beginning with alcohol, marihuana, solvents/inhalants, or codeine cough syrup at a median age of 13.2 years. The onset of sedative abuse generally occurred at a median age of 15.3 years, followed by heroin (16.8 years), cocaine (17.0 years), and illegal methadone (17.9 years). In all, these heroin users had abused an average of 9.4 different substances, including alcohol. By contrast, the nonheroin cases initiated their drug abuse careers at a median age of 14.3 years with alcohol, followed by marihuana (14.4 years), sedatives (15.8 years), and cocaine (16.8 years). Of the only 26 percent of these nonheroin cases that had experimented with narcotics at one time or another, such use began at a median age of 16.9 years, yet none considered themselves to be narcotics users at the time of interview, and narcotics had never been among their primary drugs of abuse. And finally, during their drug careers, these subjects had used an average of 4.9 different substances.

As suggested by Table 6.1, the "current" drug use of both of these groups was considerable at the time of interview. "Current," here, refers to the 90-day period prior to interview (or the 90-day period prior to institutionalization for those incarcerated or in treatment).

TABLE 6.1   Current and Regular Drug Use Among 166 Dade County, Florida, Youths (1978)

Drug group	Heroin 100.0	(70)	Nonheroin 100.0	(96)	Total 100.0	(166)
Current use[1]						
Heroin	100.0	(70)	0.0	(0)	42.2	(70)
Illegal methadone	14.3	(10)	0.0	(0)	6.0	(10)
Codeine cough syr.	2.9	(2)	4.2	(4)	3.6	(6)
Other narcotics	31.4	(22)	9.4	(9)	18.7	(31)
Barbiturates	47.1	(33)	16.7	(16)	29.5	(49)
Other sedatives	28.6	(20)	12.5	(12)	19.3	(32)
Minor tranquilizers	31.4	(22)	16.7	(16)	22.9	(38)
Major tranquilizers	18.6	(13)	4.2	(4)	10.2	(17)
Antidepressants	5.7	(4)	2.1	(2)	3.6	(6)
Cocaine	62.9	(44)	36.5	(35)	47.6	(79)
Methamphetamine	7.1	(5)	6.3	(6)	6.6	(11)
Amphetamines	20.0	(14)	5.2	(5)	11.4	(19)
Other stimulants	1.4	(1)	2.1	(2)	1.8	(3)
Other analgesics	4.3	(3)	1.0	(1)	2.4	(4)
Marihuana	91.4	(64)	72.9	(70)	80.7	(134)
LSD	12.9	(9)	4.2	(4)	7.8	(13)
Other hallucinogens	8.6	(6)	6.3	(6)	7.2	(12)
Solvent-inhalant	4.3	(3)	1.0	(1)	2.4	(4)
Alcohol	82.9	(58)	68.8	(66)	74.7	(124)
Over-the-counter drugs	5.7	(4)	3.1	(3)	4.2	(7)
Regular use[2]						
Heroin	87.1	(61)	0.0	(0)	36.7	(61)
Cocaine	31.4	(22)	27.1	(26)	28.9	(48)
Marihuana	80.0	(56)	66.7	(64)	72.3	(120)
Alcohol	57.1	(40)	57.3	(55)	57.2	(95)
Median number of drugs used	5.6		2.1		3.5	

1. "Current" = within 90 days prior to interview or prior to institutionalization. Due to multiple responses, totals add to more than 100.0 percent.
2. "Regular" = at least "several times a week."

Specifically, the heroin cases were concurrently using an average of 5.6 different substances, with the highest prevalences involving heroin (100 percent), alcohol (82.9 percent), marihuana (91.4 percent), cocaine (62.9 percent), and barbiturates (47.1 percent). In addition, the regular use (at least several times a week) of heroin, marihuana, alcohol, and cocaine was common throughout this subsample.

TABLE 6.2 Criminal Activity During Last Twelve Months Among
70 Dade County Heroin Users (1978)

Crime	Total offenses	Percentage of total offenses	Percentage of sample involved		Percentage of offenses resulting in in arrest[1]	
Total	24,670	100.0%	100.0% =	(70)	0.6%	(136)
Robbery	303	1.2	31.4	(22)	5.3	(16)
Assault	100	0.4	27.1	(19)	7.0	(7)
Burglary	565	2.3	41.4	(29)	3.9	(22)
Vehicle theft	35	0.1	17.1	(12)	5.7	(2)
Theft from vehicle	1,122	4.5	31.4	(22)	0.5	(6)
Shoplifting	2,578	10.4	62.9	(44)	0.1	(26)
Pickpocketing	223	0.9	7.1	(5)	0.0	(0)
Prostitute theft	398	1.6	17.1	(12)	0.0	(0)
Other theft[2]	84	0.3	17.1	(12)	8.3	(7)
Forgery/counterfeiting[3]	513	2.1	25.7	(18)	1.8	(9)
Con games	181	0.7	18.6	(13)	0.0	(0)
Fraud	61	0.2	7.1	(5)	1.6	(1)
Stolen goods	1,282	5.2	41.4	(29)	0.5	(6)
Arson, vandalism	30	0.1	11.4	(8)	0.0	(0)
Extortion	23	0.1	4.3	(3)	0.0	(0)
Loan-sharking	0	0.0	0.0	(0)	–	–
Prostitution	5,257	21.3	27.1	(19)	0.4	(22)
Procuring	1,869	7.6	17.1	(12)	0.1	(1)
Gambling	462	1.9	12.9	(9)	0.0	(6)
Drug sales	9,584	38.8	72.9	(51)	0.1	(11)
Mean number of offenses per subject	352					

1. That is, offenses for which an arrest was made—not necessarily the same as "number of arrests for these offenses."
2. Thefts not classifiable elsewhere, often due to insufficient information, and therefore likely to belong in one of the preceding categories.
3. Almost entirely forgery of drug prescriptions.

The nonheroin cases were somewhat less drug involved, as evidenced by their concurrent use of only 2.1 different substances. Their most commonly used drugs were marihuana, cocaine, and alcohol, and only limited proportions were using these drugs on a "regular" basis.

All of the nonheroin cases and 98.6 percent (N = 69) of the heroin cases admitted to having criminal histories, with the median ages of their first offenses occurring at 13.0 and 14.2 years, respectively. The first offenses for both groups were typically burglary, shoplifting, or

TABLE 6.3 Criminal Activity During Last Twelve Months Among 96 Dade County Nonheroin Drug Users (1978)

Crime	Total offenses	Percentage of total offenses	Percentage of sample involved		Percentage of offenses resulting in in arrest [1]	
Total	29,982	100.0%	100.0% =	(96)	0.9%	(255)
Robbery	431	1.4	26.0	(25)	3.7	(16)
Assault	75	0.3	26.0	(25)	30.7	(23)
Burglary	787	2.6	44.8	(43)	14.5	(114)
Vehicle theft	40	0.1	17.7	(17)	20.0	(8)
Theft from vehicle	1,417	4.7	15.6	(15)	0.3	(4)
Shoplifting	3,366	11.2	33.3	(32)	0.4	(13)
Pickpocketing	1,182	3.9	15.6	(15)	0.0	(0)
Prostitute theft	38	0.1	6.3	(6)	0.0	(0)
Other theft[2]	115	0.4	11.5	(11)	7.8	(9)
Forgery/counterfeiting[3]	109	0.4	16.7	(16)	8.3	(9)
Con games	599	2.0	8.3	(8)	0.3	(2)
Fraud	26	0.1	7.3	(7)	7.7	(2)
Stolen goods	910	3.0	21.9	(21)	0.9	(8)
Arson, vandalism	18	0.1	8.3	(8)	5.6	(1)
Extortion	14	< 0.1	3.1	(3)	0.0	(0)
Loan-sharking	3	< 0.1	1.0	(1)	0.0	(0)
Prostitution	8,545	28.5	15.6	(15)	0.3	(25)
Procuring	38	0.1	2.1	(2)	0.0	(0)
Gambling	1,298	4.3	10.4	(10)	0.2	(2)
Drug sales	10,971	36.6	34.4	(33)	0.2	(19)
Mean number of offenses per subject	312					

1. That is, offenses for which an arrest was made—not necessarily the same as "number of arrests for these offenses."
2. Thefts not classifiable elsewhere, often due to insufficient information, and therefore likely to belong in one of the preceding categories.
3. Almost entirely forgery of drug prescriptions.

some other theft, and arrest histories were apparent for 99 percent of the nonheroin cases and 85.7 percent of the heroin cases.

Tables 6.2 and 6.3 suggest the magnitude of the criminal involvement of these two drug-using groups. During the twelve-month period prior to interview (or twelve months prior to institutionalization), the 96 heroin cases were involved in criminal activity totaling some 24,670 offenses or an average of 352 per case—a rate of almost one crime per day per person. Interestingly, however, only 1.6 percent (N = 403) of these offenses were violent personal crimes (robbery and assault), and some 28.5 percent (N = 7095) included crimes against property or fraud, while an overwhelming 69.6 percent (N = 17,172) were victimless crimes (prostitution, procuring, gambling, and drug sales). Also striking in these data are the low levels of arrest for these self-reported offenses. Of the 24,670 criminal events, less than 1 percent resulted in arrest, or one arrest for every 181 crimes committed.

Similar distributions of criminal activity appeared among the nonheroin cases—29,982 offenses over the twelve-month period, averaging 312 crimes per respondent. Paralleling the distributions apparent among the heroin users, these offenses were primarily of a victimless nature in that 69.5 percent (N = 20,852) were instances of prostitution, procuring, gambling, and drug sales, while only 1.7 percent (N = 506) were violent crimes, and the balance circumscribed fraud and property offenses. Furthermore, less than 1 percent of these crimes resulted in an arrest, or a ratio of 1 arrest for every 118 crimes committed.

YOUTH, DRUGS AND STREET CRIME

At this point in the analysis, these data seem to have some implications for the many policy questions being asked about street crime and the youthful drug abuser. Initially, data from both the campus population and the street population suggest that drug use and crime are concomitant aspects of the youth scene. Drug use generally begins at an early age—during the fifteenth year for college students, the fourteenth year for nonheroin drug users in the street community, and the thirteenth year for primary heroin users. Similarly, crime begins during the early adolescent years—the fourteenth year for both the college students and the heroin users, and the thirteenth year for the nonheroin drug users from the street community. Furthermore, all three types of users began their drug-taking with essentially the same substances, and as many as three-fourths of the students surveyed had histories of both drug use and criminal activity. Beyond these similarities, however, the campus and street populations seem to have little in common. Only those students who are drug dealers and who use drugs on a regular basis reflect a widespread prevalence of criminality, and even among these the extent of crime is low when compared to that which occurs in the street community.

By contrast, it is clear that at least within the street population studied here, high-volume drug use and widespread criminality go hand-in-hand—regardless of whether the users are involved with heroin or not. Furthermore, despite the finding that more than two-thirds of the criminality manifested by these heroin and nonheroin drug users is of a victimless nature, the incidence of crimes against person and property is nevertheless significant—a total of 16,122 offenses over a one-year period among the two groups or almost 100 serious crimes per user. Yet do these data suggest a relationship between youth, drugs, and street crime? Are the high rates of crime apparent among the street drug users the result of a drug-taking career? Answers to these and other questions are not altogether clear, and even further analysis suggests that any relationships between drug use and youth crime may be considerably more complex than initially believed.

Among the queries often posed when investigating the drugs-crime nexus is the circular issue of which came first, the drug career or the criminal career? It has been the contention of many that at least among narcotics users, the monopolistic controls over the heroin marketplace force the otherwise noncriminal user into a life of crime in order to support his or her necessary level of drug intake (Lindesmith, 1947; Schur, 1962). This "enslavement theory of addiction" has also been put forth by several Marxist criminologists who maintain that heroin in the ghetto is an "establishment" weapon designed to control those under-privileged and dissatisfied masses who might otherwise revolt against the existing political and economic order (Chambliss, 1977).

The simple cause and effect assumption at the base of this enslave-ment theory cannot be supported by the data of this study, however, and as suggested by the median onset ages listed below, the complex texture of this issue becomes readily evident. For example, for the 70 heroin-using youths drawn from the Dade County street community sample, consider the following sequential pattern:

Event	Median age
First drug use (any drug, except alcohol)	13.2 years
First marihuana use	13.3
First alcohol use	13.5
First crime	14.2
First barbiturate use	15.3
First arrest	16.0
First heroin use	16.8
First cocaine use	17.0

This pattern suggests that the initiation of drug use occurred perhaps a year prior to the onset of criminal activity. However, the early years of these users' drug-taking careers involved only the less expensive and nonaddicting substances, typically marihuana and inhalants, as well as alcohol. Heroin use did not begin, even at the experimental level, until almost four years after the onset of drug use and almost three years subsequent to the first criminal act. As such, the heroin user's criminal career had endured for well over two years before any contact with the heroin black market became apparent.

By contrast, the nonheroin drug cases in the Dade County street sample reflected an alternative sequential pattern. For example:

Event	Median age
First crime	13.0 years
First drug use	
(any drug, except alcohol)	14.3
First alcohol use	14.3
First marihuana use	14.4
First barbiturate use	15.8
First arrest	15.9
First cocaine use	16.8

Among these drug users, where contact with the heroin marketplace is not even a significant issue, criminal activity began more than a year prior to initial experimentation with marihuana, alcohol, or any other substance, and further, crime began at a younger age than that manifest among the heroin users.

This issue becomes even more complex when one introduces data on users' various sources of income as well as the proportions of their criminal activity that are directly related to drug use support. Initially, some 92.7 percent of the heroin users reported crime as a major source of income, yet 41.8 percent of the same group of respondents also reported income from a legal occupation, 28.2 percent reported receiving money from family and/or friends, and 7.2 percent were receiving some form of public assistance. Secondly, an average of 82.5 percent of the criminality of the heroin users was reportedly for the purpose of drug-use support. One might wish to hypothesize that if heroin were legalized or if the users' heroin intake were eliminated, criminal activity would be drastically reduced. But this would not explain the presence of their criminal patterns prior to their involvement with expensive drugs. With the nonheroin drug-using cases, the distribution of income sources was almost identical. However, these users reported that less than 1 percent of their crimes were perpetrated for the purpose of drug-use support. It should be emphasized, furthermore, that the nature and extent of the criminal activity of this latter group approached the level of that of the heroin users—about 13 percent less in magnitude over the twelve-month period of inquiry.

These data, then, present some perplexing issues relative to crime and the youthful drug abuser. It appears that the Dade County cases studied became involved in crime well before drug use evolved into an advanced state. Furthermore, these data suggest that if the youthful user should eventually embrace regular heroin use, criminal activity only slightly increases, yet the income generated by it becomes utilized almost exclusively for the purpose of drug-use support. From this one could *not* hypothesize that heroin use forces the individual into a life of crime, but rather shifts his or her spending habits relative to the income generated through criminal acts.

If these findings are in any way representative of other drug-using populations, whether youthful or not, it would appear that new perspectives and questions on the drugs-crime nexus are warranted. These data indicate that at least in the early stages of a youthful drug career in the street community, substance abuse criminality may be related only indirectly, and any direct relationships may be to the sociocultural matrix within which the two phenomena independently coexist. This suggestion was documented to some degree in an earlier study which compared rates of opiate use with a series of other social casualty statuses in New York City's 30 health center districts (Inciardi, 1974b). Each district (an aggregation of socially, economically, and demographically contiguous census tracts) was ranked in terms of its rates of opiate use, poverty, unemployment, out of wedlock births, juvenile delinquency, and financial assistance. The rates of opiate use for the 30 given areas were then correlated with those of the other social and economic variables, resulting in some unusually high statistical correlations. For example:

opiate use/delinquency	$r = .75$
opiate use/financial assistance	$r = .78$
opiate use/illegitimacy	$r = .81$
opiate use/unemployment	$r = .88$
opiate use/poverty	$r = .92$

Such correlations suggest that where high rates of opiate use are apparent, high levels of poverty, delinquency, and other social problems are likely to be found. The issue then becomes not one of a relationship between drug abuse and street crime, but rather, an interpretation of the conditions under which drugs and youth crime are likely to emerge and manifest themselves.

A second issue that must be addressed is that no *single* explanation can account for the varying relationships between crime and youthful drug abuse that may exist in the numerous populations of drug users that may be active in any given area. For example, in a series of pilot studies conducted during 1977 for the purpose of assessing the differences in criminal involvement and alternative patterns of drug abuse (Inciardi, 1978), it became clear that the nature, extent, and relationships between crime and drugs varied considerably from one drug-using population to another. Among a population of black heroin addicts from the Brownsville section of Brooklyn, New York, crime had been an integral part of their life-style well before their involvement with heroin. These inner-city youths had a median age of 19.3 years, had begun using drugs regularly by age 12, and most had had juvenile arrest records prior to that time. Their criminal activities had typically included purse snatching, shoplifting, and sneak theft, and remained at a relatively low level until the onset of heroin addiction at a median age of 17.5 years. At the time of interview, their levels of predatory crime were considerable, similar to the Dade County heroin users described earlier.

In contrast to these black addicts, members of a Long Island (Suffolk County, New York) motorcycle pack interviewed in southern Delaware manifested somewhat alternative patterns in crime and drugs. This was essentially an older group having a median age of 29.1 years, and their drug use had begun during their late teens. Most had not committed any crimes prior to drug use, or prior to their initial contacts with the biker culture. At the time of interview, drug use included the heavy use of alcohol, marihuana, sedatives, and amphetamines. Their criminal activities were totally unrelated to drug use, and were generally undertaken in a group setting and connected with their membership in a major East Coast motorcycle gang. During the 30-day period prior to interview in 1977, their criminal acts tended to be more violent than other drug-using groups, and included armed robbery, hijacking, burglary, drug sales, and assaults on rival gangs.

A group of white users with mixed addictions from New York City's "West Village" had also been contacted for study during this 1977 investigation. They were for the most part males with a median age of 25.2 years, and could be best described as former members of the late 1960s "new underground" combined with several avant garde types who had entered the Greenwich Village area after the onset of its decline as a "bohemian" enclave. All of these subjects had been physically dependent on at least two substances, typically sedatives and tranquilizers, and sometimes narcotics. However, most of these addicts had no criminal involvement of any type, but the few that did committed several crimes each day for the purpose of drug-use support.

These data, when compared with the findings descriptive of the youth groups discussed earlier, further document the complexity of the issue at hand. It can be readily concluded that the relationships between drug use and crime tend to vary with the drug-using group and the sociocultural context from which they emerge. This perspective would also apply to the youthful drug abuser, whose behavior may not only be influenced by the demands of a career in drugs and a given sociocultural matrix, but also by the more general pressures indicative of the adolescent life-style.

PCP, VIOLENCE, AND THE SPECTER OF THE LIVING DEAD

Over the years, propaganda campaigns have periodically emerged which targeted specific drugs as root causes of outbreaks of violent crime among youthful users. This was dramatically apparent in Commissioner Harry J. Anslinger's war against marihuana—the "weed of madness" and "assassin of youth"—which changed the user into a diabolical killer and a member of the "living dead." Most recently, PCP has emerged as the new "killer drug," and some comment seems warranted here descriptive of its violence potential in the youthful drug scene. PCP, or more formally *phencyclidine,* is a central nervous system excitant agent with anesthetic, analgesic, and hallucinogenic properties.

The initial abuse of PCP (also known as horse tranquilizer, dust, angel dust, fairy dust, monkey dust, hog, Tic, flakes, rocket fuel, buzz, and THC), appeared in the Haight-Ashbury underground community of San Francisco and other West and East Coast cities during 1967. It was marketed as the *PeaCe Pill,* and hence, the name *PCP* quickly became popular. Characteristic of the hallucinogenic drug marketplace has been the mislabeling and promotion of one substance as some other more desirable psychedelic, and PCP for a time occupied a conspicuous position in this behalf. Samples of mescaline sold in Milwaukee, for example, were invariably found to contain phencyclidine (Reed and Kane, 1970). During the late 1960s and early 1970s, THC (tetrahydrocannabinol), the active ingredient in marihuana, was frequently sought after in its pure form as a prestige "fad" drug. Yet THC has *never* been sold on the street, for in its isolated form it becomes too unstable and quickly loses its potency. During 1970, an analysis of "street drugs" from the greater Philadelphia area revealed that PCP was a common THC substitute. In an experiment undertaken by the author in 1971, samples of alleged LSD, THC, mescaline, and PCP were secured from street suppliers in New York City's Greenwich Village. Laboratory analyses identified the THC and mescaline samples to be PCP and the PCP sample to be LSD, with only the LSD sample having accurate labeling. In a second experiment undertaken during early 1972 in Miami's Cocoanut Grove area, the author purchased 25 individual samples of alleged THC from an equal number of street drug dealers. Under laboratory analysis, 22 of the THC samples were found to be PCP, one was an oral contraceptive, another a prescription analgesic, and the last a chocolate-covered peanut. It was quickly learned that this apparent deception was aimed at those "plastic" or weekend hippies and "heads" whose social schizophrenia placed them partially in the straight world and partially in the new underground—never being fully a part of either. In both the New York and Miami drug subcultures, however, and likely in most others, THC was simply accepted as another name for PCP, explaining why the latter drug has been called "Tic" for almost a decade in many cities.

The myths describing PCP as a "killer drug" are not new, but date to its first introduction to the street community a decade ago. In 1969, a New York City Chief of Detectives told the author that one dose of PCP would cause "instant addiction," and a November 28, 1970 report in the Long Island *Press* described PCP as a synthetic drug so powerful that a person could become "high" by touching it in its powdery form—instantly absorbing it through the pores. These early reports ran counter to both medical and street experiences (Domino, 1964; Liebmann et al., 1971), and the drug quickly became relegated to the lengthening catalog of street drugs which received little public attention. Most of those using PCP were not found among the populations addicted to narcotic drugs. Rather, they were multiple drug users manifesting patterns of long-term involvement with marihuana and/or hashish combined with the experimental, sociorecreational, or spree use of hallucinogens, opiates, sedative-hypnotics, stimulants, tranquilizers, and organic solvents and inhalants (Liebmann et al., 1971).

During 1978, PCP again took on national prominence, receiving media coverage similar to that of marihuana during the era of "reefer madness." In one episode of the *60 Minutes* television series, produced by CBS News, commentator Mike Wallace described PCP as the nation's number one drug problem, reporting on bizarre yet isolated incidents of brutal violence allegedly caused by the "new" killer drug. In the September 4, 1978 issue of *People* magazine, PCP was touted as America's most dangerous new drug—the "devil's dust" (Lerner, 1978). And in these other reports, violence was always associated with PCP use, as well as its propensity to destroy the user's mind, and, hence, create new recruits to the growing army of the "living dead." During special hearings on August 8, 1978, one U.S. Senator described PCP as "one of the most dangerous and insidious drugs known to mankind," while a Congressman declared that PCP was "a threat to the national security and that children were playing with death on the installment plan" (Select Committee on Narcotics Abuse Control, 1978). And most recently in the June 2, 1979 edition of the Cincinnati *Post,* syndicated columnist Ann Landers—the seemingly self-proclaimed expert on most subjects from aardvark to zymotechnics, offered the following comment about "angel dust" (PCP) as part of her ten-year campaign against marihuana use:

> Unless a teenager is a chemist, there is no way he can be sure of what he is ingesting. The possibility of getting angel dust sprinkled in with pot should be enough to scare even the dumbest cluck off the stuff for life. Angel dust can blow your mind to smithereens [Landers, 1979].

Research during 1978 and 1979 quickly demonstrated that comments such as these were well overstated. In 1978, when PCP was labeled as the number one drug problem and responsible for more emergency room admissions than any other drug, estimates from the Drug Abuse Warning Network (DAWN, 1978) found PCP to account for only 3 percent of reported drug abuse emergencies. Furthermore, ethnographic studies among PCP users in Seattle, Miami, Philadelphia, and Chicago demonstrated that the characterizations of users' experiences were slanted and misleading (Feldman, 1979). Rather than the monster drug presented by the media as some live enemy that made the youthful users lose complete control of rationality, to be so overpowered by the drug that they helplessly and inescapably moved directly to either a psychotic episode, suicide, murder, or a state of suspended confusion that only an indefinite commitment in a mental hospital would reverse, something quite different was found. Users were typically aware that PCP was a potent drug, and except for the few that sought a heavily anethestized state, most used it cautiously. They aimed to control its effects, and although some had adverse reactions to the drug, violence was rarely a factor (Feldman, 1979). In fact, among the more than 300 PCP users contacted during the study, almost all were baffled by the connection of the drug with violent behavior. The only known episodes of violence occurred during "bad trips" when someone tried to restrain a user, and these were extremely unusual. Furthermore, the person exhibiting aggressive behavior typically had already developed a reputation for violence that was independent of PCP use.

In sum, current research suggests that the violent episodes associated with youthful PCP use were primarily media events, and that the use of this drug was not as widespread as initially believed. Among the college population reported on earlier, only two persons had experienced the effects of the drug, and none was using it regularly; among the non-heroin drug users in Dade County, only six cases were current users while none was a regular user.

CONCLUSION

To suggest any future directions of criminality among youthful drug abusers would be difficult, primarily because even their current status and situation is not yet fully known. Nevertheless, a number of possible implications might be discussed.

First, research has documented that since the 1940s, most inner-city areas have maintained large populations of drug users that are heavily involved in crime. Although the sizes of these populations tend to fluctuate and the nature of their drug use may vary, their numbers have nevertheless remained significant, and current trends suggest that this pattern will continue. In recent decades, a number of "epidemic" periods have been documented during which noticeably large numbers of new recruits to the heroin world have emerged (Hunt and Chambers, 1975). The 1967-1969 and 1973-1975 periods have been charted as the more current epidemic periods, and analyses of current populations of heroin users indicate that most were initiated during these times. Furthermore, the overwhelming majority of new users are drawn from the younger age groups. Most of the youthful heroin users studied in this essay were recruited during the 1973-1975 epidemic period. Of the

70 cases, some 62.8 percent began heroin use during those years. Furthermore, since an additional 22.9 percent initiated such use during 1977-1978, should these data be representative of other youthful heroin populations, a new epidemic period may be surfacing. This would suggest that cohorts of inner-city heroin users will continue to remain at large for some time to come, and that the criminal activity characteristic of this type of user will continue.

Second, although it has been suggested that crime and drug use, and especially heroin use, may not be directly related, but rather phenomena that exist side by side in communities characterized by high rates of unemployment, financial assistance, poverty, and other social casualty statuses, this should not imply that crime will decrease among youthful users during nonepidemic years. The data in this study have documented that nonheroin drug-using youths begin criminal activity at a young age, maintain levels of offense behavior almost as high as that of their heroin-using counterparts, and do so for purposes other than drug-use support.

Third, the history of drug use during the last twenty years has suggested that "fad" drugs come and go, and that each new "fad" brings new users to the drug street scene. During the 1960s it was marihuana and LSD, in the early 1970s it was methaqualone and cocaine, and most recently it has been PCP. Although most new users ingest drugs within an experimental or social-recreational context, significant numbers eventually become heavily involved and often dysfunctional abusers, thus adding to the ranks of the active drug subcultures. What the new fad drugs will be in years to come is not known, but a new shifting pattern is already in progress. With the close of 1979, PCP began to decline in popularity, being replaced in several cohorts by "T's and B's" (Talwain® and Pyribenzamine®). The existing warehouse of prescription sedatives, stimulants, antidepressants, analgesics, and other psychoactive drugs is so diverse, furthermore, that many types will undoubtedly emerge as new and preferred drugs of abuse, thus continuing to supply the street scene of youthful drug abuse and crime with thousands of new members.

NOTES

1. For a discussion of the drug myths and stereotypes, as well as examples of the literature in which they appeared, see Anslinger and Cooper (1937), Anslinger and Tompkins (1953), Lindesmith (1940), Michelson (1940), and Eldridge

(1962). Perhaps the best discussion of the marihuana myths is Sloman's (1979) *Reefer Madness,* which details the 1930s crusade against this drug and the beliefs that developed which described marihuana as a "killer weed" and an addicting narcotic. And on this latter point, it is curious that the notion of marihuana addiction still persists even within some segments of the medical profession. In a personal communication on May 30, 1979, between the author and an emergency care nurse affiliated with a major hospital in Columbus, Ohio, it was learned that special detoxification procedures are used at that institution for the treatment of infants born to women known to be active marihuana smokers.

2. For perspectives on heroin use within the gang culture of the 1950s, see Alksne (1959), Chein and Rosenfeld (1957), Meyer (1952), Rettig et al. (1977: 11-29), and Zimmering et al. (1951).

3. For bibliographies of the drugs-crime studies, see Austin and Lettieri (1976), Greenberg and Adler (1974, and Research Triangle Institute (1976).

4. DHEW grant #1-R01-DA-0-1827 from the Division of Research, National Institute on Drug Abuse.

5. For a discussion of the sampling and interviewing methods, see Inciardi (forthcoming).

REFERENCES

ABELSON, H. I., R. COHEN, D. SCHRAYER, and M. RAPPAPORT (1973) "Drug experience, attitudes and related behavior among adolescents," pp. 488-810 in National Commission on Marihuana and Drug Abuse, Drug Use in America: Problem in Perspective, Appendix, Vol. I. Washington, DC: Government Printing Office.

ALKSNE, H. (1959) A Follow-up Study of Treated Adolescent Narcotic Users. New York: Columbia University School of Public Health and Administrative Medicine.

ANSLINGER, H. J. and C. R. COOPER (1937) "Marijuana: assassin of youth." American Magazine 74 (July): 19, 150.

ANSLINGER, H. J. and W. F. TOMPKINS (1953) The Traffic in Narcotics. New York: Funk & Wagnalls.

AUSTIN, G. A. and D. J. LETTIERI (1976) Drugs and Crime: The Relationship of Drug Use and Concomitant Criminal Behavior. Washington, DC: Government Printing Office.

BALL, J. C. and C. D. CHAMBERS [eds.] (1970) The Epidemiology of Opiate Addiction in the United States. Springfield, IL: Charles C Thomas.

BESCHNER, G. M. and A. S. FRIEDMAN [eds.] (1979) Youth Drug Abuse: Problems, Issues and Treatment, Lexington, MA: D. C. Heath.

BLUM, R. H. and Associates (1970) Students and Drugs. San Francisco: Jossey-Bass.

CHAMBERS, C. D. (1970) An Assessment of Drug Use in the General Population of the State of New York. Albany: New York State Narcotic Addiction Control Commission.

CHAMBLISS, W. J. (1977) "Markets, profits, labor and smack." Contemporary Crises 1 (January): 53-75.

CHEIN, I. (1964) "Narcotics use among juveniles," pp. 237-252 in R. Cavan [ed.] Readings in Juvenile Delinquency. New York: J. B. Lippincott.

――― and E. ROSENFELD (1957) "Juvenile narcotic use." Law and Contemporary Problems (Winter): 52-68.

CHEIN, I., D. L. GERARD, R. S. LEE, and E. ROSENFELD (1964) The Road to H. New York: Basic Books.

CLOWARD, R. A. and L. E. OHLIN (1960) Delinquency and Opportunity. New York: Macmillan.

DAWN Quarterly Report (1978) Washington, DC: Government Printing Office.

Domestic Council Drug Abuse Task Force (1975) White Paper on Drug Abuse. Washington, DC: Government Printing Office.

DOMINO, E. F. (1964) "Neurobiology of phencyclidine (Sernyl), a drug with an unusual spectrum of pharmacological activity." Internal Review of Neurobiology 6: 303-347.

ELDRIDGE, W. B. (1962) Narcotics and the Law. Chicago: American Bar Foundation.

EPSTEIN, E. J. (1977) Agency of Fear: Opiates and Political Power in America. New York: G. P. Putnam.

FARBER, L. H. (1966) "Ours is the addicted society." New York Times Magazine 11 (December): 43.

FELDMAN, H. W. (1979) "PCP use in four cities: an overview." Presented at the Workshop for Ethnographers and State Policy Makers, Chicago, April 18-20.

――― (1968) "Ideological supports to becoming and remaining a heroin addict." Journal of Health and Social Behavior 9 (June): 131-139.

FINESTONE, H. (1957) "Cats, kicks, and color." Social Problems 5 (July): 3-13.

FORT, J. (1969) The Pleasure Seekers: The Drug Crisis, Youth and Society. New York: Grove.

GELLER, A. and M. BOAS (1969) The Drug Beat. New York: McGraw-Hill.

GOODE, E. (1970) The Marijuana Smokers. New York: Basic Books.

GREENBERG, S. W. and F. ADLER (1974) "Crime and addiction: an empirical analysis of the literature, 1920-1973." Contemporary Drug Problems 3: 221-270.

HUNT, L. (1976) "Estimates of user populations for heroin and other narcotics: available methodologies and their limitations." Presented at the Task Force Meeting, the Epidemiology of Heroin and Other Narcotics: Use, Abuse, and Addiction Conducted by the Stanford Research Institute, Menlo Park, CA.

HUNT, L. and C. D. CHAMBERS (1975) The Heroin Epidemics. New York: Spectrum.

INCIARDI, J. A. (forthcoming) "Heroin use and street crime." Crime and Delinquency.

――― (1980) "Women, heroin and property crime," in F. R. Scarpitti and S. K. Datesman (eds.) Women, Crime, and Justice, New York: Oxford.

――― (1978) Crime and Alternative Patterns of Substance Abuse: A Report Prepared for the Joint Drug Alcohol Collaborative Project. Rockville, MD: Richard Katon Associates.

――― (1974a) "Drugs, drug-taking and drug-seeking: notations on the dynamics of myth, change and reality," pp. 203-222 in J. A. Inciardi and C. D. Chambers (eds.) Drugs and the Criminal Justice System. Beverly Hills, CA: Sage.

——— (1974b) "The villification of euphoria: some perspectives on an elusive issue." Addictive Diseases 1: 241-267.

JOHNSON, B. D. (1973) Marihuana Users and Drug Subcultures. New York: John Wiley.

JOHNSON, G. (1967) The Pill Conspiracy. Los Angeles: Sherbourne.

KAPLAN, J. (1970) Marijuana—The New Prohibition. Cleveland: World.

KING, R. (1972) The Drug Hang-Up: America's Fifty-Year Folly. New York: Norton.

LAIT, J. and L. MORTIMER (1952) U.S.A. Confidential. New York: Crown.

LANDERS, A. (1979) " 'THC' determines potency of pot." Cincinnati Post (June 2): 23.

LERNER, S. (1978) "So much for cocaine and LSD—angel dust is America's most dangerous new drug." People (September 4): 46-48.

LIEBMANN, J., J. A. INCIARDI, and C. D. CHAMBERS (1971) "Angel dust." New York State Narcotic Addiction Control Commission. (unpublished)

LINDESMITH, A. R. (1947) Opiate Addiction. Bloomington: Principia.

——— (1940) " 'Dope Fiend' Mythology." Journal of Criminal Law and Criminology 31 (July-August): 199-208.

McGLOTHLIN, W., K. JAMISON, and S. ROSENBLATT (1970) "Marijuana and the use of other drugs." Nature 228 (December 19).

MEYER, A. S. (1952) Social and Psychological Factors in Opiate Addiction. New York: Columbia University Bureau of Applied Social Research.

MICHELSON, T. (1940) "Lindesmith's Mythology." Journal of Criminal Law and Criminology 31 (November-December): 375-400.

MILLER, D. T. and M. NOWAK (1977) The Fifties: The Way We Really Were. Garden City, NY: Doubleday.

National Institute on Drug Abuse (1978) Annotated Bibliography of Papers from the Addiction Research Center, 1935-1975. Washington, DC: Government Printing Office.

National Journal (1971) "Nixon's offensive on drugs treads on diverse interests." July 2.

NOWLIS, H. H. (1969) Drugs on the College Campus. New York: Doubleday-Anchor.

Pottieger, A. E. and J. A. INCIARDI (1980) "Drug use and crime on the college campus." Addictive Diseases.

PREBLE, E. and J. H. CASEY (1969) "Taking care of business: the heroin user's life on the street." International Journal of the Addictions 4 (Spring): 1-24.

REED, A. and A. W. KANE (1970) "Phencyclidine (PCP)." STASH Capsules 2 (December): 1-2.

Research Triangle Institute (1976) Drug Use and Crime: Report of the Panel on Drug Use and Criminal Behavior. Springfield, VA: National Technical Information Service.

RETTIG, R. P., M. J. TORRES, and G. R. GARRETT (1977) Manny: A Criminal-Addict's Story. Boston: Houghton Mifflin.

SCHUR, E. M. (1962) Narcotic Addiction in Britain and America. Bloomington: Indiana University Press.

Select Committee on Narcotics Abuse Control (1978) Executive Summary, Hearings on Phencyclidine. August 8. Washington, DC: Government Printing Office.

SIMMONS, J. L. and B. WINOGRAD (1966) It's Happening: A Portrait of the Youth Scene Today. Santa Barbara: Marc-Laired.

SLOMAN, L. (1979) Reefer Madness: The History of Marijuana in America. Indianapolis: Bobbs-Merrill.

SUCHMAN, E. A. (1968) "The 'hang-loose' ethic and the spirit of drug use." Journal of Health and Social Behavior 9 (June): 146-155.

SUTTER, A. G. (1966) "The world of the righteous dope fiend." Issues in Criminology 2 (Fall): 177-222.

U.S. News & World Report (1972) "Drug abuse now epidemic—what's being done about it." April 3.

WHITCOMB, I. (1974) After the Ball: Pop Music from Rag to Rock. New York: Viking.

WILNER, D. M., E. ROSENFELD, R. S. LEE, D. L. GERARD, and I. CHEIN (1957) "Heroin use and street gangs." Journal of Criminal Law, Criminology and Police Science 48 (November-December): 399-409.

ZIMMERING, P., J. TOOLAN, R. SAFRIN, and B. WORTIS (1951) "Heroin addiction in adolescent boys." Journal of Nervous and Mental Diseases (July): 19-34.

tended to look at drug use in terms of its association with the troubled atmosphere of the times. Marihuana use was found to be associated with negative attitudes toward the middle class or "establishment" life-style (Brotman et al., 1970; Suchman, 1968). Use of marihuana was also found to be closely related to low scholastic achievement (Dembo et al., 1976; Milman and Su, 1973), low motivation (Jessor et al., 1973), psychological stress (Milman and Su, 1973), and alienation from or lack of commitment to social norms and values (Jessor et al., 1973; Knight et al., 1974).

As more and more students became involved in marihuana use and as the political and social climate on campus improved, researchers reexamined some of these earlier findings. Experimentation with marihuana, according to a 1979 Gallup Poll (Boston Globe, 1979), now involves two out of every three college students. Since it is so widespread, marihuana use is losing its deviant character; experimentation is increasingly seen as a typical behavior (McCann et al., 1977; Davidson et al., 1977) which takes place in social settings, for social reasons (Kosviner and Hawks, 1977). The social character of marihuana use is also supported by Ginsberg and Greenley (1978), who found that identification with a marihuana-using peer group was a powerful determinant of subsequent marihuana use.

The prevalence of drug use on campus has been a major focus of marihuana studies in the past decade. Yet, with the exception of the National Survey on Drug Abuse of 1977, relatively little has been done to examine changes in patterns of drug use over time. It is always difficult to compare the results of studies carried out by different investigators at different locations at different points in time. Differences in data collection make it particularly difficult to document changes in patterns of drug use. For example, while some studies count as users only those who have used a substance in the past six months or year, others count all those who have *ever* used a substance. Another difficulty involves the classification of drugs. Studies do not always clarify which drugs are included in such general categories as "stimulants" or "barbiturates," if only illegally obtained drugs are included, or if supervised or unsupervised use of prescription drugs are also counted as drug use. Another factor which makes it difficult to assess change over time is that the prevalence of use of many drugs is not measured until their popular use is discovered. As a consequence, many popularly used drugs have only recently been mentioned in the literature. For example, cocaine was formerly included in either the "hard drug" or stimulant category; only recently has the incidence of cocaine use among college students been systematically assessed.

In spite of these difficulties, there seems to be some evidence that patterns of drug use among college students are changing. In the period from 1967 to 1972, researchers discovered an increase in the number of students who used not only marihuana but also other drugs such as barbiturates, amphetamines, and hallucinogens (Second Report of the National Commission on Marihuana and Drug Abuse, 1973). More recent surveys, however, have found that although the number of students who use marihuana is increasing, the incidence of use of other drugs has remained fairly stable (Boston Globe, 1979).

Figure 7.1 illustrates the change in the proportion of students who "ever used" various drugs from 1967 to 1979. In the ten-year period between 1969 and 1979, the use of marihuana increased steadily. The proportion of students who reported using marihuana almost doubled during this period, increasing from 32 percent in 1969 to 66 percent in 1979. The use of most other drugs, however, appears not to have changed. For example, the proportion of students who reported using opiates was 5 percent in 1969 and 6 percent in 1972. In 1969, 22

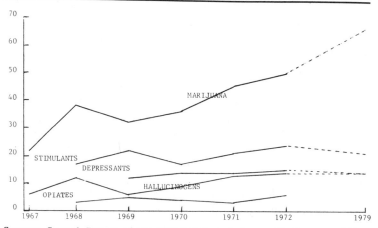

Sources: Second Report of the National Commission on Marihuana and Drug Abuse (1973). Drug use in America: Problem in perspective. Washington, D.C.: Author, p. 83.

Boston Globe (1979). "Gallup Poll." May 13, p. 23.

FIGURE 7.1   Mean Percentage of College Students Who Have Ever Used Drugs, 1967-1979

percent of the students surveyed used stimulants, and 12 percent had used depressants. Ten years later, the figures were 21 percent and 14 percent, respectively. The use of hallucinogens, however, increased from 6 percent in 1969 to 14 percent in 1979.

We have recently concluded a survey of more than 7000 students at 34 colleges in New England which will shed some light on the current patterns of drug use on campus.

METHOD

The findings reported here are based on data collected in a mail questionnaire survey of undergraduate students at 34 colleges and universities in five of the New England states (Wechsler and McFadden, forthcoming). The schools included both state-supported and private institutions in urban, suburban, and rural settings. The schools varied in size and competitiveness as measured by admission criteria and academic standards. They included both coeducational and all-women colleges.

A random sample of full-time undergraduate students was selected at each college. The sample size at each school ranged from 100 to 450, depending on total undergraduate enrollment and the ratio of men to women. The final study sample included 10,500 students (5000 men and 5500 women).

Questionnaires were sent in the spring of 1977 with a cover letter explaining the reason for the survey, the sample selection method, and the procedures used to safeguard the students' anonymity and the confidentiality of their responses. The fifteen-page questionnaire contained items on the use of marihuana and other drugs, adjustment difficulties and stresses commonly experienced by college students, reasons for drinking, problems associated with drinking, and demographic variables. A follow-up mailing was later sent to nonresponders.

Questionnaires were returned by 7170 students in response to the initial and one follow-up mailing. A third mailing, using a shortened form of the questionnaire, was sent to nonresponders at nine of the colleges, providing 175 additional responses and an overall response rate of 71 percent to the three mailings. Response rates ranged from 51 to 87 percent at the individual colleges. First, second, and third mailing responses were compared on major variables to detect possible sampling bias; no discernible difference between early and late responders was found.

For the following analyses, we report the findings of responses to the first and second mailings only. These respondents include 3185 college men and 3898 women. Cross-classification analysis, Pearson product-moment correlation coefficients, and analysis of variance were used to assess the relationships among sociodemographic variables, types of drug-using behavior, and psychological problems or stress.

FINDINGS

PATTERNS OF DRUG USE IN 1977

Students were asked if and how often they had used the following substances in the past year: marihuana, sleeping pills, tranquilizers, stimulants to study or diet, cocaine, hallucinogens, "uppers" or "downers" just for the effect, and heroin or opium. The majority of the students surveyed (67%) reported using one or more of these drugs at some time in the past year.

Marihuana was the most widely and frequently used drug. As shown in Table 7.1, 59 percent of the students surveyed had used marihuana within the past year. Of those who used marihuana, four out of ten (39 percent) reported using it at least once a week and one out of ten (10 percent) reported using it daily or nearly every day.

Few students used drugs other than marihuana. For example, only 16 percent of the students reported using stimulants, 11 percent reported using cocaine, and 10 percent reported using tranquilizers in the past year. These drugs were also used far less frequently than

TABLE 7.1   Proportion of College Students Reporting Use of Drugs Within Past Year, by Sex

Drug	Total (N ~ 7,000)	Men (N ~ 3,144)	Women (N ~ 3,857)
Marihuana	59.3	63.8	54.8
Stimulants	16.2	16.6	15.8
Cocaine	11.1	13.8[a]	8.3[a]
Tranquilizers	9.6	7.8[a]	11.4[a]
Hallucinogens	7.8	10.6[a]	5.0[a]
"Uppers"	7.0	7.9	6.1
Sleeping pills	5.1	4.3	5.9
"Downers"	4.8	5.4	4.3
Heroin or Opium	1.3	1.9[a]	0.7[a]

marihuana. Since weekly use of these substances was rare, we examined the proportions of students who reported monthly use. About one-third of the students who used stimulants (34 percent) or tranquilizers (30 percent), and 21 percent of those who used cocaine, reported taking these drugs once a month or more often. Comparatively few students reported any use of hallucinogens (8 percent), "uppers" (7 percent), sleeping pills (5 percent), "downers" (5 percent), or heroin or opium (1 percent).

MULTIPLE DRUG USE

Students were classified according to the number and type of drugs that they reported using in the past year. Of all students surveyed, 33 percent did not use any drug, 28 percent used marihuana but not any other drug, 16 percent used marihuana and one or two other drugs, and 15 percent used marihuana and three or more drugs. Only a small proportion of students (about 8 percent of the total sample) used drugs but did not use marihuana.

Of the drug users, half (51 percent) reported multiple drug use in the past year. Multiple drug use most frequently occurred in conjunction with marihuana use; 53 percent of the marihuana smokers, compared with 37 percent of the drug users who did not smoke marihuana, reported multiple drug use. Among the marihuana smokers who also used other drugs, the most commonly used substances were stimulants (46 percent), cocaine (34 percent), hallucinogens and tranquilizers (both 24 percent), and "uppers" (22 percent).

A different pattern of drug use was observed among those students who used drugs but not marihuana. Men and women in this group most commonly reported using tranquilizers (28 percent), stimulants (22 percent), and sleeping pills (18 percent). In contrast to marihuana smokers who used other drugs, less than 3 percent of the drug users who did not smoke marihuana reported using "recreational" drugs such as cocaine, hallucinogens, or "uppers" or "downers" for the effect. This suggests that while marihuana use tends to be associated with social or recreational drug use, use among marihuana nonusers may be closer to what the National Commission on Marihuana and Drug Abuse has categorized as "situational" or "circumstantial" drug use (Second Report of the National Commission on Marihuana and Drug Abuse, 1973). This type of drug use is motivated by a need to achieve an effect to help the user cope with some personal situation, such as taking tranquilizers to relax in a stressful situation, taking barbiturates to get to sleep, or amphetamines to study or stay alert for long drives.

FREQUENCY OF DRUG USE

Marihuana smokers who reported multiple drug use tended to use certain drugs more frequently than other groups. For example, weekly marihuana use was reported by more than two-thirds (67 percent) of those who used marihuana plus three or more additional drugs, compared with about half (53 percent) of those who used marihuana and one or two other drugs, and less than one-quarter (22 percent) of those students who used marihuana but no other drugs. A similar pattern was found in the use of cocaine. About 12 percent of the marihuana smokers who used three or more additional drugs and only 3 percent of those who used marihuana and one or two other drugs reported using cocaine once a month or more.

USE OF OTHER SUBSTANCES

Tobacco. Drug use was strongly associated with cigarette smoking (see Table 7.2). The overwhelming majority (87 percent) of those

TABLE 7.2   Cigarette Smoking by Sex and Use of Drugs Within the Past Year, in Percentages

			Marihuana and:		
Men	None (N = 951)	Marihuana only (953)	1-2 other drugs (205)	3 or more drugs (543)	Other (182)
Does not smoke	89.3	79.9	65.4	55.9	80.8
Less than one pack per day	6.2	13.6	20.1	21.6	7.7
Pack or more per day	4.5	6.4	14.5	22.5	11.5
x^2 = 266.86, 8 df, p < .001					
Women	(N = 1,340)	(990)	(245)	(513)	(400)
Does not smoke	85.6	62.0	50.2	37.5	72.6
Less than one pack per day	9.5	27.3	27.8	30.3	14.4
Pack or more per day	4.9	10.7	22.0	32.2	13.0
x^2 = 531.38, 8 df, p < .001					

students who did not use drugs also did not smoke cigarettes. In contrast, only 63 percent of all drug users and 52 percent of the marihuana smokers who reported multiple drug use were nonsmokers. Marihuana smokers who used other drugs were five times as likely as students who did not use drugs to report smoking a pack of cigarettes or more a day (25 percent versus 5 percent).

Alcohol. Although a large number of students reported using marihuana, alcohol is still the most widely used drug on campus: 95 percent of the students surveyed were current drinkers. Drinking, however, was strongly associated with drug use. Almost two out of three drinkers (66 percent), as compared to less than one out of five nondrinkers (18 percent) also used other drugs.

As illustrated in Table 7.3, multiple drug use was strongly related to the quantity and frequency of alcohol use. Among both men and women, marihuana smokers who used three or more additional drugs

TABLE 7.3   Drinking Typology by Sex and Use of Drugs Within the Past Year, in Percentages

Men	None (N = 948)	Marihuana only (949)	Marihuana and 1 or more other drugs (747)	Other (182)
Abstainers	9.2	0.3	0.8	4.4
Infrequent-light	30.7	8.1	5.4	25.8
Frequent-light	15.9	21.2	24.6	19.2
Intermediate	27.4	34.7	24.4	26.4
Infrequent-heavy	4.0	2.5	2.3	4.4
Frequent-heavy	12.8	33.2	42.4	19.8
x^2 = 550.12, 15 df, p < .001				
Women	(N = 1,330)	(987)	(752)	(392)
Abstainers	9.5	0.9	0.9	3.8
Infrequent-light	43.1	20.7	15.3	41.8
Frequent-light	13.8	22.0	21.2	17.4
Intermediate	27.7	41.9	38.2	29.5
Infrequent-heavy	2.0	2.0	3.4	2.8
Frequent-heavy	3.8	12.4	20.9	4.8
x^2 = 571.05, 15 df, p < .001				

NOTE: Based on a classification by two dimensions of alcohol use: usual quantity and frequency (see Wechsler and McFadden, forthcoming).

were most likely to drink heavily: 32 percent of the marihuana smokers who reported multiple drug use, compared with 23 percent of those who smoked marihuana but did not use any other drug, and 8 percent of the drug nonusers were classified as frequent-heavy drinkers. (Classification as a frequent-heavy drinker meant that the respondent reported drinking five or six cans of beer, four glasses of wine, or four drinks with liquor more than twice a week; or seven or more cans of beer, five or more glasses of wine, or five or more drinks with liquor at least once a week.)

Nearly all marihuana smokers (more than 99 percent) reported drinking alcoholic beverages. Frequency of marihuana smoking was also associated with the quantity and frequency of alcohol use. Comparing those who did not smoke marihuana with those who smoked marihuana less than once a week and those who smoked marihuana more than weekly, we found that 9 percent of the students who did not use marihuana were frequent-heavy drinkers, compared with 22 percent of the infrequent users and 36 percent of the frequent users.

Although we observed a strong relationship between the use of marihuana and alcoholic beverages, alcohol use was not highly correlated with the use of other illegal drugs. As illustrated in Table 7.4, with the exception of the association between alcohol and marihuana use, the use of illegal drugs was generally more highly correlated with the use of other illegal drugs. For example, while drinking was highly correlated (r) with the use of marihuana (.433), hallucinogens (.240), and cocaine (.233), the correlations between marihuana and these latter substances were much higher (.492 and .481, respectively).

SOCIODEMOGRAPHIC CHARACTERISTICS

While statistically significant differences were observed between men and women in the prevalence of drug use as well as in the kinds of drugs used, the magnitude of these differences was generally small. Men were somewhat more likely than women to report use of drugs in general and to report use of marihuana, cocaine, hallucinogens, and heroin in particular. Women, on the other hand, were more likely than men to fall into the category of drug users who do not use marihuana and were more likely to report tranquilizer use.

Year in college was another variable associated with drug use (see Table 7.5). Although the proportion of drug users tended to increase with each succeeding year in college, actual differences were small.

TABLE 7.4 Intercorrelations of Drug Use Within the Past Year

	Sleeping pills	Tranquilizers	Stimulants	"Uppers"	"Downers"	Cocaine	Hallucinogens	Heroin	Alcohol
Marihuana	.096	.192	.396	.404	.349	.481	.492	.254	.433
Sleeping pills		.366	.211	.171	.258	.127	.130	.166	.096
Tranquilizers			.302	.322	.441	.249	.251	.216	.104
Stimulants				.551	.413	.427	.423	.238	.206
"Uppers"					.585	.450	.499	.300	.208
"Downers"						.430	.462	.344	.169
Cocaine							.572	.353	.233
Hallucinogens								.385	.240
Heroin									.135

Patterns of drug use, however, were quite different in each college class. For example, proportionately more students used marihuana but no other drugs in the freshman (35 percent) than in the senior class (26 percent). At the same time, proportionately more seniors (22 percent) than freshmen (14 percent) reported using three or more drugs in addition to marihuana. While the data suggest that experimentation with drugs, particularly drugs other than marihuana, increases with exposure over the years, we cannot, on the basis of these data, rule out the possibility that the cohorts in each class came to college with different patterns of drug use.

Contrary to some earlier findings (Second Report of the National Commission on Marihuana and Drug Abuse, 1973; Rouse and Ewing, 1973), no relationship was observed between socioeconomic status and drug use in the 1977 college survey. Also, no relationship was found between race and drug use.

This college study did support previous findings regarding the relationship between religious affiliation and marihuana use (Ewing et al., 1970). Students with no religious affiliation and students who did not participate regularly in religious services were most likely to be drug users (see Tables 7.6 and 7.7). For example, 76 percent of the students with no religious affiliation compared with 64 percent of those with

TABLE 7.5 Use of Drugs Within the Past Year by Sex and Year in College, in Percentages

Men	*Freshman (N = 694)*	*Sophmore (679)*	*Junior (659)*	*Senior (759)*
None	38.6	32.4	32.6	30.7
Marihuana	36.0	38.9	31.0	29.4
Marihuana and 1-2 other drugs	5.2	7.1	6.7	9.6
Marihuana and 3 or more drugs	15.0	15.6	21.4	24.0
Other	5.2	6.0	8.0	6.3

$x^2 = 57.44$, 12 df, p < .001

Women	*(N = 957)*	*(839)*	*(800)*	*(844)*
None	39.8	38.4	39.8	36.3
Marihuana only	33.6	29.8	25.6	23.6
Marihuana and 1-2 other drugs	6.1	6.2	6.4	9.4
Marihuana and 3 or more drugs	12.3	13.5	15.0	18.1
Other	8.2	12.2	13.3	12.7

$x^2 = 54.18$, 12 df, p < .001

some religious affiliation reported using one or more drugs in the past year. Among the denominations, Jews were most likely to have used drugs (70 percent), followed by Protestants (60 percent), and Catholics (59 percent). In terms of attendance, 73 percent of the students who never attend religious services were current drug users, compared with 46 percent of the weekly churchgoers.

Students were asked if they participated in various extracurricular activities such as special interest clubs, intramural or varsity sports, sororities or fraternities, and student government. There were no differences in the proportion of marihuana users who participated in these activities and the proportion of marihuana users in the student body as a whole. Among drug users, however, students who reported using marihuana and one or more other drugs were less likely to take part in these activities than those who did not use drugs at all or those who used marihuana but did not use other drugs (see Table 7.8).

TABLE 7.6   Use of Drugs Within the Past Year by Sex and Religious Affiliation, in Percentages

Men	Catholic (N = 1,044)	Protestant (375)	Jewish (155)	Other (686)	None (536)
None	38.4	36.6	28.5	32.3	23.9
Marihuana only	36.3	34.0	35.2	25.2	29.7
Marihuana and 1-2 other drugs	6.2	6.9	7.2	7.7	10.1
Marihuana and 3 or more drugs	13.2	16.0	21.9	26.5	29.9
Other	5.8	6.6	7.2	8.4	6.5

x^2 = 105.67, 16 df, p < .001

Women	(N = 1,342)	(451)	(195)	(951)	(500)
None	43.3	42.9	31.9	32.8	24.8
Marihuana only	29.1	27.4	28.8	25.6	29.2
Marihuana and 1-2 other drugs	5.7	5.4	9.3	10.3	9.6
Marihuana and 3 or more drugs	10.9	12.0	18.0	20.5	25.6
Other	11.0	12.3	12.0	10.8	10.8

x^2 = 130.65, 16 df, p < .001

TABLE 7.7 Use of Drugs Within the Past Year by Sex and Frequency of Attendance at Religious Services, in Percentages

Men	Weekly (N = 605)	Monthly (254)	Holiday (677)	Never (1,271)
None	52.7	38.6	29.0	25.8
Marihuana only	30.6	39.0	40.2	30.4
Marihuana and 1-2 other drugs	2.3	6.3	7.1	10.1
Marihuana and 3 or more drugs	4.3	12.2	18.3	28.1
Other	10.1	3.9	5.5	5.7

$x^2 = 291.40$, 12 df, $p < .001$

Women	(N = 863)	(395)	(854)	(1,336)
None	55.0	44.8	35.1	27.6
Marihuana only	24.8	27.8	32.6	28.4
Marihuana and 1-2 other drugs	3.4	7.3	7.3	9.1
Marihuana and 3 or more drugs	3.7	9.4	15.8	22.8
Other	13.1	10.6	9.3	12.1

$x^2 = 287.96$, 12 df, $p < .001$

PSYCHOLOGICAL PROBLEMS

Drug use has been described as an attempt to cope with personal or psychological problems. Researchers have found that drug users tend to score higher on measures of psychological stress (Steffenhagen et al., 1972) and tend to use drugs as a response to boredom (Cheek et al., 1973).

Data from the 1977 college survey support some of these findings. Respondents were presented with a list of what were described as "concerns and feelings experienced by many college students." The list included items referring to: interpersonal problems (e.g., feeling shy, being easily hurt, feeling lonely); somatic complaints (e.g., trouble sleeping, poor appetite, headaches); anxiety (e.g., feeling tense, anxious, pressure to do well in school); and depression (e.g., feeling blue, hopeless, feeling as if everything is an effort). Students were asked to indicate if each item had been very much a problem, somewhat a

TABLE 7.8   Use of Drugs Within the Past Year by Participation in
Extracurricular Activities and Sex

	Percentage participating in student government		Percentage participating in intramural or varsity sports	
	Men	Women	Men	Women
None	11.5	12.9	53.4	24.8
Marihuana only	14.4	16.1	60.7	25.4
Marihuana and other drugs	7.0	5.9	32.9	12.3
Other	14.8	10.2	45.6	19.7
All students	11.1	11.4	48.0	20.8

	Percentage participating in: fraternity and sorority		Percentage participating in: special interest clubs	
	Men	Women	Men	Women
None	15.7	7.3	25.6	31.1
Marihuana only	22.7	6.0	25.2	28.6
Marihuana and other drugs	10.2	2.0	15.0	15.9
Other	18.6	4.0	23.0	29.7
All students	16.1	5.3	21.8	25.9

problem, a minor problem, or no problem at all in the past year. Significant differences between drug users and nonusers were observed for many of these items, and the number and type of problems mentioned were found to vary according to the pattern of drug use and the sex of the respondent.

Among women, marihuana users reported a higher incidence of problems than nonusers for 9 of the 22 items on the list. These problems were in the areas of decision-making, anger, depression, anxiety, poor concentration, tension, trouble sleeping, concern about their sex lives, and boredom. Although the incidence of these problems tended to differentiate between women who used marihuana and those who did not, they had little relationship to the frequency of marihuana use. Frequent marihuana users (those who smoked once a week or more) did not generally report a higher incidence of problems than infrequent users (those who smoked less than once a week). The one exception was that frequent marihuana smokers reported more often than infrequent smokers that being bored was a problem.

Among men, boredom was the only item which differentiated marihuana users from nonusers, with users being more likely than nonusers to report that boredom had been a problem for them in the past year. Among both men and women, then, boredom was the only psychological complaint common to both marihuana users and frequent marihuana users.

A similar pattern appeared when differences in reported problems among the following groups were compared: drug nonusers; users of marihuana but no other drugs; users of marihuana and one or two other drugs; users of marihuana and three or more other drugs; and drug users who do not smoke marihuana. Once again, the number and type of problems reported varied according to the pattern of drug use and sex of the respondent.

Significant differences among categories of drug users were observed for 8 of the 22 items among men and 13 of the 22 among women. Men and women who were not current drug users (and those who used no drug except marihuana) reported the lowest incidence of problems on all items.

Among men, those drug users who did not use marihuana reported the highest incidence of depression, tension, and headaches. Marihuana users who used three or more additional drugs were more likely than other groups to report a higher incidence of problems in areas dealing with motivation, such as trouble making decisions, boredom, and feeling hopeless about the future. Poor appetite was also reported by a greater proportion of students in this group.

A similar pattern was observed among women. Women who used marihuana and three or more other drugs reported the highest incidence of motivational problems—difficulty making decisions, trouble concentrating, boredom, feeling that everything is an effort—as well as depression, feeling hopeless, feeling lonely, tense, and having trouble sleeping. Women who use drugs but who do not smoke marihuana had a higher incidence of anxiety, anger, and headaches.

Ignoring sex differences for the moment, we find that the kinds of problems reported by students with different patterns of drug use correspond to the kinds of drugs these groups preferred. Marihuana smokers who used other drugs reported problems which could be called "motivational." These drug users were bored, had trouble concentrating and making decisions, felt that everything was an effort, and tended to feel more hopeless about the future. Although they did use stimulants, the drugs they generally used were primarily "recreational": marihuana, cocaine, and hallucinogens.

Drug users who did not use marihuana reported a higher incidence of somatic complaints such as headaches and trouble sleeping, and psychological stress such as anxiety, tension, anger, depression, loneliness, and worthlessness. Students in this group took stimulants, tranquilizers, and sleeping pills. Only rarely did they take other more "recreational" drugs.

In assessing the personal and social risk factors involved in drug use, it is important to consider not only the type and number of drugs used but also the frequency of use and the possible motivations for taking drugs. Although social or recreational use of alcohol or other drugs can lead to abuse in some individuals, the person who is under higher levels of psychological stress and who has a tendency to turn to drugs to alleviate stress is a high-risk candidate for problem drug use. Circumstantial drug use can and often does take the form of recurrent self-medication, at which point it can escalate into intensified drug use and ultimately dependency. It should be noted here that the majority (68 percent) of the drug users who do not use marihuana—our potential circumstantial users—are women.

On the basis of these survey data, we cannot definitively say if psychological stress is either a cause or a consequence of the patterns of drug use we observed. For example, it may be that marihuana smokers are taking drugs to cope with their boredom or that marihuana smoking contributes to a feeling of boredom. Drug users who do not use marihuana may be turning to drugs in order to cope with their anxiety and depression, or alternatively, their drug use may lead to that kind of stress. Nevertheless, the data do indicate that women who use drugs are more likely to experience a greater degree of psychological stress than men who use drugs and people of both sexes who do not use drugs.

SUMMARY

Data from the 1977 college survey indicate that differences between marihuana users and nonusers are declining as the incidence of marihuana use increases. However, marihuana use is associated with a particular life-style which involves the use of alcohol, tobacco, and other drugs.

Drug use appears to be an increasingly widespread phenomenon among college students. Nearly all of the students surveyed reported drinking alcoholic beverages; slightly more than two-thirds reported using one or more other drugs in the past year.

Among these other drugs, marihuana was the most widely used, with about six out of ten students reporting current use. A comparatively small number of students reported using stimulants, cocaine, hallucinogens, and tranquilizers.

For most students, drug use was an occasional practice. Weekly use of marihuana was reported by fewer than two out of five marihuana smokers. Stimulants, cocaine, tranquilizers, and hallucinogens were rarely used more than once a month.

Drug use was found to be associated with year in school, religion, and frequency of attendance at religious services. Use of any drug was also strongly associated with the use of other drugs. Nearly every drug user was also a drinker; half of the drug users reported using two or more different kinds of drugs in the past year.

A small number of students reported that they used drugs but did not use marihuana. In contrast to marihuana smokers, students in this group reported a greater use of tranquilizers and sleeping pills. They rarely used cocaine, hallucinogens, or "uppers" or "downers" just for the effect.

The most commonly reported problem among marihuana users, and the only problem area which consistently differentiated among frequent marihuana users, infrequent marihuana users, and drug nonusers was boredom. Drug users who did not smoke marihuana, however, tended to report a higher incidence of psychological problems such as depression and anxiety.

While much attention has been paid to social or recreational marihuana use among college students, the drug-taking behavior of circumstantial drug users, those who take drugs to cope with everyday problems or stresses, merits further study. Although the number of potential circumstantial drug users identified in the current study was comparatively small, students in this group might constitute a high-risk category for future drug-related problems.

REFERENCES

Boston Globe (1979) "Gallup Poll." May 13: 23.

BROTMAN, R., I. SILVERMAN, and F. SUFFET (1970) "Some social correlates of student drug use." Crime and Delinquency 16, 1: 67-74.

CHEEK, F. E., M. SARRETT-BARRIE, C. M. HOLSTEIN, S. NEWALL, and S. SMITH (1973) "Four patterns of campus marijuana use: Part 1. Drug use." International Journal of the Addictions 8, 1: 13-31.

DAVIDSON, S. T., G. D. MELLINGER, and D. MANHEIMER (1977) "Changing patterns of drug use among university males." Addictive Diseases 3, 2: 215-234.

DEMBO, R., J. SCHMEIDLER, and M. KOVAL (1976) "Demographic, value and behavior correlates of marijuana use among middle class youths." Journal of Health and Social Behavior 17 (June): 177-187.

EWING, J. A., B. A. ROUSE, M. H. KEELER, and W. E. BAKEWELL (1970) "Why students 'turn on': marijuana and other drug use in an undergraduate male population." British Journal of Social Psychology 4, 4: 255-265.

GINSBERG, I. J. and J. R. GREENLEY (1978) "Competing theories of marijuana use: a longitudinal study." Journal of Health and Social Behavior 19 (March): 22-34.

JESSOR, R., S. L. JESSOR, and J. FINNEY (1973) "A social psychology of marijuana use: longitudinal studies of high school and college youth." Journal of Personality and Social Psychology 26, 1: 1-15.

KNIGHT, R. C., J. P. SHEPOSH, and J. B. BRYSON (1974) "College student marijuana use and societal alienation." Journal of Health and Social Behavior 15 (March): 28-35.

KOSVINER, A. and D. HAWKS (1977) "Cannabis use amongst British university students. II: patterns of use and attitudes toward use." British Journal of the Addictions 72, 1: 41-57.

McCANN, H. G., R. A. STEFFENHAGEN, and G. MERRIAM (1977) "Drug use: a model for a deviant sub-culture." Journal of Alcohol and Drug Education 23, 1: 29-45.

MILMAN, D. H. and W. H. SU (1973) "Patterns of drug use among university students: very heavy use of marijuana and alcohol by undergraduates." Journal of the American College Health Association 21 (February): 181-187.

ROUSE, B. A. and J. A. EWING (1973) "Marijuana and other drug use by women college students: associate risk taking and coping activities." American Journal of Psychiatry 130, 4: 486-490.

Second Report of the National Commission on Marihuana and Drug Abuse (1973) Drug Use in America: Problem in Perspective. Washington, DC: Government Printing Office.

STEFFENHAGEN, R. A., F. E. SCHMIDT, and C. P. McAREE (1972) "Emotional stability and student drug use," pp. 129-137 in S. Einstein and S. Allen (eds.) Student Drug Surveys. Newark, NJ: Baywood.

SUCHMAN, E. A. (1968) "The 'hang-loose' ethic and the spirit of drug use." Journal of Health and Social Behavior 9 (June): 146-155.

United States Department of Health, Education, and Welfare, Public Health Service (1977) National Survey on Drug Abuse: 1977. Vol. 1. Rockville, MD: Government Printing Office.

WECHSLER, H. and M. McFADDEN (forthcoming) "Drinking among college students: extent, social correlates, and consequences of alcohol use." Journal of Studies on Alcohol.

8

THE HIPPIES
Where Are They Now?

MANUEL R. RAMOS

Perhaps no other social phenomenon during the "turbulent sixties" troubled Americans more than drug use and its characteristic life-style. The seemingly innocent emergence of the "counter culture," the "peace-and-love flower children," initially portrayed in a sympathetic fashion by both the media (Brown, 1967; Hoffman, 1968, 1969; Rubin, 1970) and the social scientific community (Yablonsky, 1968; Roszak, 1969; Reich, 1970; Keniston, 1971), suddenly evolved into a nightmarish saga: Heroin, cocaine, LSD, mescaline, amphetamines, barbiturates, hashish, and marihuana rapidly spread to a whole generation of youth.

Those with expertise in drugs and youth were admittedly puzzled. At the First Annual Rutgers Symposium on Drug Abuse, Wittenborn et al. (1969: i) noted: "A few years ago the causes, consequences, and control of drugs in America were viewed in such terms as economic handicap, social deprivation and criminal involvement." The authors added that "the increasing use of drugs among the youths of middle-income families does not lend itself to these familiar formulations."

Meanwhile, the news media prominently displayed Gallup Polls documenting the rapid increase of predominantly white middle class students who had used marihuana: 1967, 5 percent; 1969, 22 percent; 1970, 42 percent; and 1971, 51 percent (U.S. News & World Report, 1971; New York Times, 1972). Other national polls showed drugs suddenly becoming the major fear of citizens. Congress unloosened its purse strings, increasing the federal budget for enforcing narcotics laws from $3 million in 1968 to more than $224 million in 1974 (Epstein, 1977: 165-189). Between 1966 and 1976 narcotic arrests rose from 44,204 to 475,209 (FBI, 1966: 119; 1976: 185), with white youths consistently accounting for three-fourths of all narcotic arrests.

President Richard Nixon, in a June 17, 1971 message to Congress acknowledged that "the threat of narcotics frightens many Americans." He warned: "We must now candidly recognize that the ... present efforts to control drug abuse are not sufficient in themselves. The problem has assumed the dimensions of a national emergency." The American public was told that the "heroin epidemic" and the "hell of addiction," if not curbed immediately, "will surely in time destroy us." The suppliers of heroin, Nixon added, "are literally the slave traders of our time. ... They are traffickers in Living Death. ... They must be hunted to the ends of the earth" (Epstein, 1977: 165-189).

As more and more predominantly white middle-class "hippies" (as they were known to outsiders) or "freaks" (as insiders preferred to call themselves) began using heroin, altering the traditional patterns of heroin addiction (Sheppard, 1971), and as increasing numbers of parents, educators, and government officials, unschooled in the subtleties of drug use, witnesses their children becoming hippies, an understandable sense of panic and urgency arose about how to deal with "the drug problem." Why so many seemingly intelligent young people, with such promising potential, would voluntarily subscribe to a subculture extolling the virtues of drug use was indeed difficult to comprehend.

"Freaks," however, vigorously defended the use of drugs, the camaraderie, and the subculture whose hedonistic overtones so alienated "straight" America. To them drugs were "no big thing" and they were just having a good time the way they knew best. As expressed by one freak in a recent study (Ramos and Gould, 1978: 76):

> Man, you wouldn't believe how much better being a freak is. It's like we are all brothers. I mean, if you're in a strange city, need a place to crash, eat, score dope, or pick up a nice chick—if you're a freak your brothers will help you out. You gotta go where we

hang out, though, 'cause in any city there ain't many of us around and we gotta stick together even if it just means nodding our head to another brother on the street or giving him a fist sign when you pass on the highway. We have to trust each other, because when you're into a lot of dope—scoring, dealing, watching out for informers—and one brother turns on us, it's fifty quick warrants overnight on everyone's ass.

Freaks enjoyed being "outlaws," the Bonnie and Clydes, the Godfathers of the hip world, maintaining themselves in a hostile straight world of schools, parents, work, police, narcs, informers, rednecks, greasers, and bikers. Leisure time, which for many was all the time, was spent hanging out on streetcorners with other freaks, using dope, scoring with a lover, hitchhiking, dropping out, sporting long hair, dealing drugs, panhandling, crashing concerts and festivals, demonstrating in the streets, and not infrequently running afoul of "the law."

Heroin, by no means, became the drug of choice for the majority of freaks, but its role in the "natural" street-level world of drug use no doubt partly accounted for heroin's popularity among increasing numbers of hippies. Heroin became what Finestone (1957: 3-13) in his early study on black adolescent addicts called "the ultimate 'kick.' " "No substance," observed Finestone, "was more profoundly tabooed by the conventional middle-class society. Regular heroin use provides a sense of maximal social differentiation from the 'square.' " Euphoric drugs, including heroin, also fit very neatly into the hippie ideology (Simmons and Winograd, 1966; Suchman, 1968; Davis and Munoz, 1968; Feldman, 1968).

Valuable insights into the diverse, complex, and heterogeneous worlds of drug subcultures have been provided by recent street ethnographers who have had to overcome considerable ethical, legal, and methodological obstacles (Weppner, 1977). Especially after most authorities, including government officials, conceded that few addicts came to the attention of statisticians (Epstein, 1977: 165-172), it became imperative to know what was the fate of drug abusers who successfully avoided detection.

For instance, Sutter (1966: 205) was the first to note the existence of the "garbage junkie," those drug users who sought "help" for their drug use; street people did not consider them as part of their world, but researchers had traditionally used the "garbage junkies" and only "garbage junkies" as their study populations. Recalls Sutter: "Once a drug user was known to have asked for 'help' at a Synanon House, where he would be associating with some alcoholics and garbage junkies, the opinion of his clique was that he 'hit rock bottom and copped out' on his soul as a dope fiend."

In a "natural" street group of hippies, Ramos and Gould (1978) found that although 78 percent of their sample had regularly used heroin or LSD for several years, only 9 percent of their entire sample ever received drug treatment. Similarly, two-thirds of the sample successfully avoided arrest or detection.

It has become apparent that the freaks who achieved the highest street status of all—the junkies (Ramos and Gould, 1978: 78) and the "righteous dope fiend" described by Sutter (1966, 1969)—have been conspicuously absent or considerably underrepresented in traditional follow-up studies on drug abusers. Using treated or incarcerated addicts in their sample, these early studies unhesitantly concluded that the long-range prognosis for drug addicts was very poor: Relapse rates to drug use following treatment or imprisonment were very high—over 90 percent in two studies (Hunt and Ordoff, 1962; Duvall et al., 1963) and over 50 percent in others (O'Donnell, 1964; Vaillant, 1966a, 1966b, 1966c; Boyd, 1971; Langenauer and Bowden, 1971; Stephens and Cottell, 1972). Death rates were also high and general social adjustment poor. "Once an addict, always an addict," was a common epithet for addiction, and all illicit drug use became suspect.

Street ethnographies, such as those by Polsky (1967) on Greenwich Village in the early sixties, Sutter (1966, 1969) on the Bay Area in the mid-sixties, Partridge (1973) on the hippies of a Florida college town in the late sixties, and Walker's (Gould et al., 1974) rendering of New Haven's urban drug scene in the early seventies, have substantially furthered our knowledge of drug use and its characteristic life-style by showing that the treated or incarcerated drug user is by no means representative of those in their "natural" street environment.

Nonetheless, while a number of studies have documented the striking tendency for juvenile delinquents and young adult criminals to discontinue criminal and other forms of deviant behavior as they mature (Whyte, 1955; Miller, 1962; Johnson, 1968: 68-72), the "snapshot" portrait of users offered by street ethnographers, who at the most spend a year or two with their subjects, is unable to satisfactorily capture the extent to which drug users on the street, especially those using narcotic drugs, continue or discontinue their use as they mature and perhaps even leave the subculture of drug use. The "movie" on the state of most drug users is conspicuously absent from the literature.

It appears that both traditional follow-up studies of users and the more recent ethnographies of user groups have shortcomings. Follow-up studies do attempt to present the important longitudinal perspective on users, but there is the implicit assumption that most users inevitably become patients or prisoners, thereby allowing one to unhesitantly extrapolate the poor fate of incarcerated and treated users to user groups in general. Street ethnographers assume just the opposite: Most users are not detected and one has to leave the prisons and the treatment clinics to receive a true picture of user groups. More representative "natural" groups of users have been successfully sought out, but no one has attempted to follow-up their study population many years after the ethnographic "snapshot" has been taken. What is the long-term social impact of drugs on predominantly youthful users?

Partridge (1973: 80), for example, insisted that hippies were not participating in a "therapeutic sojourn," stating, "One might reach this conclusion if residents returned to the university or in some other way joined the larger society." Only as an aside does Polsky (1967: 150) mention, "A significant minority of beats are in their thirties or forties." Sutter (1969: 811) does address the issue, but only briefly, noting that most drug users "share in the general round of conventional adolescent life. His personal traits equip him well for such participation, and there is good reason to believe that he will use his ingenuity to 'advance himself,' continue with his education, marry, get a conventional job and raise a family."

Walker (Gould et al., 1974: 65), another street ethnographer, concludes his observations by noting:

> The streets are geared to suit the needs of dope fiends, hustlers, and other outlaws. So the guy who has cleaned up generally feels pretty uncomfortable there. In addition he usually finds that there are a lot of people he had been tight with that he can't relate to once he is straight. So it doesn't happen very often that a person quits dope and then remains on the street where all his dope friends can ask him about how he did it and how he feels. . . . It's usually only when a person drops out of sight that he might be staying clean, but then practically nobody notices.

"Nobody notices" that young "dope fiends" or hippies may eventually leave the streets and go straight because those who do leave are not missed; they are continually replaced by succeeding generations of new upcoming younger "beats," "dope fiends," "freaks," "hippies," delinquent gangs, or "punk rockers." The fate of the individual hippie or delinquent gone straight goes unnoticed to peers and social scientists alike.

Many of the shortcomings found in traditional follow-up studies of users and the ethnographic "snapshot" of user groups were overcome in Ramos and Gould's unique five-year follow-up of a "natural" street group of hippies (Ramos, 1974, 1976: Ramos and Gould, 1978). Only through a somewhat serendipitous chain of events was Ramos, a former participant in a large, urban street drug scene during the late sixties, able to spend a year to locate and document the fate of 95 street friends and acquaintances. Ramos's and Gould's efforts ensured that the fate of at least one group of "natural" street drug users would not go unnoticed.

The following section offers both a qualitative and quantitative look at how some individuals participating in the characteristic hippie life-style of the sixties, when found some five, six, seven years later, were no longer freaks, but were pursuing a myriad of other challenges and life-styles. Indeed, in retrospect, it is rather remarkable how only a short time ago Steve (The Mountain Man), Zona (Mother Sans Memories), Liz (Glitter Girl), Peter (Suburbanman), Leslie (Actress), Ron (The Dealer), Jim (Quiet Teacher), Gary (Prisoner), Chris (Navy), Troy, (The Apostle), Bill and Cathy (Gay Warriors), and Harry (Reporter) could have ever had anything in common, yet alone something as seemingly significant as participating in the same hippie/drug subculture. These profiles (only names and other identifying characteristics have been changed) and the more comprehensive statistical analysis of the follow-up data do much to question accepted notions on drug use and its possible long-term consequences on youth.

HIPPIES: THEN AND NOW

THE MOUNTAIN MAN

It was somewhat of a surprise that Steve was one of the first to leave East City and never return, heading west to a commune in Colorado he had read about in *Life* magazine. Although, at age twelve, he was one of the first to smoke marihuana, and then a few years later to use heroin on a regular basis, Steve was always too easygoing to be much of a leader. The high point of the sixties for him, as it was for many people, was Woodstock: "Man, I never balled so many chicks and did so many different drugs during five days in my life."

"Hell man, dirt is organic," Steve would often remind the rare visitor to his secluded Colorado mountain cabin he shared with his common-law wife and daughter. Organic? "We're just humble animals, no different than the ones out here in the woods," Steve explains, "organic, you know, like being naked, having all over tans, not shaving, smelling a little, burping, farting, pissing, getting crabs, clap, balling, pissing, shitting, making babies, and getting high, you know, natural, it's no big thing, right?" After living here for four years with no electricity, running water, or even a battery radio, and spending the summers hunting, cutting wood for the long winter, protecting his marihuana plants from the chickens and maybe leaving occasionally for some summer migrant work to subsidize his family's food stamps and his wife's welfare monies, Steve had indeed moved a long way from the world of crowded street corners and shooting needles filled with heroin into his collapsing veins.

He now despised "the city" and the "city people" who would come up in the summers to pollute the swimming holes, scare the animals, and just not appreciate "my woods." Steve just wanted to "mellow," play his guitar, and be left alone. "Where else could a tenth-grade dropout like me live the way he wants to," he proudly said. "Nah. After four years of being a mountain man, there ain't nothing like organic living. Nothing."

MOTHER SANS MEMORIES

While changing diapers on the youngest of her three children, Zona, now call her Suzanne, remarked, "Sure I like to visit old friends, but it's like—Why are you bringing these old memories with you? Memories you want to forget. No one is interested in the past anymore." The memories for Suzanne were perhaps more painful than for others going through the sixties: running away from home, a couple of abortions before again getting pregnant and having a child at sixteen, hepatitis from dirty needles, and a bad "death trip" on LSD.

Today she prides herself on just being a good mother and wife. "I don't want my kids going through what I went through," she said at one point. Her husband, a truck driver, provides them with a comfortable suburban home near her parents with whom she has long since reconciled. "I find myself telling my kids the same thing they used to tell me."

Suzanne mentioned how she has since become "more practical," noting how she cut her long, blonde hair and does not necessarily wear "the 'in,' 'hip' clothes I thought were so important once." Before excusing herself to make dinner, "I've got to feed everybody before *Hollywood Squares* comes on at 7:30," she felt compelled to explain: "I'm really not trying to be cool anymore."

GLITTER GIRL

If there was anyone who came closest to fitting that stereotypic junkie role it was Liz. She began using heroin at fifteen and now seven years later she was still trying to quit. She had dropped out of school, lived with several men, worked in a massage parlor as a prostitute, dealt heroin, was raped twice, and almost died of an overdose, but "I love heroin," she exclaimed.

Using heroin, however, seemed to be the only thing that remained the same for Liz during the seventies. Cleaning up her life-style somewhat, she now enjoyed living in style. "Most of my friends are rich faggots, fancy dressers," Liz explained over drinks at a local gay bar she patronized. Not unlike the others present, Liz, her hair meticulously cut in a shag, wore glitter makeup, sweet perfume, and high-heeled platform shoes. "I got very few friends though, just acquaintances I cop from and get down with all the time. But, I really do want to quit. The physical part of it," she explained, "is really not that hard. I could probably just go ahead and kick without going through this [methadone] program. But, maybe a psychiatrist can tell me why I have no willpower, why I'm in a rut, why I like to get down so often, why I crave junk so much."

SUBURBANMAN

Peter was called "hippie" back then because of his waist-length, straight black hair. Money was the least important thing in his life. "Man, nobody has to get into that '9 to 5' trip if they're smart," he was fond of saying. Today, Peter, married, a father of two children, renting a two-bedroom apartment in the suburbs, acknowledges, even jokes about the changes he and others have gone through. Every morning, Monday through Saturday, at 5:30 he wakes up to arrive at his surveyor job by 7:00. "I don't have to work Saturdays, but I wouldn't get overtime pay if I didn't."

"Shit, I guess we were fucking good at postponing the inevitable. I don't have any regrets. We had a better time than most. But, man you just gotta fucking go and work eventually. For sure, it didn't happen overnight, but eventually I just lost touch with the people on the streets. Then when I cut my hair to get a better job, it was like 'who are you?' I mean when you're putting 40 to 50 hours on the job, you're just not into hanging out no more. Anyway we know a couple of dealers here in the suburbs whenever we want to cop." But, Peter admits, too, that "my getting wrecked days are pretty much over. I don't have all the time I used to waste by getting stoned all the time. I can't work when I'm wrecked and I need all the time I can find. But, sometimes my old lady and I, we smoke a number, lie back, watch the boob tube for a while, and crash out."

THE ACTRESS

No one would have ever thought, including Leslie, that she would one day be an international movie star. After drifting away from the urban street scene and working as a secretary for two years, she went to Europe with her boyfriend for a vacation. They broke up while in Paris. She decided to stay, learned French, met two young French movie directors, moved in with them, and now she jets around the globe making movies. "I used to do these movies in Hong Kong; those Kung Fu movies where they needed three European girls to be kidnapped, but I'm starting to get a few things in Hollywood now."

She felt that "America" had changed dramatically during the last four years. Her surprising French accent suited her new, rather sophisticated, attractive appearance, especially when she was angry. And she was distraught about a recent incident: "My sister and I went to this deli down the street, you know where Blimpies used to be, and you should have seen those American kids. They were taking up all the seats, carrying on, making fun of others there, and they weren't buying anything. They were really obnoxious."

Apparently she had forgotten the times she used to hassle the straight people who would come in Blimpies. "Oh. We were never that bad. These kids were horrible," she insisted.

THE DEALER

Ron used to always be kidded about being a "juvenile delinquent." He had been arrested for stealing cars, burglarizing homes, and getting into fights. There were also the small drug scams, the heroin, and the time he had to "cold turkey" in the city jail: "Man, you wouldn't have believed it. That holding cell was filled with puke, shit, piss from all the drunks and faggots and they put me there so I could kick."

It was a pleasant change from that holding cell to the international wheeling and dealing of cocaine he was involved with now. Making on the average of $11,000 a month for each pound of cocaine he smuggled in from Bolivia, he made it look easy. Since he had grown up with little, he bought everything: bikes, cars, a house on the Pacific Ocean, trips to the Caribbean, a sailboat, and the best guitar money could buy, even though he did not know the first thing about playing it. He bought his parents, brothers, and sisters expensive appliances for Christmas. His own family, his beautiful common-law wife and handsome children similarly were not found wanting.

"It's simply a business," said Ron, looking more and more like a businessman, his beard and long hair gone, slacks and patent leather shoes replacing the faded, torn Levi and barefoot look of years past. There were risks, "but man, there's risks in any business. The bigger the risks the more you have to gain. And man, when you have the bucks you can do whatever you fucking please." He dreams, waits for when "I can just sit back and pay people to run the stuff for me. The bigger you are the less chance you'll get busted. And even if you do, like when Jack got busted with $150,000 worth of coke, you go into court with your six lawyers, two private detectives and $100,000 later you're back in Bolivia making up your business losses."

QUIET TEACHER

As a high school teacher at a predominantly black ghetto school, Jim encounters many students who are regularly using heroin. It had only been six years since he, too, was using heroin after dropping out of high school.

Asked if he is ever tempted to tell his classroom junkies that he understood what they were going through, Jim replies:

> I really don't know if I understand, you know. I mean, yea, I was into it once, but there's no way anyone could have helped me kick when I didn't want to. You want to kick, you kick. But, I don't even tell my wife (who is also a schoolteacher) that I was strung out once. People still get kind of weird if they find out you used to be a junkie. It's like they're never really sure of you, like you're going to blow it again one day if things get too heavy. I really don't want anyone to know. It could cost me my job.

Couldn't you see it, "Former Drug Addict Is Teaching Local Schoolchildren." To everyone who knows me now, I'm a good person: A high school teacher who maybe goes with his nice wife to drink at parties, and maybe even smokes pot with other radical ghetto teachers, but that's all right nowadays.

We really don't party that much. Sometimes. Usually I just like to kick back with Joyce, watch TV, maybe just read a book, grade some papers. Shit, there's really no need to go out seeking a wild time anymore.

PRISONER

Gary, one of the few who had been through the Haight-Ashbury scene, always seemed to complain about how much better life was in California: better drugs, music, and more sex. But life in East City improved for Gary the more lucrative his drug dealing became. For a while there, all was going well. He had many friends, lovers, drugs, and he was very generous with his inventory of cocaine and Colombian.

But one night he was set-up. His connection had advanced him $5000 worth of Colombian and a trusted customer and friend in trouble helped the federal agents set a trap for him. "It was an open and shut case," Gary later said. "One fucking mistake ended the good life for me and started the bummer of my life."

Not only was prison life an overwhelming experience—"the first night here this black dude lights his mattress on fire and jumps right into it. I never smelled a burning body before. . . . The guards were putting this 300 pound faggot, he looked like King Kong, anyway those guards were putting him in a different cell every night so he could rape someone"—but Gary was bitter that "all my friends, ex-friends I should say, deserted me." Gary was given the opportunity by the federal narcotics agents to walk away, have the charges dismissed, if he would only cooperate and help them get his "main man." He refused. But, friends were suspicious. "If they don't trust me," Gary exclaimed, "Well, fuck them. I don't need friends like that. Not one person, except you or Sharon, has come by to visit me since I got busted; I mean, not even picked the phone up to fucking see how I was doing."

NAVY

Unlike many of his friends who did not even bother to register, Chris, spurred on by the strong likelihood of getting drafted, joined the

Navy. "It's not so bad," he observed while on a recent visit to see his parents in East City. He had been in now for almost three years. "It was pretty rough at first, but I was real lucky. I ended up over in Italy, on this small island where they have a Navy hospital. It was really beautiful the two years I spent there. The local people would take me out fishing in their launches. I didn't know Italian and they didn't know English, but we got along fine."

It was in Italy where he met his wife, an American schoolteacher who taught at the base. His experience at the Navy hospital convinced him that when he got out he wanted to work in a hospital. Although not a good student in high school and without college experience, he was determined: "Don't laugh, but I know I'm going to be a doctor someday. I'm going to bust ass, go through college in a couple of years with the GI bill, and damn it I'll get in a medical school; if not here, I'll go back to Italy or Mexico. Crazy isn't it?" (In the five years since Chris has left the Navy he has done just what he intended. A father of two now, he is finishing his second year at a good medical school in New England.)

"Remember when we used to listen to WHIP," Chris, looking somewhat uncomfortable in the presence of a former street friend, began, "Remember how our parents used to yell, 'turn that noise down?' They couldn't understand why all the songs sounded the same. Anyway. It was beautiful. Lori [his little sister] turns on the radio in the car and puts on this really awful music. I started complaining and she says, 'Chris, this is WHIP, the same station you and your friends used to listen to.' "

THE APOSTLE

Troy had gained much notoriety for his substantial role in the movie *Woodstock*. With his skinny, 6'10" frame, extremely long Afro, and thick, bushy beard, he was easily recognized on the streets of East City by friends and strangers alike.

Suddenly, however, there was no sign of his electrifying appearance. The former junkie and revolutionary was still on the streets, but now he was peddling Jesus and not drugs. Joseph was his name, his Christian name now, and it did match his new appearance: a shaved head, clean-shaven face, and added weight.

He knew the scriptures well and would quote the Bible whenever his former friends failed in their attempts to avoid him. "We're in danger.

The Day of Judgment is fast approaching. Look at all the recent catastrophes. The wars, the famines, the earthquakes, and the impending nuclear devastatioñ. The Bible prophesied it all. In Matthew 24:7 it says, 'And there shall be famines and plagues in different places.' In Luke 21:11 ..."

Joseph seemed to have gone from one extreme to the other. He explained how "drugs aren't good for you at all. Like so many other things we used to get into, its of the flesh. An evil that leads us through so much unhappiness. Jesus is the best high I've ever been on and I'll always Praise the Lord for it."

GAY WARRIORS

Bill and Cathy were always at the front of all the antiwar demonstrations, screaming such slogans as *"Ho. Ho. Ho Chi Minh. The NLF is gonna win."* When that battle was won, they moved to a ghetto apartment on New York City's Lower East Side and were just as enthusiastic and committed in freeing Americans from the chains of sexism as they were about liberating the Vietnamese from the chains of imperialism.

Despite their homosexual politics, Bill and Cathy still held on to much of their past hippie ideology: the frumpy, freaky, ultranatural hair styles, secondhand clothes, and irreverent mannerisms. There were the welfare checks, "crazy money," because "when you're gay it's really easy to convince the straight government psychiatrists that you're too crazy to work." The checks payed for the color TV, the elaborate, wheel-to-wheel tape deck, the health-food juicer, and the sparse furniture, which included straw mats in the bedroom that served as beds.

"Fucking women and eating meat," Bill proclaimed, "are straight men's desperate attempt to salvage their masculinity without appreciating their own feminine qualities within them." Cathy adds: "If the majority of straight men were not hung up on being all man, then maybe we could have some People Liberation, not just simply Gay Liberation. People should be liberated to see each other as people, and not just simply as a good fuck."

REPORTER

Toward the end of the sixties heroin was the great divider: Many persons like Harry did not want anything to do with "those strung-out junkies who'd kill their mother for a fix," even if they had been friends at one time. Harry's drugs, both for his own use and for selling to his college friends in East City were grass, hashish, and LSD.

After graduating from college, Harry moved to the Southwest and began working for a large, well-known, metropolitan newspaper. "You'd be surprised," he said almost apologetically, "how different people react to you when you have short hair. You even start feeling like a different person." Harry was indistinguishable from the many reporters milling about the large, open newsroom. He enjoyed his new job and while finding his colleagues rather conservative at first, "the more you get to know them, the more you realize how this whole hippie thing caught on in Middle America. I mean stuff like a couple of my bosses' wives asking me to sleep with them. Also there's some people here you wouldn't believe would ever toke up at parties. It's like they're 'closet hippies' or something, but hell you can't blame them if they want to have a good time."

As to whether Harry was still using LSD and smoking grass, he responded that "I'm more into this German beer Sandy [his live-in lover] and I got turned on to when we went to Europe last summer. Dope is really too expensive here. You know they want fifty, five-zero, dollars for a two-finger lid of good Colombian! Why, man, I'd rather buy fifty bottles of Meinz beer than buy one little half-ounce of Colombian that's probably cut with Mexican anyway."

GROUP CHARACTERISTICS

Overall, it was found (Ramos and Gould, 1978) that the original group had disbanded, all 95 individuals had given up their "freak" identities, and nearly 70 percent were living, a short five years later, what would have to be described as conventional, straight lives at the time of the follow-up. Jobs, not drugs or the streets, had become the focal point in life. This group included teachers, truck drivers, waitresses, musicians, servicemen, Playboy bunnies, nurses, artists, newspaper reporters, housewives, store managers, electricians, secretaries, construction workers, actresses, carpenters, and parents.

Not everyone, however, abandoned deviance as a style of life. Approximately 30 percent (N = 27) continued to participate in a nonconformist life-style. Ten members of the population became adult criminals and at the time of the follow-up were either in prison (4), still using heroin (2), or dealing drugs at the wholesale or import-smuggling levels (4). There were 17 people actively involved with other deviant or quasi-deviant, but not criminal, groups; 8 were living in rural communes, 2 were actively involved with gay activist organizations, and 7 were involved with various religious sects.

The mean age of the 48 males and 47 females, the study population, during the height of the group's activities, late 1969, was eighteen years. Recent indications are that the 30 percent in the "still deviant" category have substantially decreased in number since the original follow-up. As they now approach thirty years of age, these individuals appear to have followed the paths of their former street comrades in pursuing more conventional endeavors. For instance, the lives of Steve (Mountain Man), now a construction worker living with his wife and two children in "the city," Ron (The Dealer), now working in an exclusive nightclub after being arrested by federal narcotics agents and serving three years in a federal penitentiary, Gary (The Prisoner), now supporting his wife and young son, working as a stereo and TV technician, and Cathy (Gay Warriors) who is now finishing her second year of law school in a large southern city, all, like other ex-freaks who have gone straight, exhibit a present life-style that is more easily understood as a manifestation of their current social situation—their jobs, their families, and their friends from work—and not as vestigial characteristics of their deviant past.

Likewise, present drug-use patterns are not too dissimilar from those found to be of acceptable levels for the society at large. It would be inaccurate to compare the use of drugs found among ex-freaks without noting the prevalent nature of drug use, both licit and illicit, existing in conventional society (Brecher, 1973). The public's attitude toward drug use has undergone some swift and "revolutionary" changes. At the height of the group's activities in late 1969, even the slightest residue of marihuana sent violators to prison for lengthy terms. Today, however, several states, through state statutes or local police guidelines, have in effect legalized the use of marihuana.

During their days on the streets, drug users in the study population (Ramos and Gould, 1978: 78-79) classified each other into three basic social types, each, to be sure, only approximating actual drug-use patterns: mellow freaks, chemical freaks, and junkies. Mellow freaks used marihuana, and occasionally hashish, experimenting with other drugs, but settling on cannabis. The chemical freaks used pills (barbiturates and amphetamines, psychedelics, LSD, mescaline, or peyote), and sometimes cocaine. Chemical freaks used heroin, although not necessarily on a regular basis; those who did use regularly received the highest street status of all—they were junkies. Of the study population thus classified, 22 percent were mellow freaks, 44 percent were chemical freaks, and 34 percent were junkies.

Among the 95 persons we could locate or find information about five years later, only 3 could still be classified as junkies (of the 3, 1 had died in the interim of a heroin overdose), none still continued to use chemicals (although a few used cocaine occasionally), 11 used no drugs at all (not even alcohol), and the overwhelming majority, 80 individuals (84 percent), continued to use cannabis on occasion. No one who had not used heroin before progressed to its use later.

It would be misleading, however, to say that the majority of former hippies studied were now mellow freaks, first because none identified any longer with the streets and the freak life-style, and second because drugs now played a decidedly less central role in their lives. Typically, cannabis was now a "social" or occasional drug for this group. It would be accepted if offered at a party and might even be used on occasion for pleasure or relaxation, but in no case did we find it to be the main focus of people's lives nor would many go out of their way to purchase large amounts for their own use, preferring instead to purchase alcohol, a more convenient and perhaps still a somewhat more acceptable drug.

The most deleterious aspect of youthful deviant involvement, at least for the hippies studied, was the relationship this had with arrest, incarceration, and the attendant consequences. Although a majority of this population, 60 percent, escaped arrest, both as juveniles and as adults, nearly two-thirds of those who were arrested as juveniles were later rearrested as adults and more than half of this number spent time in jail or prison.

Again, were it possible to conduct a ten-year follow-up of this study population, we would expect to find individuals increasingly more conventional in regard to their life-style, drug use, and involvement with the law. That which prevents a subsequent follow-up—the dissolution of even the slightest remnants of the once strong social network— also ensures that these former street people, once away from each other's peer influence, (over half of the study population has moved from East City), would drop back into a society they perhaps never completely left. One can only speculate what long-term consequences their brief participation in the world of drug use and the streets had over an entire lifetime, but surely a second look at the fate of hippies from the late sixties cautions against any quick and simple conclusions.

GOING STRAIGHT: WHEN AND WHY

Studies on the more familiar juvenile delinquent groups of the fifties and more recent follow-up studies of narcotics users substantiate the hypothesis that hippies would inevitably go straight and "reform." Indeed it was only a myopic view of drugs, viewing drugs and their effects apart from their social and situational context that prompted many to disregard insights gained by traditional studies of adolescent delinquent behavior. By characterizing hippies as drug-using, middle-class juvenile delinquents, and tying the cessation of deviant behavior to the dissolution of the adolescent reference group, one can subsequently understand why drug use in the sixties, including narcotic addiction, did not seal the fate of an entire generation.

Several studies have come a long way in correcting many of the myths, half-truths, and outright fabrications surrounding drug use. Drug use did not appear to be that consequential for addicted doctors (Bloomquist, 1958), a natural population of addicted, inner-city black males (Robins and Murphy, 1967), addicted Vietnam veterans (Robins, 1974), and former hippies who were regular heroin users (Ramos and Gould, 1978)—each documenting relapse rates of only 15 percent, 14 percent, 3.7 percent, and 8 percent, respectively.

Criticizing earlier follow-up studies for overlooking the extent to which socioeconomic and cultural characteristics may have, alone, influenced negative findings and conclusions on drug use, Musto and Ramos (forthcoming) found that a group of early twentieth-century American opiate addicts, when compared against the "general population," died substantially earlier and at a disproportionately higher rate from tuberculosis, pneumonia, venereal disease, alcoholism, accidents, and suicides. When compared to the "lower-class population," however, the fate of the predominantly lower-class addicts increasingly resembled and in fact differed little from that of their nonaddicted, but lower-class neighbors.

It has long been argued that the type of person who uses drugs and not the type or amount of drugs used determines the extent to which that person can and will go straight. Ray (1961: 132) suggested long ago that social and psychological conditions are more important in explaining persistence in drug use than is mere psysiological dependence on drugs. "A cure from physiological dependence on opiates," he wrote, "may be secured within a relatively short period, and carefully controlled studies indicate that use of these drugs does not cause psychosis, organic intellectual detention, or any permanent impairment of intellectual function. But despite these facts, addicts display a high rate of recidivism."

Vaillant (1966b: 1287) offers some insight into the apparent paradox of high relapse rates among addicts traditionally studied. After studying New York heroin addicts he found that the average addict was addicted for only 20 percent of his adult life and yet was socially disabled for 80 percent of it. Vaillant suggests that "one might say with justification, 'What is wrong with the addict is not that he uses drugs but that he is a healthy, intelligent person who is unable to hold sustained employment.'"

The fact that hippies of the late sixties were predominantly white middle-class adolescents assumes considerable significance in light of findings by Waldorf (1970: 242) that the "ability to deal with one's family and society *before* the use of heroin assists a person to make an adjustment after he is off heroin"; Vaillant (1966b: 1288) maintains that "it was their ability to sustain employment (at school and in the community) *before* addiction, rather than length or strength of addiction, that determined whether the addicts in the study eventually became abstinent"; and Winick (1964: 178) points out that physician addicts' high recovery rates can be attributed to "their recollection of the agreeable way of life that they enjoyed *before* addiction" (emphasis added).

Still, the question remains as to what facilitates the discontinuation of drug use; especially that which is, like the hippie phenomenon, so strongly reinforced and encouraged by peers in a subcultural drug setting? It is at this juncture that some significant parallels have been found between the middle-class drug-using hippies and the more traditionally studied lower-class juvenile delinquents. Yablonsky (1970: 8), who has studied both delinquent gangs and hippies, notes: "The parallel patterns include a clear sense of alienation from the larger society, similarities in group structure, parallels in personality structure, and a strong sense of distrust of the establishment." Similarly, those who have studied addicts have noticed how "in general, the addict resembles the alcoholic delinquent far more than he resembles any conventional 'psychiatric' patient" (Vaillant, 1966b: 1287) and that "the addicts' life cycle may be analogous to that of a typical delinquent" (Winick, 1962: 5).

The typical life cycle of a young drug user, not unlike that of a juvenile delinquent, occurs within an ongoing cultural and social system. He or she is less a member in a group *of* drug users and more a participant in a group *for* drug use. In their classic delinquency work, Matza and Sykes (1961: 717-719) warned against characterizing "the dominant society as being fully and unquestioningly attached to the virtue of hard work and careful savings" when evaluating the deviant juvenile delinquent's behavior which may at worst only caricature society's "subterranean values" and leisure ethic. Unfortunately, all ethnographers, whether studying aborigines in New Guinea or heroin addicts on the street, have a tendency to skip the more similar, mundane, boring, and seemingly unnoteworthy behavior and attitudes of the deviant group being studied. It is almost inevitable that the behavior which interests the researcher, the reason for studying the individuals in the first place, will take priority over details describing the extent to which the group does not differ from the researcher's more conventional world.

Most drug users, indeed, drift between the hip world of their peers and the more straight world of their parents, displaying different but appropriate behavior and attitude patterns to each: He or she is one thing to a lover, another to a parent, and still another to a teacher, policeman, sociologist, or psychiatrist. Like the delinquents of the fifties, drug users, including addicts, also "transiently exist in limbo between convention and crime, responding in turn to the demands of each, flirting now with one, now with the other, but postponing commitment, evading decisions" (Matza, 1964: 28-29).

Matza (1964: 22) further speculated that "60 to 85 percent of delinquents do not become adult violators" and emphasized that "this reform seems to occur irrespective of intervention of correctional agencies and irrespective of the quality of correctional service."

A generation later Ramos and Gould (1978: 82-83) similarly found that nearly 70 percent of hippies were leading rather conventional lives as adults and they too emphasized:

> Freaks left the streets and drugs, however, not necessarily because of the ever increasing efforts by social control agencies to "stop the drug problem" (60 percent of the study population was never arrested), nor because drugs were found to be dangerous (78 percent had regularly used LSD or heroin for years), but rather because of subtler, more natural processes: old friends could not be found on the streets, the camaraderie waned, and the social and psychological conditions necessary for maintaining the freak way of life were no longer present. Heavy drug use and the street

life abated and other challenges were pursued. Some refused to go straight, but for all the special world of the streets and the freak life-style was over.

It appears to be just as fruitless to treat and attempt to "cure" the adolescent hippie drug user as it is to treat the adolescent juvenile delinquent. McCord and McCord (1969: 89-96) in evaluating the effectiveness of the Cambridge-Somerville Youth Study concluded that "treatment consisting in guidance to the family, medical and academic assistance for the boys, co-ordination of community agencies, and supplementary entertainment of the boys had been no more effective in crime prevention." With maturity there was a tendency toward decreased criminality, but the McCords found that "comparison of the treatment and the control groups shows clearly that this decrease was not a function of treatment." Yale University researchers (Harford et al., forthcoming), following up both treated and untreated drug abusers, likewise noted that with maturity there was also a substantial turn away from criminality. This recent study also questions the efficacy of treating drug addicts for their addiction since "heroin use, criminality and unemployment abated equally" in both treated and untreated addicts.

Although few would probably endorse the assertion that many young hippies, drug users, and even drug addicts reform *despite* incarceration or various therapeutic treatment modalities, it is nonetheless important not to underestimate the extent to which drug users naturally reform once the adolescent peer group supporting the deviant behavior matures, weakens, and inevitably disbands. When this occurs, it no longer acts as an impediment to the discontinuation of potentially destructive antisocial and deviant behavior patterns.

Given the negative connotations of youthful "deviance" and the inherent problem/solution orientation that either explicitly or implicitly underlies any discussion of drugs and youth, there is a strong temptation to suspect that former juvenile delinquents, ex-hippies, or other former adolescent deviants have been emotionally scarred or will somehow have to pay a price down the line for their youthful indulgences. Indeed, it is difficult for police officers, drug counselors, physicians, social workers, professors, parents, and the general public who see, hear, or read, time after time, only the cases which merit attention—for example, Sutter's (1966:205) "garbage junkie"—to appreciate the extent to which, if left alone, most drug users, including addicts, will simply "mellow out." Once they do become part of the straight world it is very unlikely that these former "freaks" will boast about the old days when they ran around dealing and using heroin. Their legacy could very well be of a positive nature, but it is only the negative consequences that make the headlines, thereby characterizing as negative the entire youthful deviant behavior which for the most part, when viewed over the long run, was not that significant or at all catastrophic.

Also, there is the curious manner in which social scientists, not unlike lay persons, must find consistencies between an individual's past and present behavior. The seemingly irreconcilable behaviorial and attitudinal changes found among hippies of the sixties dramatically illustrate the complexity and plasticity of human behavior. Such natural reform underscores and perhaps further substantiates claims by a few behaviorists who contend that individual behavior is less influenced by "free will" and personality characteristics than previously thought (Zimbardo, 1972; Morris and Hawkins, 1972; Milgram, 1975). Zimbardo (1972: 7) suggests that in fact "we underestimate the power and pervasiveness of situational controls over behavior. . . . [Because] they are often non-obvious and subtle, we can avoid entering situations where we might be so controlled, and we label as 'weak' or 'deviant' people in these situations who do behave differently from how we believe we would." One does not have to completely embrace Zimbardo's thesis that "individual behavior is largely under the control of social forces and environmental contingencies rather than personality traits, character, will power or other empirically unvalidated constructs" to appreciate the extent to which former freaks, who increasingly found themselves spending more time at work with fellow construction workers, students, or businesspeople and less time on the streets, gradually changed, in time becoming indistinguishable and displaying the same behaviorial and attitudinal traits as their straight friends.

Researchers have coined different phrases for the naturally occurring changes that apparently influence each generation of youthful deviants to go straight. Matza (1964) described how juvenile delinquents eventually "drifted away" from their deviance. Winick (1962: 6), who was the first to speculate that "addiction may be a self-limiting process for perhaps two-thirds of addicts," developed a "maturing out" hypothesis. In his excellent study, Sutter (1969: 827) writes: "In light of the world of street-level opiate use (with its related criminal behavior), most addicts as well as hustlers 'burn out' with increasing age. It is clear that the hustling world is for young athletes or hunters not for older men and women."

Whether former hippies and street freaks from the sixties "drifted-out," "matured-out," "burned out," or "mellowed-out" is more than a matter of semantics and may simply be reflective of other, perhaps more important, nondeviant, nondrug demographic characteristics of the sample. Predominantly white middle-class hippies certainly appeared to have "mellowed-out" well before they reached their thirties; each one serving as living testimony to the vagaries and capriciousness of youth rather than becoming an ominous reminder of the severe price one pays for using heroin, cocaine, LSD, mescaline, amphetamines, barbiturates, hashish, and marihuana as adolescents.

Granted, the perspective on drugs and the youthful user developed here to explain the fate of hippies from the late sixties does little to assist those—the drug counselor, the psychiatrist, the aggrieved parent, the law and order politician—searching for a way to control drug use and prevent young people from getting caught up in a "hippie" or delinquent type world. Yet it is of some consolation, no doubt, to recognize that as far as youthful drug users are concerned, going straight, not staying deviant, is the rule rather than the exception.

As society continues, however ineffectively, to deal with the "drug problem," one thing is certain: The perseverance of adolescent deviant behavior, be it drug use, delinquent gangs, burglary rings, or car thefts, to the extent that it is encouraged and supported by an adolescent peer group, becomes suspect. When young criminals and youthful deviants do leave the confines and influence of their peer-oriented, nonconventional world, their baggage—the characteristic deviant and antisocial attitudes, behaviors, and beliefs—are also left behind for the next generation of young criminals and youthful deviants. Our well-founded concern and zealousness to somehow change the script should not render us impervious to the fact that young deviant actors are rather adept and do change, performing the straight script with the same enthusiasm and professionalism once displayed in their former freak/hippie role.

REFERENCES

BLOOMQUIST, E. (1958) "The doctor, the nurse, and narcotic addiction." General Psychiatry 18: 124-129.

BOYD, P. (1971) "Treatment and follow-up of adolescents addicted to heroin." British Medical Journal (4 December): 604-605.

BRECHER, E. (1973) Licit and Illicit Drugs. Boston: Little, Brown.

BROWN, J. [ed.] (1967) The Hippies. New York: Time.

DAVIS, F. and L. MUNOZ (1968) "Patterns and meaning of drug use among hippies." Journal of Health and Social Behavior 9: 156-164.

DUVALL, H., B. LOCKE, and L. BRILL (1963) "Follow-up study of narcotic addicts five years after hospitalization." Public Health Reports 78: 185-193.

EPSTEIN, E. (1977) Agency of Fear. New York: G. P. Putnam.

Federal Bureau of Investigation [FBI] (1966 and 1976) Uniform Crime Reports. Washington, DC: Government Printing Office.

FELDMAN, H. (1968) "Ideological supports to becoming and remaining a heroin addict." Journal of Health and Social Behavior 9: 131-134.

FINESTONE, H. (1957) "Cats, kicks, and color." Social Problems 5: 3-13.

GOULD, L., C. LIDZ, and A. WALKER (1974) Connections: Notes from the Heroin World. New Haven, CT: Yale University Press.

HARFORD, R. J., H. KLEBER, C. FORREST, and L. GOULD (forthcoming) "Treated and untreated drug abusers: comparative pro-social changes."

HOFFMAN, A. (1969) Woodstock Nation. New York: Vintage Books.

——— (1968) Revolution for the Hell of It. New York: Dial.

HUNT, G. and M. ORDOFF (1962) "A follow-up of narcotic addicts after hospitalization." Public Health Reports 77: 41-54.

JOHNSON, E. H. (1968) Crime, Correction and Society. Homewood, IL: Irwin.

KENISTON, K. (1971) Youth and Dissent. New York: Harcourt Brace, Jovanovich.

LANGENAUER, B. and C. BOWDEN (1971) "A follow-up of narcotic addicts in the NARA program." American Journal of Psychiatry 128: 41-46.

LEVY, B. (1972) "Five years after: a follow-up of 50 narcotic addicts." American Journal of Psychiatry 128: 868-872.

MATZA, D. (1964) Delinquency and Drift. New York: John Wiley.

——— and G. SYKES (1961) "Juvenile delinquency and subterranean values." American Sociological Review 26: 715-719.

McCORD, J. and W. McCORD (1969) "Prevention of juvenile delinquency: a follow-up report on the Cambridge-Somerville Youth Study." Annals of the American Academy of Political and Social Sciences (March): 89-96.

MILGRAM, S. (1975) Obedience to Authority. New York: Harper & Row.

MILLER, W. B. (1962) "The impact of a 'total community' delinquency control project." Social Problems 10: 168-191.

MORRIS, N. and G. HAWKINS (1972) The Honest Politician's Guide to Crime Control. Chicago: University of Chicago Press.

MUSTO, D. F. and M. R. RAMOS (forthcoming) "Socio-economic, cultural and historical correlates of opiate addiction: a follow-up of registrants in the New Haven morphine maintenance clinic (1918-1920)."

New York Times (1972) "Gallup finds a continued rise in the use of marijuana and LSD on campuses." (February 10).

O'DONNELL, J. A. (1964) "A follow-up of narcotic addicts." American Journal of Ortho-Psychiatry 34: 948-954.

PARTRIDGE, W. (1973) The Hippie Ghetto. New York: Holt, Rinehart & Winston.

POLSKY, N. (1967) Hustlers, Beats and Others. Chicago: AVC.

RAMOS, M. R. (1976) "Hippies' fates: sagas of the seventies." Washington Post Sunday Magazine (4 January): 14-27.

——— (1974) "Going straight or staying deviant?: the social evolution of a natural group of drug users." B.A. dissertation, Yale University.

——— and L. C. GOULD (1978) "Where have all the flower children gone? A five-year follow-up of a natural group of drug users." Journal of Drug Issues 8 (Winter): 75-84.

RAY, M. (1961) "The cycle of abstinence and relapse among heroin addicts." Social Problems 9: 132-140.

REICH, C. (1970) The Greening of America. New York: Random House.

ROBINS, L. N. (1974) The Vietnam Drug User Returns. Washington, DC: Government Printing Office.

ROBINS, L. N. and G. E. MURPHY (1967) "Drug use in a normal population of young Negro men." American Journal of Public Health 57: 1580-1596.

ROSZAK, T. (1969) The Making of a Counter Culture. New York: Doubleday.

RUBIN, J. (1970) Do It: Scenarios of the Revolution. New York: Simon & Schuster.

SHEPPARD, C. (1971) "The changing patterns of heroin addiction in the Haight-Ashbury subculture." Journal of Psychedelic Drugs 3: 21-29.

SIMMONS, H. and B. WINOGRAD (1966) It's Happening: A Portrait of the Youth Scene Today. Santa Barbara, CA: Marc-Laird.

STEPHENS, R. and E. COTTEL (1972) "A follow-up of 200 narcotic addicts committed for treatment under the NARA." British Journal of Addiction 67: 45-53.

SUCHMAN, E. A. (1968) "The 'hang-loose' ethic and the spirit of drug use." Journal of Health and Social Behavior 9: 146-155.

SUTTER, A. (1969) "Worlds of drug use on the street scene," in D. Cressey and D. Ward (eds.) Delinquency, Crime and Social Process. New York: Harper & Row.

——— (1966) "The world of the righteous dope fiend." Issues in Criminology 2: 177-222.

U.S. News & World Report (1971) "Latest findings on marijuana." (February 1).

VAILLANT, G. (1966a) "A twelve-year follow-up of New York addicts: I. The relation of treatment to outcome." American Journal of Psychiatry 122: 735-740.

——— (1966b) "A twelve-year follow-up of New York addicts: II. The natural history of a chronic disease." New England Journal of Medicine 275: 1282-1288.

——— (1966c) "A twelve-year follow-up of New York addicts: IV. Some characteristics and determinants of abstinence." American Journal of Psychiatry 123: 573-584.

WALDORF, D. (1970) "Life without heroin: some adjustments during long-term periods of voluntary abstention." Social Problems 18: 228-243.

WEPPNER, R. S. [ed.] (1977) Street Ethnography: Selected Studies of Crime and Drug Use in Natural Settings. Beverly Hills, CA: Sage.

WHYTE, W. F. (1955) Street Corner Society. Chicago: University of Chicago Press.

WINICK, C. (1964) "The physician narcotic addicts." Social Problems 9: 174-186.

——— (1962) "Maturing out of narcotic addiction." Bulletin on Narcotics 14: 1-6.

WITTENBORN, J. R., H. BRILL, J. P. SMITH, and S. WITTENBORN [eds.]
(1969) Drugs and Youth: Proceedings of the Rutgers Symposium on Drug
Abuse. Springfield, IL: Charles C Thomas.
YABLONSKY, L. (1970) The Violent Gang. New York: Viking.
——— (1968) The Hippie Trip. New York: Pegasus.
ZIMBARDO, P. (1972) "Pathology of imprisonment." Transaction 9: 1-11.

PART III

PREVENTION AND CONTROL OF DRUG USE

9

DRUG EDUCATION
Does It Work?

DAVID J. HANSON

INTRODUCTION

Drug use and abuse are not new phenomena and the American experience is marked by frequent examples of drug-related problems. These include morphine dependence following the Civil War, opium use of the Chinese during the building of the West, and the attempt to prohibit alcohol consumption during the early part of this century (McCune, 1973).

However, extensive evidence of widespread and growing use of drugs among youth in all segments of society has led to the call for a massive drug abuse education program to combat the problem. In 1970, the President of the United States asserted that drug abuse education, as a preventive measure of the highest national priority, must reach all publicly educated children from kindergarten through the twelfth grade (Einstein et al., 1971). Subsequently, federal expenditures for drug education, information, and training increased dramatically and an enormous bureaucracy for the delivery of drug education was developed.

251

Just as the early abolitionists assumed that teaching the "evils of alcohol" in schools would lead to abstinence (Milgram, 1976), so it was believed that if youth were taught the facts about various drugs they would tend to abstain. However, it has been argued that drug education has failed to prevent or even reduce the consumption or abuse of drugs and might actually stimulate interest in such substances (Bard, 1975; Halleck, 1970; Hammond, 1973; Jaffe, 1974; Levy and Brown, 1973; Mason, 1972; Zazzaro, 1973). The National Commission on Marihuana and Drug Abuse recognized the lack of knowledge regarding the impact of drug education and recommended a moratorium on all drug education programs in the schools, at least until existing programs could be evaluated. It asserted that "no drug education program in this country, or elsewhere, has proven sufficiently successful to warrant our recommending it," and speculated that "the avalanche of drug education in recent years has been counterproductive, and that it may have stimulated rebellion or simply raised interest in the forbidden (National Commission on Marihuana and Drug Abuse, 1973: 356-367).

Increasing attention has been directed toward the consequences of drug education (Berberian et al., 1976a, 1976b; Boldt et al., 1976; Goodstadt, 1974; Randall and Wong, 1976; Smart and Fejer, 1974; Swisher, 1974; Warner, 1975) and this chapter examines the existing evidence regarding its effectiveness. For this purpose, studies are organized in terms of (1) those that have investigated drug knowledge, (2) those that have examined drug attitudes, (3) those that have considered both knowledge and attitudes, and (4) those that have explored drug use.

THE RESEARCH

DRUG KNOWLEDGE

While there is little reason to believe that knowledge is clearly or directly related to behavior (Dorn, 1975), several studies have focused entirely upon the cognitive dimension of drug education. O'Rourke (1973) examined the effectiveness of the New York State Drug Curriculum Guide in four high schools in Nassau County, New York. Students in two schools used the new revised curriculum for six months (experimental group), while those in the two others followed their regular health education programs which included some information on drugs and alcohol, but no special guidelines about them. Students exposed to the new curriculum guide received a higher mean score on a multiple-choice drug knowledge test than did the students not exposed to the new guide. Unfortunately, as there was no pretest of drug knowledge, one cannot know whether or not the observed differences would have occurred in the absence of the new curriculum guide.

Eiseman (1971) evaluated a "student research approach" to drug education at the college level. Students were given course material on drugs and then broken into groups to conduct their own research on the subject. Pre- and posttests of knowledge revealed that students experienced significant gains, but that this was unrelated to the research conducted. Regrettably, the lack of a control group makes difficult the interpretation of findings.

The values-clarification and cognitive approaches to drug education were evaluated by Smith (1973), who randomly assigned students to the two experimental and to a drug-uneducated control group. In the values-clarification approach, small groups of students met together to raise questions and discuss their views on the drug problem. In the cognitive approach, the teacher followed the traditional role of presenting factual material to a class that listened and took tests. On the basis of knowledge scores, the values-clarification group learned more. However, there were no differences between the cognitive and control groups. A similar study compared a values clarification with a traditional lecture method among approximately 500 sixth graders who were randomly assigned to the experimental or to the no-treatment control classes (Sadler and Dillard, 1978). Pre- and posttest data revealed that while neither approach was superior to the other, both were associated with significant knowledge gains over the no-treatment control environment.

A study (Dorman, 1974) of the effects of in-service teacher training upon the drug education achievement of pupils involved 36 teachers who were randomly assigned to experimental and control groups. Pre- and posttest data indicated that students of teachers who had received the training failed to perform significantly better on a drug-knowledge test than did the other students. Shetler (1973) found that classroom teachers who had experienced in-service drug education exhibited higher levels of drug knowledge. A similar study found that teachers exposed to a two-week special training program performed significantly better on a posttest of drug knowledge than did teachers who had experienced no special training. Also, the students of the "trained" teachers also did significantly better (Stephens, 1971). Teachers in a

25-hour course demonstrated small but significant increases in drug knowledge (Wong and Zimmerman, 1974).

The effects of a 30-hour lecture-discussion course for police were investigated at the University of Nebraska. Pre- and posttests were administered to the class officers and an officer control group composed of officers chosen by the class members as those men on the force most similar in terms of police experience and outlook on life. The investigators (Piper and Rivers, 1975) reported significant improvement in drug knowledge among the class officers.

ATTITUDES

Studies Reporting Positive Findings

It should be emphasized that much research has demonstrated low correlations between attitudes and behaviors in areas as diverse as race relations, child-rearing, and industrial relations. Nevertheless, a number of studies have attempted to discover if drug education leads to attitude change.

A short series of presentations and discussions on drugs was presented to 196 elementary school children. Attitudes toward marihuana were found to be "considerably more" negative after the course than before it (Galvin and Starkey, n.d.).

To determine if a program about "narcotics" would change drug-related attitudes, Amendolara (1973) studied eight classes of seventh graders in a New Jersey public junior high school. Four of the classes were exposed to 15 weekly one-and-a-half hour sessions while four constituted a no-treatment group. The experimental group demonstrated significantly greater gains in antidrug attitudes than did the control group. Unfortunately, the scale measuring attitudes included a number of items tapping knowledge.

Examining the effects of a self-directed drug education program was a study (Blackwell, 1972), in which an experimental class of 36 college students was taught using self-directed learning activities while a control class of 25 students was taught using conventional procedures. Pre- and posttest data revealed that changes in attitudes occurred in the experimental group that did not occur in the control group.

Using an extensive attitude inventory as a pre- and posttest, Emmel (1974) attempted to determine whether or not attitude change toward drugs would occur among participants of one section of a college-level health course with 32 members. At the end of the course students perceived drugs as safer than at the beginning of the course, but they also expressed a decreased inclination to use them. They were less likely to approve of drug use by friends and viewed their fellow students as also having less favorable attitudes toward drug users.

Friedman (1973) studied the effects of his affective drug education program upon seventh- and eighth-grade New York City junior high school students' attitudes toward drug abuse. Ten classes in a Brooklyn junior high were given the affective program one period each week for 14 weeks. Ten classes in a Queens junior high school served as the control group. There were no significant differences in pretest drug attitude scores between the experimental and control groups. However, at the completion of the program, significant differences favored the experimental over the control group.

The ability of drug education films to change students' attitudes was studied by English (1972) using four male high school physical education classes. One viewed an emotion-oriented film, a second viewed a fact-oriented film, a third viewed a nondrug-related newsreel, while the fourth viewed no film. According to self-report questionnaires completed immediately after the film viewings, both groups of students who had seen drug films had less favorable attitudes toward certain drug-using groups then did the two control groups. Regrettably, as there was neither pretesting nor random assignment to groups, it cannot be assumed that both groups were equal in attitude at the beginning of the experiment.

Leary (1972) found that 135 drug education workshop participants demonstrated significantly different attitudes toward selected drug abuse concepts than did 112 participants in a nontrained control group.

Emphasizing alternatives to drugs was a study (Warner et al., 1973) in which 119 ninth graders were randomly assigned to experimental or control groups. A behavioral counseling program reinforced alternatives, a cognitive dissonance program aroused dissonance between pro-drug attitudes and other values, and a "placebo" program involved listening to and accepting student comments in a nonjudgmental fashion. Each program consisted of a 45-minute session each week for six weeks. The results of pre- and posttests revealed that significantly greater attitudinal improvement occurred in the "alternatives" program than in any other group.

To determine if inducing cognitive dissonance can lead to changes in drug attitudes, 34 undergraduates were randomly assigned (Swisher and Horan, 1972) to experimental or control groups. Cognitive dissonance was created by making explicit the discrepancy between favorable attitudes toward drugs among those students who valued "direct experiences" (e.g., play your favorite sport) rather than "mediated experiences" (e.g., watch your favorite sport on TV). Although the sample was small, the results suggested that drug attitudes can be changed through inducing cognitive dissonance.

Studies Reporting Negative Findings

A number of studies have reported negative findings. Richardson et al. (1972) studied two classes comprising a total of 50 fifth-grade students. One class received a ten-hour drug course over a two-week period, while the other class received no drug instruction. Pre- and posttest measures revealed no program effect. The difficulty of the program and the small sample size may have contributed to the insignificant outcome. To examine possible attitude change, Brower (1971) presented a drug education program to a class of twelfth-grade psychology students, while a second such class received no special instruction. Comparison of pre- and posttest results revealed that the program did not lead to a change in attitudes. In their study of Boston, Chicago, Detroit, and New York, Brown and Klein (1975) found support for their hypothesis that mass media communication used in drug education programs had no effect on changing the attitude of the audience to which it was presented. Unfortunately, their study lacked a control group.

The effectiveness of the New Jersey state-mandated drug education program was studied (Degnan, 1971) among 881 ninth graders in three suburban schools who completed both pre- and posttests. It was concluded that this informational program had little or no effect on attitudes toward drugs. Similarly, a three-week instruction package consisting primarily of a programmed text complemented by color films failed to change drug abuse attitudes among 80 seventh graders as measured by pre- and posttests (Vogt, 1977).

Comparing two forms of drug education was an early study by Cox and Smart (1970). One form was structured information-giving while the other was unstructured discussion. Each had a control group receiving no drug instruction. Analysis of pre- and posttests revealed few differences and several which favored the controls. To assess the relative effectiveness in changing attitudes of (1) lecture versus discussion methods or presentation and (2) large class versus small class size, 475 army trainees were exposed to a one-hour drug prevention program. A control group was made up of 36 trainees. Comparison of pre- and posttests indicated that neither group size nor method of presentation had a significant effect upon attitude change (Kriner and Vaughan, 1975).

An intensive 40-hour training program for teachers involving lecture-discussions and small-group sessions was studied (Fiman et al., 1974) by administering pre- and posttests to 100 teachers and administrators who enrolled in a graduate drug education course. While participants overwhelmingly endorsed the course as a valuable experience, there was no evidence of any significant change in the manner they perceived drugs and the drug user. An intensive eight-week training program including daily 3-hour seminar-lecture series and on-site visits for twenty health professionals failed to bring about attitude change as measured by pre- and posttests (Waring, 1975).

A total of 589 adult participants in ten-day drug education courses held at the National Center for Drug Education in Oklahoma were tested before and after each course to assess changes in their attitudes toward drug use and abuse resulting from the course. No statistically significant changes were produced (Bruhn et al., 1975a).

Examining the effectiveness of behavioral group counseling in changing attitudes was a study (Warner et al., 1973) in which 119 ninth graders were randomly assigned to groups experiencing behavioral group counseling, other forms of group counseling, or no counseling. Pre- and posttest results demonstrated that although the behavioral counseling groups showed the greatest gain in "healthy" drug attitudes, these changes were not significantly better than those exhibited by the no-treatment control.

In two British studies involving 86 male students aged 14-17, no evidence was found to suggest that informal talks made the pupils more "sympathetic to drug use" (Morgan et al., 1976).

A study (Adams, 1976) of a juvenile court education program for alcohol offenders compared 79 such offenders with a control group of 30 teenagers. Attitudes toward alcohol were not altered by the program.

Studies Reporting Mixed Findings

In his study of seventh-grade students, Johnson (1972) identified the pre- and posttest drug attitudes of 204 experimental and 22 control respondents. The findings indicated that the drug education program to which the students were exposed was effective in altering attitudes.

However, the influence was multidirectional. It appears that attitudes which initially were very conservative tended to be liberalized by new and accurate drug abuse information, while attitudes which were initially highly liberal tended to become more conservative when exposed to the program.

An English study (Swift et al., 1974) compared four types of lessons. One was a teacher presentation, while the others were films emphasizing shock value, personality, or pharmacology. Each lesson ranged from 40 to 90 minutes in duration and was usually followed by a discussion. Results of pre- and posttests administered to 1300 students revealed that antidrug attitudes increased slightly but so did favorable attitudes toward drug users. It should be noted that there was no control group not receiving drug education.

A study was made of the effectiveness of a revised New York State Curriculum Guide in changing attitudes among 234 high school students compared to 199 comparable students receiving a traditional program (O'Rourke and Barr, 1974). Results indicated a significantly higher score for the experimental group. However, closer analysis revealed that the program seemed to be effective for males but not for females.

Byrne (1974) investigated the following modalities: (1) group counseling, (2) interaction groups led by teachers, (3) classroom instruction emphasizing drug information, and (4) classroom instruction emphasizing components of affective education. Pre- and posttesting of attitudes occurred for both experimental groups and a control group for each treatment condition. In the study of group counseling, both the experimental and control groups regressed over the ten-week time period of the program. However, the experimental group experienced less deterioration of desirable attitudes related to drug use. In the study concerning interaction groups, there was no significant change between pretesting and posttesting. In the study involving classroom instruction, the class which emphasized informational aspects about drugs changed in its attitudes in a reverse direction when compared to a control group. The group involving classroom instruction augmented by affective education experienced no significant change in attitude when compared to its control group. Unfortunately, students in the various groups were self-selected. Byrne concluded that drug education programs of a strictly factual nature are ineffective in altering attitudes related to drugs and that the most promising were group interaction and affective classroom procedures.

KNOWLEDGE—ATTITUDES

Investigations of drug attitudes often examine both drug knowledge and drug attitudes as independent variables. To determine the effects of a week-long drug seminar, 175 randomly selected school personnel completed pre- and posttests (Taylor, 1976). The results indicated that participants made statistically significant gains in drug knowledge and favorable changes in drug attitudes. A high school drug curriculum emphasizing the development of human potential was tested by randomly assigning students to experimental and control groups and by administering pre- and posttests. Data from 1031 experimental students demonstrated significant positive effects upon both drug knowledge and attitudes (Myers, 1974). A curriculum incorporating television instruction among 167 students similarly led to the same findings (Wong and Barbatsis, 1976). A one-day program for university students and staff involving films and discussion led by drug abuse experts was studied by Swisher and Horman (1970). On the basis of pre- and posttest scores, a significant increase in knowledge was found among the experimental group, but not among a comparable control group. Significant shifts to more conservative drug attitudes were found among the student (but not staff) participants.

While a study of approximately 250 eighth- and twelfth-grade students found significant increases in drug knowledge, it also found increased curiosity about drugs and an increase in attitudes favorable to their use (Mason, 1972).

One investigation (Swanson, 1973) compared a values-oriented approach to a more traditional process of education among 78 elementary school teachers who participated in a 3½-day intensive live-in training session. Pre- and posttest data revealed that while both approaches produced significant knowledge gains, there was a significant advantage in favor of those trained by the traditional method. Both groups made significant shifts toward a "healthy" attitude about drugs. Evaluation of a humanistically oriented seminar on preventing drug abuse indicated that participating classroom teachers gained significantly in drug knowledge and changed significantly in attitudes concerning drug abuse (Lotecka, 1974).

A number of studies have reported greater changes in knowledge than in attitude. For example, in a study comparing lecture and small discussion group approaches, Connor (1974) randomly assigned 100 participants to the two modalities. Pre- and posttest results revealed a significant gain in knowledge among those using the small discussion group method. The writer concluded that while it is a relatively easy task to change levels of information, attitude change is a more complex and involved phenomenon. A similar result and conclusion has been reported by Benberg (1973), who randomly assigned 301 fifth-grade students to either a "planned" or an "unplanned" drug prevention program. Those in the planned program exhibited a significant increase in knowledge between pre- and postests. He concluded that it is much easier to achieve positive results in the cognitive as compared to the affective domain. Also reporting a greater magnitude of change in knowledge compared to attitude has been Mascoll (1976), who administered pre- and posttests to eighth-grade students in three school districts as well as to control groups. Students exposed to the alcohol programs in the three systems demonstrated significant increases in knowledge and more positive attitudes. However, the magnitude of change in knowledge was greater than that of attitude.

Consistent with the above relationship are the findings of a study of 217 adults who participated in a drug education program (Rosen, 1970). While they demonstrated increases in knowledge and desired attitude change compared to a control group, a follow-up one year later revealed that attitudes (but not knowledge) tended to regress.

An evaluation (Cobb et al., 1970) of a five-day workshop for students and school personnel comparing pre- and posttest measures of knowledge and attitudes revealed significant gains in knowledge. However, attitudes demonstrated shifts toward both extremes of opinion.

Several studies have reported changes in knowledge unaccompanied by changes in attitude. Jones (1974) randomly assigned 60 tenth-grade students to an instructional unit on drug education and 60 students to a control group. Pre- and posttest scores revealed no significant increase in drug knowledge among those in the experimental group. Similarly, Hanna (1973) randomly assigned 88 seventh-grade students to an experimental six-week unit on drugs. A randomly selected control group consisted of an equal number of students. Data from pre- and posttests revealed that while the experimental group experienced a significant increase in knowledge, there was no significant difference between the groups in drug attitudes. Comparing a sample of 59 teenage alcohol offenders who participated in an educational program with 30 control teenagers, Adams (1976) found that the program increased drug knowledge but did not alter drug attitudes. A government-funded, student-conducted drug education program aimed primarily at pharmacy, nursing, law, and medical students has been evaluated (Anthony et al., 1974) at thirteen college sites using extensive pre- and posttests of knowledge and attitudes. While overall results revealed a significant increase in knowledge, the program did not appear to affect attitudes. Finally, a 60-hour training course for 14 paraprofessional counselors produced significant increases in drug knowledge (which were maintained over a seven-month period) but no changes in attitudes (Gluckstern, 1972).

Reporting the reverse of the above findings was a study by Virgillio (1971) which compared the effects of two different three-week drug programs. Eighteen sections of high school students were randomly assigned to one program, while eighteen were randomly assigned to another. Pre- and posttests revealed no significant difference in knowledge but did reveal that the lecture-discussion program resulted in significant attitude change. Several studies have found no changes in either knowledge or attitude. In an attempt to evaluate the relative effectiveness of four drug education programs, 50 college freshmen were randomly assigned to each of the four treatment groups. The investigator (Toennies, 1971) concluded that prolonged classes are no more effective in inculcating drug knowledge than a two-hour discussion group, and that none of the programs were effective in influencing drug attitudes.

Finding no significant change in either knowledge or attitudes was a study of 120 ninth graders in four classes (Pethel, 1971). Two classes served as control groups while one experienced a student-oriented method of instruction and one experienced the traditional method. Based upon pre- and posttest data, neither method produced significant changes. Also reporting no change in either knowledge or attitudes as measured by pre- and posttests was an investigation of the affects of a 26-hour workshop upon 12 graduate students (Friedman and Meyers, 1975).

To evaluate (Barresi and Gigliotti, 1975) the effectiveness of expert speakers in bringing about change in drug knowledge and attitudes, 224 tenth graders were randomly assigned to either a control group or to groups exposed to a speaker on the legal, the pharmacological, or the social-psychological effects of drug abuse. Results of a questionnaire administered prior to the experts' 50-minute presentation and nine days later indicated that the use of such speakers had no effects.

In an attempt to determine if "drug-educated" parents would teach their children drug knowledge and attitudes more effectively than other parents (Thomas et al., 1971), eighteen families were randomly assigned to an experimental group involving formal lecture, group discussion, and informational pamphlets. Children in the experimental families exhibited similar knowledge and attitudes when compared to children in eighteen randomly assigned control families.

Former drug users have been used in a number of studies investigating drug knowledge and attitudes. Hawk (1972) conducted a study of 216 high school students who were randomly assigned to drug education groups. In some groups, former drug users were present; in other groups, knowledgeable individuals who had never used drugs were present; and in other groups, no models were present. All groups received a drug unit taught in health class. Pre- and posttest results revealed no significant changes in drug knowledge or attitude between the groups. Similarly, in a study (McCleaf, 1974) of fifteen randomly assigned selected groups of eighth graders, it was concluded that the students' knowledge and attitudes were not affected by their perceptions of the social role and prior use or nonuse of drugs by the speaker.

However, different findings were reported by Geis (1969), from a study conducted in a depressed Mexican-American section of Los Angeles. In two junior high schools, former addicts instructed teachers in workshops prior to the program in the educational program itself. In two nearby schools, the traditional unit on narcotics was presented. Although comparable on pretests of both knowledge and attitude, the experimental schools demonstrated significantly higher gains on knowledge and favorable (i.e., antidrug) attitude change.

USE

By far the most rigorous test of educational effectiveness involves subsequent student drug use. This section reviews studies which have examined that educational outcome, often in combination with drug knowledge and/or attitudes.

Studies Reporting Decreased Use

Several studies have found drug usage to be reduced following drug education. Favorable results were reported (Kline, 1972) in an evaluation of a two-week program among 650 junior high school students. According to retrospective self-reports, 75 percent of the professed drug users claimed to have stopped. Unfortunately, the lack of a pretest and a control group reduce the credibility of the finding.

A three-year values-clarification approach among students in grades 4 through 12 was analyzed (Carney, 1971) by means of pre- and posttests. Compared to control drug education classes, the values-oriented classes tended to be lower in drug abuse. Evaluation (McClellan, 1975) of a drug education program for high school drug abusers involving a daily semester-long "alternatives class" (focusing on Gestalt self-awareness, sensory awareness, communication skills, and interpersonal relationships) revealed that although students reported continued drug use, they tended to use fewer drugs and drugs with lower abuse potential. The effects of twelve weeks of nondirective techniques and sensitivity training among two nonrandomly selected groups of twelve students each has been reported (Dearden and Jekel, 1971). According to self-reports, three of the six students in the first group who had been drug users had stopped using and the remaining three had reduced their use. In the second group, one of the four drug users had stopped using and the other three had reduced their use.

Students in 36 randomly selected classes in grades 7 through 9 were administered a questionnaire concerning tobacco knowledge, attitudes, and behavior (Rabinowitz and Zimmerli, 1974). Those students who were given health care education demonstrated significant increases in tobacco knowledge, significant changes in attitude, and an appreciable but statistically nonsignificant reduction in smoking.

Adult participants who had completed ten-day drug education courses were mailed questionnaires one year later. Of the 41 percent who responded, from one-fourth to one-third reported decreased or discontinued use of caffeine, tobacco, and alcohol. Practically no differences were observed with respect to hallucinogens, amphetamines, barbiturates, and opiates (Bruhn et al., 1975b).

Although not reporting a decrease in drug use, analysis of a values-clarification program among 104 sixth graders revealed that those who had received the program demonstrated a significantly lower rate of increase in the use of licit drugs than did the control students (Gerbasi, 1976).

Studies Reporting No Change in Use or Nonuse

By far, the largest number of studies have found no effects of drug education upon use. In a cross-sectional survey of 1716 men on sixteen Army posts, as well as a separate sample pre- and posttest evaluation of a drug education program at one post (Cook and Morton, 1975), drug education programs in the Army were consistently found to be ineffective in preventing or reducing drug use. This failure occurred regardless of the particular educational process or technique employed. In a questionnaire study (Lawrence and Velleman, 1974) of 1416 upper-middle-class school children in a New York City suburb, drug education was found unrelated to either attitudes or use. An experimental study (Jackson, 1975) of a drug education program in two high schools also found that there were no significant differences between the experimental and control students on drug knowledge or drug usage.

Similarly, a 50-hour self-development approach to drug education including values-clarification, empathy training, and drug information was evaluated (Jackson and Calsyn, 1977) by randomly assigning 29 students to drug treatment groups and 43 students to control groups. On the basis of pre- and posttests, no differences between the experimental and control groups were found in drug knowledge or drug usage.

A study (Bruett, 1972) which randomly assigned 250 college freshmen to one of five groups (three experimental and two control) and administered pre- and posttests found no significant difference in drug knowledge, attitudes, or usage as a consequence of the experimental program.

Finally, in a study (Sine, 1976) comparing the effect of a values to a factual approach to drug education, 50 college students were randomly assigned to the two groups where they received drug instruction over a four-week period. Results of pre- and posttests revealed that neither approach was successful in reducing drug use.

Very extensive studies have similarly found no effects of drug education. A study (de Haes and Schuurman, 1975) of three approaches (mild horror, factual, and individual adjustment) in a Rotterdam school involved 1035 pupils. Pretest, posttest, and follow-up data were collected. The results indicated that the increases in knowledge tended to disappear over time and while users do not tend to stop, some nonusers may decide to try drugs. "The general conclusion tends to be that drug education, as such and independently of the method, has no effects at best, or has mixed or negative effects at worst" (de Haes and Schuurman, 1975). A similar study (Sillem, 1974) tested four drug education methods in Amsterdam among pupils, teachers, and parents. Minimal or nonexistent effects were found.

Data on drug attitudes and behaviors of students in 33 junior and senior high schools in New Haven were collected yearly over a three-year period and were analyzed (Berberian et al., 1976b) in relation to the drug education program in the schools. Basic program modalities identities were assemblies, regular course work, special courses, staff training, and two or three modalities, plus staff training. The researchers (Berberian et al., 1976b: 366) concluded that "The *overall impression* from the analyses dealing with possible *effects of drug education* is that drug education in general (or a particular modality) *did not have a strong, across-the-board, consistent influence on drug use rates, or on attitudes and beliefs.*" Furthermore, the presence of any form of drug education was generally associated with increases in the proportion of students who reported that they knew where to obtain illegal drugs.

A number of reports indicate that while drug knowledge and/or attitudes may be changed, drug use has not. A study (McCune, 1970) of drug programs in eleven California school districts involving a diversity of educational approaches (e.g., commercially developed packages, peer-run programs, television-based programs, and "innovative" programs) led to the conclusion that no program was more effective than the others. Most had positive effects on knowledge and attitudes, but little, if any, on drug use.

Pipher (1977) evaluated the impact of an experimental alcohol education course on 81 junior high school students enrolled in a required health class. Pre- and posttest results, as well as follow-up test data, indicated that the course had effected only limited change in terms of attitudes and knowledge and no change in drinking behavior. A three-to-four-hour high school drug program utilizing rehabilitated users (Swisher and Crawford, 1971) and pre- and posttests found increased knowledge but no change in either attitudes or use.

A community team workshop was found (Shapiro, 1971) to be effective in increasing knowledge, but ineffective in changing either attitudes or use. While there was no control group, pre- and posttests were used.

Experimental research has often led to the same finding. One study (Swisher et al., 1972) randomly assigned high school students to one of four treatment conditions. As measured by self-reports on pre- and posttests, all four approaches were equally effective in increasing knowledge and equally ineffective in changing attitudes and behavior. A similar study (Swisher et al., 1973) involved 374 college students who were randomly assigned to four different drug education programs and a control group. Pre- and posttest data revealed significant increases in knowledge but no significant differences between the five groups. Unlike the earlier study, there were significant attitude changes (pro-drug) in the four experimental groups, but not in the control group. Again, there were no significant differences in drug use.

A total of 216 high school students stratified for intelligence were randomly assigned to one of four experimental groups (Swisher et al., 1972). On the basis of pre- and posttests it was found that all four groups significantly increased their knowledge, but did not differ from each other. No changes in attitudes or use were discovered.

Immediate and six-month follow-up examination of ninth graders who received six student-taught drug education classes, and controls who received no classroom instruction, revealed that the peer-run program led to more knowledge about drugs, but no differences in drug attitudes or usage (Smart et al., 1976).

To determine the effects of one presentation of a drug education film, 166 college students were randomly assigned to an experimental and a control group (Sohn, 1976). While an increase in drug knowledge among the experimental group was measured immediately following this film, such knowledge was dramatically eroded when assessed two weeks after the film. At the same two-week point in time, there was no difference between the experimental and control groups in reported drug use.

Studies Reporting Increased Use

Some studies have found drug education to be associated with increased drug use. A college course evaluation (Korn and Goldstein, 1973) involving 129 students who completed pre- and posttests revealed a nonsignificant increase in drug usage following a semester-long drug education course. Unfortunately, there was no control group.

To compare the drug use of students in a ten-session drug education program (either teacher or student-led, and with major drug content, minor content, or both) with those in a control group not receiving drug education, 935 seventh and ninth graders completed pre-, post-, and follow-up tests (Stuart, 1974). Students who experienced the program demonstrated significant increases in both drug knowledge and use. It was also observed that "worry about drug effects" decreased in the experimental group.

A group of 452 eighth graders in one school was given a three-week drug education course while 380 eighth graders in another school served as the control group (Weaver and Tennant, 1973). Unfortunately, students were not randomly assigned and there was no pretest. At the conclusion of the course, the experimental group displayed more drug knowledge than the controls did, as well as a higher rate of drug use (12.5 percent versus 4.1 percent). Nine months after the program, a follow-up testing of the experimental group revealed increased drug use. As no follow-up was made of the control group, no comparison with it is possible.

In a study (McCune, 1973) of 4604 junior and senior high school students from seven school districts, pre- and posttests revealed that in only three of the districts did attitudes change significantly in a positive direction. More importantly, after instruction there were increases in uses of marihuana, barbiturates, amphetamines, hallucinogens, opiates, and inhalants. Finally, a study by the National Association of Youth Clubs (Lane, n.d.) concluded that drug education programs stimulate interest in drug use among many young people.

A survey study (Goldstein, 1972) of university students found that of those who experienced organized high school drug programs, 78 percent reported drug use while of those with no drug education experience, 59 percent reported drug use. These findings appear to suggest that drug education leads to drug use, but may actually reflect the consequences of student self-selection in courses. For example, surveys administered (Linder et al., 1973) to 839 college students who had never taken a drug course were compared to 209 who completed the questionnaire on the first day of such a course. More students who elected to enroll in a course on drug abuse reported using drugs than those who had not. Unfortunately, it is not known why drug users chose to take such a course.

Studies Reporting Mixed Findings

With regard to drug use, some studies have reported findings which can be described as "mixed." In an early study (Williams et al., 1968) designed to evaluate a program stressing tolerance for abstention or moderate use of alcohol but intolerance for excessive use, 205 male eleventh graders were assigned to experimental and control groups. The educational program met daily for a week and placed major emphasis on small-group discussions led by an adult. In addition to the pretest, a posttest was administered one month following the program and again in one year. The experimental group demonstrated consistently significantly higher knowledge scores. While significant changes in attitudes toward temperate use occurred in both groups, significant changes in atttitudes toward intemperate use occurred only in the control group. Importantly, while slightly more experimental students got intoxicated in the year following the program, they did so less often than did the controls. An evaluation of a two-day high school drug abuse program has been reported (Lewis et al., 1972), in which pre- and posttest findings revealed a nonsignificant difference in drug use between the experimental and control school. However, there was a 9 percent increase in alcohol use at the program school.

A drug education class was given by a physician to 947 soldiers, 50.5 percent of whom admitted on an anonymous questionnaire to prior illegal drug use at the time the class was given (Tennant et al., 1974). In order to determine whether class members decreased in their use, an anonymous questionnaire was administered three months after the class. A total of 39 percent of LSD users, 24 percent of amphetamine users, 25 percent of sedative-hypnotic users, and 45 percent of opiate users reported discontinuation or decrease in their drug consumption (which they attributed to the class). Drug-related hospitalizations decreased from 22 in the twelve months prior to the class to 11 during the following twelve months. However, a small percentage of soldiers stated that they actually started smoking hashish as a result of the drug education class.

The use of medical and nursing students in a drug program for seventh-grade students was found to be effective in significantly increasing knowledge. There was no correlation between information about alcohol, marihuana, or amphetamines and students' predictions of their future drug use. However, those students with the most knowledge about heroin and psychedelics tended to be the ones expressing the least desire to use them (Rosenblitt and Nagey, 1973).

Four approaches to drug education (values-clarification, self-actualization by reinforcement, behavioral alternatives, and factual information) were studied among 1159 students in grades kindergarten through 12 (Swisher and Piniuk, 1973). Pre- and postmeasures were made of behaviors, values, knowledge, and attitudes. While program effectiveness varied by grade level, it can be noted that elementary students in the values-clarification program became significantly more liberal in their attitudes toward drug use. Among high school students the behavioral alternatives, values-clarification, and factual information approaches all led to significant increases in knowledge and significantly more liberal attitudes toward drugs. Only those in the values-clarification program reported a significant reduction in drug use.

Four studies (Tennant et al., 1973) have led to the conclusion that drug education programs are not effective and can possibly be harmful. In one study a high school drug education program was given in one town but not in two nearby towns. While no precourse data are available, drug-related hospital admissions in the experimental town were lower than in the control towns. In another study of lecture-discussions, 20 percent of the high school students believed that the programs would reduce their drug use, while 23 percent felt that they would use more drugs. The third secondary school program involved the use of a mobile drug abuse education van. While no systematic evaluation was made, it was reported that a group of students experimented with drugs as a consequence of visiting the van. As one student reported, "The drugs in the van looked so good that we wanted to try them" (Tennant et al., 1973: 249). The final program involved elementary (grade 5 and 6) students in ten one-hour weekly classes presented by a specially trained teacher. On the basis of pre- and posttest results, it was found that after the program significantly fewer students expressed an intention to use drugs.

Over 9000 elementary, junior, and senior high school students were involved in a 2½-year study (Blum et al., 1976) by being randomly assigned to didactic (information-giving), process education (values-clarification, norm-setting discussion), and control groups. A wide diversity of measures were administered each fall and spring and attempts were made to control for classroom size, frequency of presentation, teacher differences, school milieu, and so on. The researchers found that there were two forms of educational impact. One is destabilization: More student users increased their levels of drug use as they experienced drug education. Stability, on the other hand, was most dramatic for those experiencing the least drug education. The other form of impact was extent of "spread." Expansion in intensity and variety of drug use was least among those exposed to didactic education, greater among process-educated students, and highest among those in the control group. About 25 percent of the didactic group were "destablished" by drug education in comparison with the more stable controls, while over 30 percent more control students than didactic students greatly increased their levels of drug use once they did begin to change.

Drug education was found to be simultaneously productive, nonproductive, and counterproductive.

> Drug education is productive insofar as its goal is to retard the increase in intensity and variety of nonmedical psychoactive drug use which occurs as part of the normal social development of metropolitan children. It restricts the extreme spread of use among those youngsters whose drug use is expanding anyway.

That impact is limited among our Californian youngsters to elementary school pupils. Successful drug education is associated both with information giving and with discussion (value clarification, decision making) in the classroom, but more strikingly with the former.

Drug education is nonproductive. It makes no noticeable impact on young children in grades 2 and 3 or among older ones in grades 9-12.

And drug education is counterproductive. It destabilizes existing drug habits, including abstinence, and leads to a greater variety and intensity of use. This effect is also centered in the elementary grades, being most evident among youngsters in grades 6-8. These are the same years when the first great leap forward occurs in drug use [Blum et al., 1976: 169].

MISCELLANEOUS

Subjective Evaluations

Some studies have reported authors' subjective evaluations. Reporting a four-session collegiate program in England, Hornibrook (1977: 171) reported her impression that "some students increased their awareness of how and why they used drugs and therefore increased their potential for change." The principal (Nelson, 1973) of an elementary school in California subjectively evaluated as effective a program involving a slide show with synchronized sound and flashing lights followed by two weeks of daily discussions, research, and role-playing. Finally, Tashjian and Crabtree (1972) have described a group consultation method that utilizes psychiatrists, other staff (teachers, nurses, attendants, recreational therapists), and patients from an adolescent treatment center in an attempt to engage high school students in the "personal arena of shared experience and to foment such interpersonal events as openness, honesty and active participation." The authors' impressions are that nonusers and occasional users feel more confident in their personal commitment against significant drug use, that the students are more serious and cautious about even occasional use of narcotics and other hard drugs, and that there has been no alteration of attitude toward the use of marihuana.

Many other studies have examined the reactions of students to drug education. Johnson (1968) evaluated a two-day "seminar" for thirteen and fourteen year olds which included panel presentations by experts, a film, and student discussions. The majority (83 percent of the eighth graders and 66 percent of the ninth graders) reported that the program had added to their knowledge of drugs and approximately the same percentage felt that it had influenced them against using drugs. A similar program in a large high school was evaluated by Blauat and Flocco (1971) who found that 59 percent of those who had experimented with drugs felt that they were influenced not to take drugs in the future. Of all students surveyed in the school, 65 percent felt the same way. In a study by Martin and O'Rourke (1972) college students were asked to rank the effectiveness of various programs (e.g., radio ads, religious programs, "tough laws," and so on) and certain categories of people (physicians, clergy, parents, and the like) in preventing or stopping the use of drugs. The most effective program was perceived to be "good personal example by friends," while church programs were seen as least effective. Former users were viewed as the most effective resource persons while members of the clergy were seen as the least effective. The responses of the 120 students who had taken a drug course were not different from the 75 who had not.

A total of 1026 students ranging from the fifth grade to senior high school and representing a wide range of socioeconomic levels evaluated an educational program using panel presentations and intensive small-group encounters which were developed and implemented by ex-addicts (Kline and Wilson, 1972). Students who condemned the use of drugs and alcohol overwhelmingly approved of the program and the majority of those who approved the use of drugs and/or alcohol also reacted favorably and approved of the program, although less enthusiastically.

A drug program lasting several days and including films, lectures, and small-group discussions was studied by Nowalk (1969) who found that 75 percent of the 1044 high school students responding rated the overall value of the program as excellent or very good. The discussion-with-experts part of the program was evaluated as preferable to the lecture and film components. In a survey of 1029 high school and college students, small-group discussions were indicated by a majority of students as the most effective approach to drug abuse education (Fagerberg and Fagerberg, 1976). Similarly, a study in eleven metropolitan high schools revealed that students viewed as largely unsuccessful programs that emphasized the pharmacological aspects of drugs and were more in favor of counseling and/or group therapy programs (Farkas, 1974). Among his sample of 502 Marine officers and noncommissioned officers, Adkins (1973) found small-group discussion to be favored for disseminating information about drugs.

A survey of 10,131 students in grades 7 through 12 (Zimering, 1974) revealed that about one-quarter of those who had experienced health education believed that they had learned a great deal about alcohol and drugs. They reported learning most about medical facts, the harmful effects of drug use, and arguments against taking them. Almost 75 percent of the students thought the information presented was either "accurate" or "very accurate" and most of them believed that their teachers "told it like it is." However, a large number believed their teacher overemphasized the harmful effects of drugs and attempted to use scare techniques. While most considered themselves to be as in formed as their teachers about drugs and their effects, the number of students who reported that they valued their teachers' opinions far outweighed those who did not. Respondents rated discussions led by an ex-addict, special films, and class debates to be the most interesting approaches, while textbooks, pamphlets, and discussions led by doctors or nurses were rated the least interesting.

Walpole (1973) surveyed a random sample of 646 high school students and found that 63 percent responded that drug information obtained at school had a preventative effect. In the sample, 38 percent of the abusers and 58 percent of the experimental users responded that school-dispensed information would keep them from using some drugs but not others.

Knowledge and Use

Nearly a decade ago it was suggested (Halleck, 1970) that young people might be interested in drug education because they were already using drugs and wanted to obtain as much information as they could so as to enjoy the most pleasurable drug experience and be informed on how they might deal with any undesirable reactions. Recent support for this view is provided by a survey of 682 students in grades 7 through 12 (Dembo and Miran, 1976). Drug users preferred programs that explained how to live better with drugs and how to handle bad drug experiences. Nonusers were not interested in these topics but were interested in learning the physical dangers of drug use, the psychological consequences of drug use, the immorality of drug use, and family damage of drug use. Conversely, drug users were not interested in these themes. Thus, program preferences appear to be consistent with drug use behavior.

Considerable evidence exists that drug users possess greater drug knowledge or information than do nonusers. Among a group of 69 military offenders, those who reported drug use histories exhibited a significantly higher degree of drug knowledge (Ratcliff, 1977). Similarly, an examination of junior and senior high school students found drug users to have higher drug information scores than nonusers (Shuman, 1972). There was also a strong relationship between drug information and frequency of past drug use. A survey of 14,000 high school students found that those most heavily involved in drugs were the most knowledgeable about the pharmacological and legal consequences of drug use (Schaps et al., 1974). Drug users were also found to possess more drug knowledge in a survey of 137 teenagers (Stock and Ruiz, 1977) and in a study of 124 adults and high school students (McKee, 1973). A survey of 2454 high school students in Toronto found drug users to have more drug education than nonusers (Fejer and Smart, 1973), and another survey of 4693 high school students in the same city revealed that users had higher knowledge scores than did nonusers (Smart and Fejer, 1974). Similarly, a survey of 1060 seniors in Washington state found that problem drinkers exhibited higher alcohol knowledge scores than did those who were not problem drinkers (Burkett and White, 1976).

It should also be noted that Korn and Goldstein's study (1973) of 129 college students and Stuart's study (1974) of 935 junior high school students (both of which are described earlier in this chapter) also found knowledge to be associated with usage.

SUMMARY

Research has demonstrated that while it is relatively easy to increase drug knowledge, it is more difficult to modify attitudes. A number of studies have reported greater changes in knowledge than in attitude, or have reported changes in knowledge unaccompanied by changes in attitude. Clearly the most rigorous test of educational effectiveness involves subsequent drug usage. By far the largest number of studies have found no effects of drug education upon use. A few have found drug usage to be reduced while others have found it to be increased following drug education.

While there is much correlational evidence that drug users possess greater drug knowledge than do nonusers, there is no evidence that increases in such knowledge stimulate use. It has been suggested (Stuart, 1974) that drug education might stimulate use by (1) providing students with facts that overcome beliefs which inhibit use, (2) changing attitudes that prevent use, (3) encouraging students to think of themselves as potential users by virtue of having been included in drug education programs, and (4) providing specific information which serves to facilitate the use of drugs. On the other hand, it is also plausible that greater knowledge results from use rather than vice versa.

A massive expenditure of funds and energy is being used throughout the United States to deploy a diversity of theories, techniques, and materials in attempts to influence drug beliefs, attitudes, and behaviors. It would appear that the burden of proof rests upon those who advocate such programs to demonstrate their efficacy, particularly in view of the fact that some evidence exists that they may be counterproductive.

As pointed out earlier, the National Commission on Marihuana and Drug Abuse decried that lack of knowledge regarding the impact of drug education and recommended a moratorium on these programs until such time as adequate evidence might be available. Writing in 1973, the Commission concluded that no drug education program had proven sufficiently successful to warrant recommendation and speculated that such programs could be counterproductive. The evidence reviewed in this chapter appears to confirm the Commission's position.

REFERENCES

ADAMS, D. B. (1976) "Evaluation of an education program for juvenile alcohol offenders and their parents." Ph.D. dissertation, University of Utah.

ADKINS, S. C. (1973) "An assessment of attitudes toward drug abuse and preventative programs held by Marine officers and non-commissioned officers." Ed.D. dissertation, University of Virginia.

AMENDOLARA, F. R. (1973) "Modifying attitudes towards drugs in seventh grade students." Journal of Drug Education 3 (Spring): 71-78.

ANTHONY, J. C., D. C. RANDALL, M. KOENEN, and M. JANSEN (1974) "Evaluation of Project SPEED curriculum model." Final Report, University of Minnesota. (unpublished)

BARD, B. (1975) "The failure of our school abuse programs." Phi Delta Kappan 57 (December): 251-255.

BARRESI, C. M. and R. J. GIGLIOTTI (1975) "Are drug programs effective?" Journal of Drug Education 5, 4: 301-316.

BENBERG, T. E. (1973) "The effects of a planned curriculum on correlates of drug-abusing behavior." Ed.D. dissertation, East Texas State University.

BERBERIAN, R. M., C. GROSS, J. LOVEJOY, and S. PAPARELLA (1976a) "The effectiveness of drug education programs: a critical review." Health Education Monographs 4 (Winter): 377-398.

BERBERIAN, R. M., W. D. THOMPSON, S. V. KASL, L. C. GOULD, and H. D. KLEBER (1976b) "The relationship between drug education programs in the greater New Haven schools and changes in drug use and drug-related beliefs and perceptions." Health Education Monographs 4 (Winter): 327-376.

BLACKWELL, J. T., Jr. (1972) "The effects of a self-directed drug abuse education program on attitudes of college students." Ed.D. dissertation, Auburn University.

BLAUAT, H. and W. FLOCCO (1971) "A survey of a workable drug abuse program." Phi Delta Kappan 52 (May): 532-533.

BLUM, H., E. BLUM, and E. GARFIELD (1976) Drug Education: Results and Recommendations. Lexington, MA: D. C. Heath.

BOLDT, R. F., R. R. REILLY, and P. W. HABERMAN (1976) "A survey and assessment of drug-related programs and policies in elementary and secondary schools," pp. 39-63 in R. E. Ostman (ed.) Communication Research and Drug Education. Beverly Hills, CA: Sage.

BRANSON, J. O. (1974) "An analysis of principals' attitudes regarding drug abuse prevention education programs in selected public schools in Michigan." Ph.D. dissertation, Michigan State University.

BROWER, L. (1971) "An investigation of the effects of a drug education program on the attitudes of students toward drug abuse." M.A. thesis, Idaho State University.

BROWN, E. H. and A. L. KLEIN (1975) "The effects of drug education programs on attitude changes." Journal of Drug Education 5, 1: 51-56.

BRUETT, T. L. (1972) "Predicting drug abuse and evaluating selected educational approaches to preventing drug abuse." Ed.D. dissertation, University of Georgia.

BRUHN, J. G., B. V. PHILIPS, and H. D. GORUIN (1975a) "The effects of drug education courses on additional change in adult participants." International Journal of the Addictions 10, 1: 65-96.

——— (1975b) "Follow-up of adult participants in drug education courses." International Journal of the Addictions 10, 2: 241-249.

BURKETT, S. R. and M. WHITE (1976) "School adjustment, drinking and the impact of alcohol education programs." Urban Education 11 (April): 79-94.

BYRNE, J. (1974) "The effectiveness of group interaction and classroom instruction in changing patterns of drug use." Ed.D. dissertation, Columbia University.

CARNEY, R. E. (1971) "An evaluation of the 1970-71 Coronado, California Drug Abuse Education Program using the risk-taking attitude questionnaire." (unpublished report)

COBB, H., J. BLAND, R. BULOW, and J. LEADER (1970) "Washington, D.C. seminar for school personnel and students report." Washington, DC: Department of Research and Evaluation.

CONNOR, B. C. (1974) "An evaluation of alcohol education methods." Ed.D. dissertation, University of Pittsburgh.

COOK, R. F. and A. S. MORTON (1975) "An assessment of drug education-prevention programs in the United States Army." Technical Paper 261 ERIC Document Reproduction Service No. ED 106 708. Washington, DC: United States Army Research Institute for the Behavioral and Social Sciences.

COX, C. and R. G. SMART (1970) "A failed comparison of structured and unstructured approaches to drug education. Substudy 2-33. Toronto: Addication Research Foundation.

DEARDEN, M. and J. F. JEKEL (1971) "A pilot program in high school drug education utilizing nondirective techniques and sensitive training." Journal of School Health 41, 3: 118-124.

DEGNAN, E. J. (1971) "An exploration into the relationship between depression and a positive attitude toward drugs in young adolescents and an evaluation of a drug education program." Ed.D. dissertation, Rutgers University.

de HAES, W. and J. SCHUURMAN (1975) "Results of an evaluation study of three drug education methods." International Journal of Health Education 18 (October-December): 1-16.

DEMBO, R. and M. MIRAN (1976) "Evaluation of drug prevention programs by youths in middle-class community." International Journal of the Addictions 11, 5: 881-903.

DORMAN, R. C. (1974) "The effects of a drug education inservice program on the achievement of the students of participants. Ed.D. dissertation, Florida Atlantic University.

DORN, N. (1975) "Notes on prediction of behavioural change in evaluation of drug education." Drug and Alcohol Dependence 1 (September): 15-25.

EINSTEIN, S., M. LAVENHAR, E. WOLFSON, D. LOURIA, M. QUINONES, and G. McATEER, (1971) "The training of teachers for drug abuse education programs: preliminary considerations." Journal of Drug Education 1 (December): 323-345.

EISEMAN, S. (1971) "Teaching about narcotics and dangerous drugs: further findings about the student research approach." International Journal of Health Education 38, 1: 139-144.

EMMEL, B. D. (1974) "A study of the effects of a college health course on student attitudes." M.S. thesis, Moorehead State College.

ENGLISH, G. E. (1972) "The effectiveness of emotional-appeal versus fact-giving drug educational films." Journal of School Health 42 (November): 540-541.

FAGERBERG, S. and K. FAGERBERG (1976) "Student attitudes concerning drug abuse education and prevention." Journal of Drug Education 6, 2: 141-152.

FARKAS, M. I. (1974) "Students' views of school drug use." Journal of Drug Education 4 (Winter): 457-468.

FEJER, D. and R. G. SMART (1973) "The knowledge about drugs, attitudes towards them and drug use rates of high school students." Journal of Drug Education 3 (Winter): 377-387.

FIMAN, B. G., L. MAXWELL, and V. H. COHN (1974) "An evaluation of a teacher training program in drug education: results and implications." Journal of Drug Education 4 (Spring): 69-82.

FRIEDMAN, S. M. (1973) "A drug education program emphasizing effective approaches and its influence upon intermediate school student and teacher attitudes." Ph.D. dissertation, Fordham University.

FRIEDMAN, M. P. and J. MEYERS (1975) "A workshop model for training the school psychologist in drug education and intervention techniques." Journal of School Psychology 13 (Spring): 63-67.

GALVIN, B. and J. STARKEY (n.d.) "A study of attitude change concerning marijuana in the fourth grade." ERIC Document Reproduction Service No. ED 062 640. DeKalb: Northern Illinois University.

GEIS, G. (1969) "Addicts in the classroom: the impact of an experimental narcotics program on junior high school students." ERIC Document Reproduction Service No. ED 062 640.

GERBASI, K. F. (1976) "Drug education and evaluation: an application of social psychological commitment theory and an examination of the values clarification hypothesis." Ph.D. dissertation, University of Rochester.

GLOBETTI, G., M. ALSIKAFI, and E. G. CHRISTY (1977) "Permissive attitudes toward alcohol abuse among young military dependents." Journal of Drug Education 7, 2: 99-107.

GLOBETTI, G. and D. E. HARRISON (1970) "Attitudes of high school students toward alcohol education." Journal of School Health 40 (January): 36-39.

GLUCKSTERN, N. B. (1972) "Parents as lay counselors: the development of a systematic community program for drug counseling." Ed.D. dissertation, University of Massachusetts.

GOLDSTEIN, J. W. (1972) "Drug education worthy of the name." Impact 1 (Summer): 18-24, 64.

GOODSTADT, M. S. (1974) "Myths and methodology in drug education: a critical review of the research evidence," pp. 113-145 in M. Goodstadt (ed.) Research on Methods and Programs of Drug Education. Toronto: Addiction Research Foundation.

HALLECK, S. (1970) "The great drug education hoax." Progressive 34 (July): 34-37.

HAMMOND, P. G. (1978) "The abuse of drug information." School Library Journal 25 (April): 17-21.

HANNA, S. B. (1973) "The effects of drug education on attitudes and achievement in seventh grade life science students." M.S. thesis, Pennsylvania State University.

HAWK, R. S. (1972) "Four approaches to drug abuse education: an investigation of high school counselors' ability to withhold reinforcement in behavioral counseling." Ed.D. dissertation, Pennsylvania State University.

HORNIBROOK, J. (1977) "A health education programme in a country technical college." Journal of Drug Education 7, 2: 171-178.

JACKSON, J. A. (1975) "An evaluation of the students, teachers and residents involved in Drug Education (S.T.R.I.D.E.) Program." Ph.D. dissertation, Michigan State University.

JACKSON, J. and R. J. CALSYN (1977) "Evaluation of a self-development approach to drug education: some mixed results." Journal of Drug Education 7, 1: 15-26.

JAFFE, A. (1974) "SPARK: school rehabilitation through drug prevention programs." Drug Forum 3 (Winter): 137-147.

JOHNSON, B. A. (1968) "A junior high school seminar on dangerous drugs and narcotics." Journal of School Health 38, 2: 84-87.

JOHNSON, D. P. (1973) "A study of relationships between drug abuse education and attitudes toward six classes of abused drugs." D.S.W. dissertation, Tulane University.

JONES, W. L. (1974) "A study of tenth grade student attitudes toward, and knowledge of, drug abuse when related to a drug education program." Ed.D. dissertation, University of Southern Mississippi.

KLINE, J. A. (1972) "Evaluation of a multimedia drug education program." Journal of Drug Education 2 (September): 229-239.

——— and W. WILSON (1972) "Ex-addicts in drug abuse prevention education." Drug Forum 1 (July): 357-366.

KORN, J. H. and J. W. GOLDSTEIN (1973) "Psychoactive drugs: a course evaluation." Journal of Drug Education 3 (Winter): 353-368.

KRINER, R. E. and M. R. VAUGHAN (1975) "The effects of group size and presentation." Technical Report 75-11. ERIC Document Reproduction Service No. ED 112 325. Alexandria, VA: Human Resources Research Organization.

LANE, D. A. (n.d.) "Drugs education: questions and answers." (unpublished)

LAWRENCE, T. S. and J. D. VELLEMAN (1974) "Correlates of student drug use in a suburban high school." Psychiatry 37 (May): 129-136.

LEARY, W. (1972) "The affective attitudes of drug abuse education workshop participants toward selected concepts of narcotic and drug abuse." Ph.D. dissertation, University of Pittsburgh.

LEVY, R. M. and A. R. BROWN (1973) "Untoward effects of drug education." American Journal of Public Health 63 (December): 1071-1073.

LEWIS, J. M., J. T. GASSETT, and V. A. PHILLIPS (1972) "Evaluation of a Drug Prevention Program." Hospital & Community Psychiatry 23, 4: 124-126.

LINDER, R. L., S. E. LERNER, and J. C. DROLET (1973) "Drug use by students of drug abuse." Journal of Drug Education 3 (Fall): 309-314.

LOTECKA, L. (1974) "A project advocating humanistic education: an evaluation of its effects on public school teachers." Journal of Drug Education 4 (Summer): 141-149.

MARTIN, G. L. and T. W. O'ROURKE (1972) "The perceived effectiveness of selected programs and sources with respect to preventing the use of dangerous drugs." Journal of Drug Education 2 (Winter): 329-335.

MASCOLL, S. H. (1976) "The effect of alcohol education programs on the knowledge, attitudes, and intended behavior of eighth grade students." Ed.D. dissertation, Columbia University.

MASON, M. L. (1972) "Drug education effects." ERIC Document Reproduction Service No. ED 071 011. Gainesville, FL: Young Adult Services.

McCLEAF, J. E. (1974) "The effect of students' perceptions of a speaker's role on their recall of drug facts and their opinions and attitudes about drugs." Ph.D. dissertation, University of Maryland.

McCLELLAN, P. P. (1975) "The Pulaski Project: an innovative drug abuse prevention program in an urban high school." Journal of Psychedelic Drugs 7 (October-December): 355-362.

McCUNE, D. A. (1973) "An analysis of the role of the state in drug education," pp. 392-401 in National Commission on Marihuana and Drug Abuse, Drug Use in America: Problem in Perspective. Vol. 2, Social Responses to Drug Use. Washington, DC: Government Printing Office.

——— (1970) "A study of more effective education relative to narcotics, other harmful drugs and hallucinogenic substances: a progress report submitted to the California legislature." Sacramento: California State Department of Education.

McKEE, M. R. (1973) "Main Street, USA: fact and fiction about drug abuse." Journal of Drug Education 3 (Fall): 275-295.

MILGRAM, G. (1976) "A historical review of alcohol education research and comments." Journal of Alcohol and Drug Education 21 (Winter): 1-16.

MORGAN, H. G. and A. HAYWARD (1976) "The effects of drug talks to school children." British Journal of Addiction 71, 3: 285-288.

MYERS, E. (1974) "The effects of a drug education curriculum based on a causal approach to human behavior." Journal of Drug Education 4 (Fall): 309-316.

National Commission on Marihuana and Drug Abuse (1973) Drug Use in America: Problem in Perspective. Washington, DC: Government Printing Office.

NELSON, H. (1973) "Media program combats student drug problem." School Management 17 (October) 26-27.

NOWALK, D. (1969) "Innovation in drug education." Journal of School Health 39 (April): 236-239.

O'ROURKE, T. W. (1973) "Assessment of the effectiveness of the New York State Drug Curriculum Guide with respect to drug knowledge." Journal of Drug Education 3 (Spring): 57-66.

––– and S. L. BARR (1974) "Assessment of the effectiveness of the New York State Drug Curriculum Guide with respect to drug attitudes." Journal of Drug Education 4 (Fall): 347-356.

PETHEL, D. L. (1971) "Comparison of two approaches to instruction on drug abuse." School Health Review 2 (April): 9-11.

PIPHER, J. R. (1977) "An evaluation of an alcohol course for junior high school students, and examination of differential course effectiveness as annotated with subject characteristics." Ph.D. dissertation, University of Nebraska.

PIPER, J. and P. C. RIVERS (1975) "A course on alcohol abuse and alcoholism for police: a descriptive summary." Journal of Alcohol and Drug Education 20, 2: 18-26.

PIERCE, J., D. HIEATT, M. GOODSTADT, L. LONERO, H. PANG, and A. CUNLIFFE (1974) "An experimental evaluation of a community based campaign against drinking and driving." Presented at the Sixth International Congress on Alcohol, Drugs and Traffic Safety, Toronto, Ontario.

RABINOWITZ, H. S. and W. H. ZIMMERLI (1974) "Effects of a health education program on junior high school students' knowledge, attitudes, and behavior concerning tobacco use." Journal of School Health 44 (June): 324-330.

RANDALL, D. and M. R. WONG (1976) "Drug education to date: a review." Journal of Drug Education 6, 1: 1-21.

RATCLIFF, B. W. (1977) "Comparison of attitudes, knowledge and drug abuse among military offenders." Journal of Drug Education 7, 2: 109-115.

RICHARDSON, D. W., P. R. NADER, K. J. ROGHMANN, and S. B. FRIEDMAN (1972) "Attitudes of fifth grade students to illicit psychoactive drugs." Journal of School Health 42 (September): 389-391.

ROSEN, M. J. (1970) "An evaluative study comparing the cognitive and attitudinal effects of two versions of an educational program about mind-affecting drugs." ERIC Document Reproduction Service No. ED 044 564. Los Angeles: Evaluation and Research Associates.

ROSENBLITT, D. L. and D. A. NAGEY (1973) "The use of medical manpower in a seventh grade drug education program." Journal of Drug Education 3 (Spring): 39-56.

SADLER, O. W. and N. R. DILLARD (1978) "A description and evaluation of TRENDS: a substance abuse education program for sixth graders." Journal of Educational Research 71 (January-February): 171-175.

SCHAPS, E., C. R. SANDERS and P. H. HUGHES (1974) "Student preferences on the design of drug education programs: drug users and nonusers compared." Journal of Psychedelic Drugs 6 (October-December): 425-434.

SHAPIRO, M. (1971) "An evaluation of a drug education workshop." M.A. thesis, Pennsylvania State University.

SHETLER, R. H. (1973) "A study of the value of in-service drug education training for teachers." M.S. thesis, Glassboro State College.

SHUMAN, M. C. (1972) "Patterns of drug use and drug information in junior and senior high school students." Ph.D. dissertation, University of Michigan.

SILLEM, A. (1974) Experimentel underzoeh naar effecten van drugvoorlichting. Amsterdam: Stichting voor Alcohol en Drugonderzoek.

SINE, R. (1976) "The comparative effect of a values approach with a factual approach on the drug abuse and smoking behavior of college students. Journal of the American College Health Association 25 (December): 113-116.

SMART, R. G., C. BENNETT, and D. FEJER (1976) "A controlled study of the peer group approach to drug education." Journal of Drug Education 6, 4: 305-311.

SMART, R. G. and D. FEJER (1974) Drug education: current issues, future directions. Toronto: Addiction Research Foundation of Ontario.

SMITH, B. C. (1973) "Values clarification in drug education: a comparative study." Journal of Drug Education 3 (Winter): 369-376.

SOHN, M. F. (1976) "Change in factual knowledge and reported use of illicit drugs resulting from the viewing of a motion picture." Ph.D. dissertation, University of Maryland.

STEPHENS, B. S. (1971) "The effects of drug abuse training upon teacher awareness." M.A. thesis, California State College.

STOCK, W. P. and E. M. RUIZ (1977) "Drug abuse: bridging the multidimensional ignorance gap." Drug Forum 5, 4: 335-344.

STUART, R. B. (1974) "Teaching facts about drugs: pushing preventing?" Journal of Educational Psychology 66 (April): 189-201.

SWANSON, J. C. "Drug abuse: an in-service education program." Journal of School Health 43 (June): 391-393.

SWIFT, B., N. DORN, and A. THOMPSON (1974) Evaluation of drug education: findings of a national research study of effects on secondary school students of five types on lesson given by teacher. London: Institute for the Study of Drug Dependence.

SWISHER, J. D. (1974) "The effectiveness of drug education: conclusions based on experimental evaluation," pp. 147-160 in M. Goodstadt (ed.) Research on Methods and Programs of Drug Education. Toronto: Addiction Research Foundation of Ontario.

――― and J. L. CRAWFORD (1971) "An evaluation of a short-term drug education program." School Counselor 18 (March): 265-277.

SWISHER, J. D. and J. J. HORAN (1972) "Effecting drug attitude change in college students via induced cognitive dissonance." Journal of Student Personnel and Teacher Education 11 (September): 26-31.

SWISHER, J. D. and R. T. HORMAN (1970) "Drug abuse prevention." Journal of College Student Personnel 18 (September): 337-341.

SWISHER, J. D. and A. J. PINIUK (1973) "An evaluation of Keystone Central

School District's Drug Education Program." Harrisburg: Pennsylvania Governors Justice Commission.

SWISHER, J. D., R. W. WARNER, and E. L. HERR (1972) "Experimental comparison of four approaches to drug abuse prevention among ninth and eleventh graders." Journal of Counseling Psychology 19 (June): 328-332.

SWISHER, J. D., R. W. WARNER, Jr., C. C. SPENCE, and M. L. UPCROFT (1973) "Four approaches to drug abuse prevention among college students." Journal of College Student Personnel 14, 3: 231-235.

TASHJIAN, L. D. and L. H. CRABTREE, Jr. (1972) "A group method of altering adolescent attitudes toward drug use." Psychotherapy: Theory, Research and Practice 9 (Winter): 314-316.

TAYLOR, G. R. (1976) "Innovation in drug education: an interdisciplinary approach." Southern Journal of Educational Research 10 (Winter): 51-58.

TENNANT, F. S., P. J. MOHLER, D. H. DRACHLER, and H. D. SILSBY (1974) "Effectiveness of drug education classes." American Journal of Public Health 64 (May): 422-426.

TENNANT, F. S., S. C. WEAVER, and C. E. LEWIS (1973) "Outcomes of drug education: four case studies." Pediatrics 52 (August): 245-251.

THOMAS, P., G. FRISONE, and D. LIPSON (1971) "An evaluation of parent drug education." Mental Hygiene 55, 4: 456-460.

TOENNIES, J. E. (1971) "Effectiveness of selected treatments on drug education programs for university freshmen." H.S.D. dissertation, Indiana University.

VIRGILLIO, D. (1971) "A comparison of the effects of the school health education study (SHES) approach and the lecture-discussion approach upon drug knowledge and attitudes of high school students." Ed.D. dissertation, Boston University.

VOGT, A. T. (1977) "Will classroom instruction change attitudes toward drug abuse?" Psychological Reports 41 (December): 973-974.

WALPOLE, J. W. (1973) "A survey of drug use and an examination of the relationship of self-perceptions and adjustment to adolescent drug abuse." Ed.D. dissertation, University of Northern Colorado.

WARING, M. L. (1975) "The impact of specialized training in alcoholism on management-level professionals." Journal of Studies on Alcohol 36 (March): 406-415.

WARNER, R. W., Jr. (1975) "Evaluation of drug abuse prevention programs," pp. 83-91 in B. W. Corder et al. (eds.) Drug Abuse Prevention: Perspectives and Approaches for Education. Dubuque, IA: Wm. C. Brown.

WARNER, R. W., J. D. SWISHER, and J. J. HORAN (1973) "Drug abuse prevention: a behavioral approach." Bulletin, National Association of Secondary School Principals 57, 372: 49-54.

WEAVER, S. C. and F. S. TENNANT (1973) "Effectiveness of drug education programs for secondary school students." American Journal of Psychiatry 130 (July): 812-814.

WILLIAMS, A. F., L. M. DICICCO, and J. UNTERBERGER (1968) "Philosophy and evaluation of an alcohol education program." Quarterly Journal of Studies on Alcohol 29, 3: 685-702.

WONG, M. R. and G. S. BARBATSIS (1976) "Attitude and information change effects by drug education via broadcast television and group viewing." ERIC

Document Reproduction Service No. ED 128 705. Presented at the annual
meeting of the American Educational Research Association, San Francisco,
California.

WONG, M. R. and R. ZIMMERMAN (1974) "Changes in teachers' attitudes
toward drugs associated with a 'social seminar' course." Journal of Drug
Education 4, 4: 361-367.

ZAZZARO, J. (1973) "Drug education: is ignorance bliss?" Nations' Schools 92
(August): 29-33.

ZIMMERING, S. (1974) "Health and drug education—how effective?" Journal of
Drug Education 4 (Fall): 269-279.

10

TREATING THE YOUNG DRUG USER

DAVID J. HUBERTY

Treatment concepts and programs clearly grew out of the demands of the times—most recently in response to the explosive rates of addiction of the past twenty years and the comparative failure of more traditional means of coping with drug dependency. As the style and rate of drug usage itself has an identifiable history as described in Part I of this volume, so too does the treatment scene.

EARLY NARCOTIC TREATMENT

The turn of the century brought the medicinal use of heroin which had just been derived from morphine in 1898. This "hero" drug had been hailed as a "cure" for morphine addiction and was perhaps a first attempt at "treatment"—a mistake all too understandable within the context of medical expertise at the time, which was oriented toward

AUTHOR'S NOTE: I wish to acknowledge special friends who are so much a part of this chapter—Cathy, my wife, and Nick, Fred, Gary, and Jeff.

treatment of symptoms rather than causes. Most of the 264,000 narcotic addicts at the turn of the century had become addicted as a result of opiates being used as pain medication without adequate medical understanding of the physiology of addiction. The hypodermic syringe had been invented just prior to the Civil War and had been used extensively to inject morphine to kill the pain of war wounds. Following the Civil War, thousands of veterans developed the so-called "soldiers disease" of morphine addiction and most remained addicted for the rest of their lives. However, by 1900 as the memory of the war dimmed with the passage of addicted grandparents, the attitudes toward the use of narcotics changed from sympathy associated with symptomatic treatment of a patriotic disease to an aversion of needles associated with the hedonism of self-injections. In a few short years, the prevailing social attitude toward abuse of narcotics went from use as a physical analgesic or pain killer to abuse as a mental analgesic or psychic pain killer. Treatment concepts and public policy responded in accordance with public social attitudes which reflected more control than treatment.

HARRISON ACT OF 1914

The Harrison Narcotic Act (1914) reflected this changing national attitude toward increased control through efforts to limit the production and trade of opiates to what was necessary for medical and scientific purposes. Persons and firms handling narcotic drugs were required to register and pay small fees. Violation was punishable by up to ten-year maximum sentences. The act itself made no direct mention of the 264,000 addicts—many of them clearly youthful—whose addiction and treatment was to be so greatly affected.

From 1919 until 1922, there was a brief effort at treatment through establishing 44 narcotic clinics which distributed narcotics to registered addicts; in theory this was not dissimilar from methadone maintenance clinics of the late 1960s and the 1970s. However, as Lindesmith (1965: 139-140) quotes from government reports in 1920:

> As a result of the decisions of the Supreme Court . . . it was held that the furnishing of narcotic drugs to an addict merely to satisfy his addiction, is not bonafide medical treatment of disease or addiction . . . that such clinics accomplish no good and that the cure of narcotic addiction is an impossibility unless accompanied by institutional treatment. Steps are now being taken to

close these clinics, which are not only a menace to society but a means of perpetuating addiction.

Once again, these objections are not dissimilar to those of critics of today's methadone clinics. By 1922, because of judicial interpretations of the Harrison Act and closure of the narcotic clinics, persons addicted to narcotics had to obtain all narcotic drugs illegally regardless of whether they were continuing and increasing their dosage or attempting self-treatment or withdrawal by decreasing their doses gradually. The only exception was if the addict was in an institutional setting and if the narcotic was given in diminishing doses. Since addicts were generally not accepted in hospitals, this so-called treatment exception was mainly theoretical. Prevailing law and social attitudes prescribed *no treatment*.

Predictable was the mushrooming of black-market narcotic drug traffic in the early 1920s. Protests from the medical profession over the restricted prescription of narcotics by physicians resulted in the brief softening of this trend. The unanimous Supreme Court opinion in Linder v. United States (1925) termed addicts "diseased and in need of medical treatment." This medical orientation toward addiction even suggested a "right to treatment" concept in holding that an addict who had been denied medical care by earlier court decisions was actually a *diseased* person entitled to such care. Despite this interpretation and because of legal confusion in subsequent court cases, most doctors and hospitals did not even attempt to treat addicts. Lindesmith (1965: 11-12) cites blatant ignorance of the Linder case on the part of prosecutors and police officers as adding greatly to the reluctance to treat the narcotic addict, which resulted in the only alternative available to most communities—that is, incarceration. This rapid reversal from near wholesale "hero" (heroin) treatment just a decade earlier illustrates the ambivalence and inconsistency prevalent in responding to drug use of that time. This issue of *treatment* of the addict versus *control* of the addict has continued to surface nearly every decade since that time, including the more recent 1960s and 1970s.

FEDERAL NARCOTIC FARMS–LEXINGTON 1935

In response to the Linder case, the lack of community treatment facilities, and the community's desire to get the addict off the street, the American Medical Association recommended, and federal legislation was passed in 1929, which led to construction of two federal hospitals for treatment of federal prisoners who were narcotic addicts. This first Federal Narcotic Farm opened in 1935 at Lexington, Kentucky, and the second, three years later, in Fort Worth, Texas. For the next 30 years, these two hospitals were the main *treatment* centers for narcotic addiction in the country. "Treatment" consisted mainly of physical withdrawal from narcotics, work assignments, limited individual psychotherapy, and, because the locations were far away from the addiction setting of the urban ghettos, the obvious attitude that just being away—"down on the farm"—must be healthy and wholesome.

After 30 years of treating the relatively new illness of addiction, the two centers claimed a 90 percent relapse rate and a complementary rate of 10 percent for total "cure"—measured by complete abstinence (National Institute of Mental Health, 1963: 11). However, as Vaillant (1966a: 727) observed, "to be meaningful, relapse rates must embrace more than one point in time." In his twelve-year follow-up of 100 New York City male addicts first admitted to the Lexington Hospital between August 1952 and January 1953, he discovered that while at some time 90 percent return to drug use, 46 percent were drug-free and in the community by the end of the twelve-year study. In addition (Vaillant, 1966c; Vaillant and Raser, 1966), 65 percent of these, or 30 percent of the research population, had been abstinent for from three to twelve years. Also, 67 percent of those who had been in prison for at least nine months and on parole for a year had been abstinent for one year or more. Vaillant (1966a: 736) concluded: "The most significant variable in determining abstinence in the confirmed addict appeared to be the presence or absence of constructive but enforced compulsory supervision." The majority of the addicts studied by Vaillant were under age 30 and certainly youthful, if not adolescent, at the time of their initial addiction. Vaillant (1966b: 1282) reintroduced the disease concept detailing "the natural history of a chronic disease" of narcotic addiction and stated "like other chronic processes, addiction leads to multiple hospitalizations, multiple remissions and multiple relapses." However, except for a brief "camelot" in 1925 in the Linder case, the history of treatment for the addict from 1914 until 1966 wholly ignored the view that the addict was a diseased person in need of treatment: Emphasis had been on control through rigorous enforcement of federal and state laws with increasing penalties. By 1956, the Narcotic Drug Control Act required *mandatory* penalties of 10 to 40 years with no provision for probation or parole for a third offense for *possession* or for a second offense for sale of narcotics. For the addict of the time—youthful or elderly—"treatment" meant control, which meant essentially punishment!

ALCOHOLISM: ATTITUDES-CONTROL-TREATMENT

Somewhat different from the punitive and highly legalistic approach to narcotic addiction in the first half of this century, "just getting drunk" on alcohol was comparatively free from the social aversion of needles and intervention of federal programs. Social attitudes toward alcohol were, nevertheless, ambivalent, contradictory, and confused. On the one hand, early efforts at control were evident through temperance movements in the 1830s which claimed beverage alcohol in all forms was evil and that only evil could come from its use. Anderson (1967: 705-723) observes that "these groups insisted that total abstinence was the only way to civilize and Christianize the barbaric frontier west of the Appalachian Mountains." He further notes that "between 1874 and 1919, 33 states had adopted prohibition of some kind; 68 percent of the population lived in 'dry areas' and 95 percent of the territory of the United States was legally dry."

On the other hand, Anderson shows that during the same years and even earlier, treatment and care were introduced: George Washington, Dr. Benjamin Rush, and Abraham Lincoln recognized quite clearly that the "inebriate" was a person who frequently was not responsible for his condition. As early as 1841 in Boston, a home for inebriates had been established. Passage of Prohibition in 1919 (the 18th Amendment to the Constitution, or the Volstead Act) and its repeal in 1933 (21st Amendment), with the "speakeasy's" and moonshine industries in between, attest to the attitudinal contradictions prevalent during those years. It was not until 1935, less than two years following the repeal of Prohibition, with the founding of the Alcoholics Anonymous (AA) movement by Bill W. and Dr. Bob, that alcoholism began to become recognized as legitimate illness—that is, a condition beyond the individual's immediate control.

The juxtaposition of Prohibition, its repeal, and Alcoholics Anonymous indicates movement from high moral blame in 1919 to comparative low moral blame associated with alcoholism in 1935 within this short span of fifteen years. This compares with the similar transition of social attitudes from high moral blame toward narcotic addiction beginning in 1914, continuing strongly into the late 1950s, and softening to low moral blame in the 1960s. One study (Pattison et al., 1968:

164-166) summarized that "public recommendations for coping with narcotic addiction lag at least a decade behind the recommendations for coping with alcoholism and, we may estimate, perhaps two decades behind public recommendations about mental illness."

At the time of his writing in 1968, Pattison noted that "for both narcotic addiction and alcoholism there is reasonable public support for medical and psychiatric treatment but little support for socially-oriented treatment." The solutions recommended by the public for the addiction problem shifted in emphasis from legalistic and punative measures to medical help and social reforms. Despite this postulated shift in *public* social attitudes, Pattison (1968: 166) charged that "psychiatry has not yet resolved its own conflicts over its professional view of the nature of the narcotic addict and other character disorders. Moralistic images of the character disorders still persist in psychiatry, hampering treatment programs." Such attitudes of psychiatrists and psychologists relating specifically to alcoholism also continue to prevail into the 1970s. Knox (1970: 1675) reported that they "rejected the disease concept in reference to characterizing alcoholism as a behavioral problem, symptom complex, or escape mechanism. Both groups were inconsistent in advocating neuro-psychiatric hospitalization while considering treatment benefits very limited. Members of both groups were reluctant to participate personally to any degree in rendering this treatment."

SYNANON—THE THERAPEUTIC COMMUNITY MOVEMENT

In 1958, Synanon—the "granddaddy" of the therapeutic communities—spearheaded a challenge to the strictly medical and psychiatric treatment approaches of earlier decades. No longer was physiological detoxification and withdrawal the main concern. No longer were earlier childhood events or resurrected "oedipal" conflicts of adolescence allowed as an excuse for an initial or continued drug abuse, as implied by the psychoanalytic framework. While self-help programming had existed throughout Alcoholics Anonymous since 1935, AA had never claimed to be a full-scale treatment program and never became involved in a financial, property-owning political structure as did Synanon. Described by some as "attack therapy," the therapeutic community approach is predicated on placing the addict in a 24-hour residential setting directed by ex-addicts who serve as role models. Through group encounters, seminars, ventilating sessions, and marathons (extended encounters lasting 18 to 24 hours designed to cut through defense mechanisms and resistance), the addict's values and way of life are extensively questioned.

As Weppner (1973b: 74-75) describes, therapeutic communities are oriented to a moral code which is more rigid than any in the middle class. There is a severance of ties to the outside which serves to strengthen the self-help organization's primary group nature. Newcomers must totally submerge themselves in the activities and philosophies of the group and subscribe completely to its rules, which range from a prohibition of "street talk" to a requirement of long, hard hours of work. In all self-help groups, the therapeutic techniques are the same, with an emphasis on the "game" which is a leaderless type of *confrontation* therapy. The closeness that develops may accurately be described as an "extended family," with a system of rewards and punishments built in as a means of social control. Therapeutic communinities may be described as individual change through self-help requiring a unique communal living milieu:

> Its historical prototype is ancient, existing in all communal forms of healing and support which have appeared as self-help responses to human dysfunction. . . . Examples include ancient tribal surrogate families, and within religious history, the cell-like communities of monks seeking to re-establish the purity of Christian ideals in a community setting. . . . The emphasis is on fellowship and personal openness, honesty, and public confession, interpersonal responsibility, involvement, and concern—relating to guilt and alienation by forgiveness, healing and restitution [Mowrer, 1976: 7].

Synanon encompassed the above microcosm of society and became the modern progenitor of the familiar, traditional, therapeutic community. However, while Synanon required and still requires a lifetime commitment, most contemporary therapeutic communities have not fully accepted this Synanon model. With the comparative abundance of federal dollars, newer therapeutic communities emerged with an ambitious goal of full rehabilitation of the individual to a new and healthy start in life. Daytop Village, Phoenix House, Odyssey House (New York), The Village South (Florida), Gateway Houses (Chicago), Marathon House (Rhode Island), Delancy Street (San Francisco), Eden House and Pharm House (Minneapolis), SHAR (Self-Help Addiction Re-orientation Foundation—Detroit) represent a wide variety of styles, lengths of stay, funding resources, and program stability. Nevertheless, each subscribed to the fundamental concept of therapeutic communities, that being the *necessity* for a 24-hour, total influence to render stable changes in lifelong self- and socially destructive patterns of behavior. Panelists further described therapeutic communities at a Conference of the Therapeutic Communities of America:

> It's primary staff, clinical and custodial, are para-professionals, consisting of ex-offenders or ex-drug addicts successfully rehabilitated in therapeutic community programs. The daily regime is full and varied, including encounter group therapy, tutorial-learning sessions, remedial and formal educational classes, special projects, residential job functions, and in later stages, conventional occupations for clients in a living-out situation. . . . Today most urban therapeutic communities offer ancillary treatment or training services such as occupational counseling, family therapy, individual counseling, and various forms of outpatient treatment (night groups and ambulatory services). . . . Compared to the religious life-long vows of the monks and the life-time commitment by Synanon members, most therapeutic communities founded in the mid-1960's required a shorter stay of 15 to 24 months prior to re-entry into independent living in society. However, the post-1975 styled therapeutic communities began to experiment with even shorter periods of stays of six to 15 months. These recent models have assumed a new responsibility of "treatment" within the system of institutionalized medicine without having fully or directly changed either the form, concept, or function derived from their initial role of "healing" through concerned human fellowship [DeLeon and Beschner, 1976: 9, 22].

Weppner (1973b: 75) documents the declining age of therapeutic community admissions. In his report on Matrix House, the average age was 21.9 years and in a visit to Synanon he was told that "the overall age was dropping." This seemed to relate to the change in the drug scene of the early 1970s: The hard narcotic user was being replaced by younger "acid heads" (LSD users) and "speed freaks" (methamphetamine abusers). While there has certainly been criticism of the cost of therapeutic communities, others cite their cost-effectiveness:

> The impression that the therapeutic community is expensive (as a residential treatment) is inaccurate. The cost of maintaining a client in a therapeutic community is modest compared to other institutions that provide residential or inpatient care. Moreover, clinical impressions of those who graduate a program, long-term

success rates appear high, indicating that this modality is effective for those individuals who complete the program. Many of those who do not complete the treatment (dropouts) may, in fact, be much improved as a result of their therapeutic community experience and reflect a positive change in drug abuse, criminal behavior and employability post-treatment. For this "improved" group of former therapeutic community residents, the long-term drain on social costs will be greatly reduced [DeLeon and Beschner, 1976: 10-11].

On the other hand, Brill (n.d.: 4) asserts that while a close family atmosphere, a rigid system of rewards and punishment, and severance of ties to the outside world is effective for some addicts, therapeutic communities have been criticized for failing to return substantial numbers of rehabilitated residents to the community.

EX-ADDICT AS COUNSELOR

Nevertheless, in terms of treatment, two new important concepts emerged out of the therapeutic community movement: (1) the use of the ex-addict as therapist/counselor and (2) long-term (lifetime) expectation of remaining drug-free. While AA held a goal of total abstinence for their more typically middle-aged alcoholics neither medicine, psychiatry, nor corrections included such goals in their control and treatment of youthful dependency in earlier years. Both concepts are widely used and accepted throughout youthful drug treatment modalities currently.

Weppner (1973a: 102-103) summarizes the advantages of using the ex-drug abuser in treatment and rehabilitation:

(1) The first and most important is that of the ex-addict as a *role-model.* He is able to relate to the drug abusing patient because he too "has been there." Thus, a life-style of abstinence from drugs seems more attainable to the patient when he meets such an individual.

(2) The ex-addict or recovering alcoholic does not necessarily relate better, but just quicker! Establishing an immediate trust relationship is critically important in the uncertain initial period when a drug abuser is as liable to flee a program as to accept it.

(3) The ex-drug abuser knows the belief and value system of the addict or alcoholic and he is conversant with the "street code" of addicts or the "street jargon." The ex-addict counselor intuitively knows the reasons for using drugs such as the enjoyable

effects, peer pressure, status seeking, or escape from a meaningless life-style and can understand the drug abuser's self-reported
motivations. Therefore, he does not communicate the negative
attitude of those who may see chemical dependency only as
deviate, illegal, wrong, or psychopathological.

(4) The ex-drug abuser also knows many of the cons, hustles, and
manipulations which addicts and alcoholics use to manipulate
others. He may also be able to prevent or stop these manipulations. An example of this is the prevention of phony "insights"
in therapy groups.

(5) The recovering chemically dependent person in a counselor role
is able to act as an intermediary between professional treatment
staff and the patients in a way which has a valuable buffering
effect in many programs.

Deitch (1971: 134) capsulizes the disadvantages of the ex-addict role
as counselor. Like the word "psychiatry, the term ex-addict had attributed to it magical and curative powers." It was as if having the
credentials of a psychiatrist at one time enabled one to be magical and
thereby cure and treat anybody. Along similar lines, many people began
to think of the new vogue of ex-addicts as treaters: "If one is a former
addict, that label in and of itself equips one to treat, gives one magical
powers which will make treatment effective. . . . In reality, people are
only good if they are competently trained and if they personally are
capable of doing a given job, as in any other profession." Despite
whatever cautions there may be, the use of the ex-addict and recovering
alcoholic as treatment personnel brings a vital ingredient to the treatment team and a perspective that was not sanctioned, for example, in
terms of paid employment by the federal government until four such
ex-addicts were hired at the Federal Narcotics Hospital at Lexington,
Kentucky in 1971—thirteen years after the founding of Synanon.
Therapeutic communities continue to flourish as evidenced by the
incorporation of the "Therapeutic Communities of America, an organization which speaks for 100 agencies with a client population exceed-
ing 15,000 *young* people, 2,200 treatment workers, and 230 facilities in
37 States and Canada" (Stephens, 1979: 3).

COMMUNITY-BASED TREATMENT

Therapeutic communities challenged earlier attempts by local communities to get rid of addicts by sending them to faroff institutions.
Next in historical sequence in treating youthful drug abusers came

community-centered demonstration projects in the early 1960s, primarily in New York City. Nonnarcotic drug abuse was not yet rampant and therefore such projects were concerned with narcotic addiction in a city with such a narcotic addiction problem that it could not be ignored, nor could large numbers of addicts be shipped off to the federal "narcotics farms."

INTENSIVE CASEWORK

One such demonstration project (Brill, 1963), under funding from the National Institute of Mental Health, worked primarily with the 21 to 30 age group, covered a five-year period from 1957 through 1961, and essentially provided intense coordination of community social services for follow-up after detoxification or inpatient psychiatric treatment. It was a time of severe gaps in knowledge of addiction and rehabilitation. Research results pointed to the futility of attempting to rehabilitate patients without effecting changes in their *family* environments. Most significantly, project findings dramatically underscored the importance of integrated *long-term community* programs and services to provide this step-by-step support that the returned addict desperately needs.

CIVIL COMMITMENT

With a similar approach of long-term aftercare coordination of existing resources by a case manager or treatment coordinator, but with the added lever of "compulsory supervision," California implemented a civil commitment program in 1962 and New York state followed with similar but improved provisions in their legislation in 1966. The civil commitment procedure emerged as national policy when the federal government passed the Narcotic Addict Rehabilitation Act (NARA) of 1966. From 1966 until about 1974, the similarities in the legislation illustrated what may be termed a national trend in treating and controlling narcotic addicts (Huberty, 1972: 106). The civil commitment of a narcotic addict was applicable to two phases of treatment—inpatient and outpatient. Length of inpatient treatment varied from the California program requiring a six-month *minimum* to the federal program which was limited to a *maximum* of six months. Outpatient aftercare treatment could last up to seven years under the California law but only three years under the federal program. Treatment during either phase could include any or all of the following: individual psychotherapy, group therapy, milieu therapy, vocational and educational rehabilitation, family counseling, and other social services. On the other hand, treatment sometimes simply consisted of urinalysis to check for reverting to drugs.

The key to the treatment structure of the civil commitment programs was in what Brill and Lieberman (1969) had investigated as techniques of "rational authority" and "reaching out." They described rational authority as providing a firm structuring of the treatment relationship involving the setting of limits, controls, and sanctions through which the acting-out behavior of the addicts could be curbed and minimized. Reaching out included visiting addicts in their homes involving their families, following them into hospitals, jails, and courts, and simply not letting go until a relationship could be established that would more actively involve them in the rehabilitation process. Kiley and Huberty (1975) suggested that this treatment relationship included a gradual process of teaching addicts to use community resources effectively; at the same time it was imperative to curtail their manipulation of one community agency against the other, resulting in what they termed molding the community into a therapeutic milieu." In studies of civilly committed addicts under the federal NARA program, 98 percent had experienced their first drug use prior to age 20 (Bowden and Langenauer, 1972), 8 percent were under age 21, and 38 percent were under age 25 at the time of their commitment (Gold and Chatham, 1973).

With amazing expediency, in about seven years the national trend toward civil commitment as a combined method of treatment and control was reversed. By 1974 it had been replaced by more comprehensive and varied community-based programs with less direct federal funding and more state involvement. However, before its demise, the NARA program had provided training and had established experienced addiction counselors in nearly every major city across the country. The spread of these aftercare agencies helped increase public awareness of the epidemic proportions of drug abuse in their home communities. For the first time, a continuum of consistent treatment from inpatient to outpatient care had been made available. Previous lack of aftercare treatment had been one of the most valid criticisms of almost all drug treatment prior to this time.

POLYDRUG ABUSE

While social attitudes, laws, and treatment programming had separated addiction from alcoholism for decades, developments in the 1970s began to blur these previous separations. One major development, as covered in earlier chapters, was the spread of a wider variety of pharmocological chemical substances. Early history of treatment had primarily concerned narcotics and alcohol. Substances emerging into concern in the 1960s and 1970s included hallucinogens (LSD, STP), barbiturates (Secobarbital, Pentobarbital, Phenobarbital), nonbarbiturate sedative-hypnotics (meprobamates such as Miltown and Equanil; chlordiazepoxide such as Librium and most notably, Valium), amphetamines (Benzadrine, Dexedrine, Methadrine), and inhalants or sniffing agents (spot removers, gasoline, paint thinners, aerosol propellants, and other volatile solvents).

As more nonnarcotic drugs of abuse gained greater accessibility and wider acceptability among youth, along with marihuana, the age of onset of abuse and dependency seemed to drop to younger and younger levels. However, it is worthwhile to note that twenty years earlier, in its 1956 report on narcotic addiction by the Counsel on Mental Health of the American Medical Association, the statement was included that "addiction in persons under 21 years has also increased since World War II. The extent of *adolescent* addiction, however, does not justify the degree of public alarm which has risen. Adolescent addiction is not a new phenomenon." Other reports from the ghetto revealed widespread adolescent narcotic drug abuse and addiction since the late 1940s, but the movement of adolescent drug experimentation and abuse to the suburbs created a new alarm response in the white middle-class community in the late 1960s (Deitch, 1971). Despite the fact that youthful alcohol abuse had existed for decades, concern regarding youthful—and more specifically, adolescent—alcoholism did not develop until national attention switched from the heroin epidemic in 1971 to the polydrug or multidependent drug abusers of the middle 1970s, which then included alcoholism. This evolution to more and different drugs of abuse by younger and younger white middle-class youths resulted in money supplied to implement new treatment modalities and programs in the 1970s. A part of this evolution included the "flower children" or "hippies" in the mid-to-late 1960s, as they ushered in media fascination with the concept of "recreational" drug use.

THE VIETNAM DRUG EXPERIENCE

As the "flower children" were singing the praises of "blowing grass" and "getting high," the war in Vietnam drew increased numbers of youthful servicemen to Southeast Asia. While there was clearly increased use of marihuana between 1965 and 1970 by military personnel in Vietnam, this simply reflected similar practices in stateside use. In fact, about 75 percent of the marihuana users in Vietnam had first used in the states, so that only a remaining 25 percent of marihuana users in Vietnam were first-time users. Of course, these soldier/users were largely under 21 and almost totally under 25 years of age. The increases of marihuana use by the "hippies" in the states paralleled the increase of heavy (twenty times or more) use in Vietnam, up from 7 percent in 1967 to 34 percent in 1971 (Stanton, 1976). Just as there had been few community-based treatment programs in the United States at that time, similarly the Army had no bonafide drug treatment programs before 1969, although they had included some drug education components in brief preparatory courses for groups departing for overseas assignments in 1967.

In 1970, an influx of highly potent heroin entered Vietnam and upwards of 20 percent of enlisted servicemen became addicted to the cheap but 90 to 96 percent pure heroin. A respectable habit could be maintained for $8-$10 a day and there was relaxation of peer taboos against drug abuse both in Vietnam and in America. Unlike marihuana, with which so many soldiers had a pre-Vietnam experience, heroin use was clearly a Vietnam phenomenon. Pre-Vietnam heroin use had been uncommon by servicemen, but by the fall of 1970 34 percent of military enlisted men had used heroin in Vietnam. Stanton (1976) describes the denial or sidestepping of the drug issue by the military at Pentagon level, whereby they claimed it did not exist or existed only among a few select soldiers who had been heavy users prior to military experience.

Traditionally, drug offenders were "treated" by punishment and/or discharged, as the military did not want the responsibility of long-term rehabilitation. This conflicted with emerging congressional views that rather than turning drug addicts loose on the street, the military had a responsibility to eliminate addiction in those who developed it under military auspices. Within the first six months of 1971, many Army voluntary treatment programs in Vietnam emerged and dissolved. Stanton concludes that these programs were, for the most part, ineffectual, partly because of the inexperience of the people designated to carry them out. This inexperience paralleled the lack of addiction treatment experience stateside as described earlier. Denial of a significant drug problem by military personnel in Vietnam paralleled the denial by family members back home. Psychodynamically, it is well accepted that family members tend to emotionally deny an addiction process within the family. And, just as forgiveness is usually hard for family members, amnesty was difficult for the Army. The result in families is unnecessary delays in treatment; so it was for the Army too.

Bombarded by the epidemic in Vietnam and fueled by the public's horror of high-grade heroin being smuggled back into the United States in the corpses of the young who had died in Vietnam, President Nixon declared a "war on drug abuse" in June 1971. Prior to discharge from Vietnam, treatment began through physical exams, collecting drug histories, and urinalysis. By mid-1971, the Army had initiated approximately 35 drug and alcohol programs in stateside Veteran's Administration installations. By 1979 these had nearly tripled, making treatment more accessible and acceptable. While the war on drug abuse was aimed at military veterans and most specifically the heroin epidemic, it was perhaps the best "shot in the arm" that polydrug abuse treatment programs (including alcoholism treatment) received in the states.

Stanton (1976) summarized studies of drug experiences of young Vietnam returnees. They had almost a 95 percent remission rate by 1974; half of those who injected heroin for the first time in Vietnam never used narcotics again after Vietnam and only 16 percent became readdicted. Those veterans who were addicted in Vietnam seemed to have a more favorable prognosis, less psychopathology as measured by the MMPI (Minnesota Multiphasic Personality Inventory), and lower arrest rates than comparable nonveteran addicts. Just as the increasing heroin problem in the states resulted in community-based training and experience for agencies and counselors, the Vietnam epidemic resulted in very positive effects in the field of drug abuse treatment and research. Military drug abuse treatment through the President's Special Action Office for Drug Abuse Prevention (SAODAP) became a testing ground for drug programs in the nation as a whole. As Stanton (1976: 568) further observes, "The Viet Nam experience dispelled many myths and misconceptions about, for example, heroin addiction, and it was found that physiological addiction was neither as persistent nor as untreatable as had previously been believed. . . . These findings helped to reduce cynicism and instill hope for treatment success in a field that had been choking for years on 90 percent failure rates."

COMBINED ADDICT/ALCOHOLIC TREATMENT MODES

Returning Vietnam veterans in the early 1970s noticed that addiction at home was no longer limited to heroin and that nonmedical polydrug abuse had become much more of a widespread phenomenon than when they had left for Vietnam in 1966. In an effort to treat this new wave of young narcotic addicts and polydrug abusers uncovered in the early 1970s, some adult alcoholism treatment programs began to experiment with joint treatment of addicts and alcoholics. Hazelden Foundation[1] and Eagleville Hospital and Rehabilitation Center[2] were two nationally renowned facilities that courageously moved to joint addict/alcoholic treatment.

CHEMICAL DEPENDENCY THEORY

These combined treatment programs took the alcoholic treatment philosophy of Alcoholics Anonymous, didactic lecture or seminar presentations, group therapy and individual counseling, and asked the youthful addict to adapt to those concepts and techniques. Assumptions were made that the emotional dynamics of addiction were the primary common denominators and that psychopharmacology and life-styles were secondary, if not nearly irrelevant, in treatment. Since alcohol, narcotics, and the other polydrugs of abuse all qualified as mood-altering substances, it was a logical and valid comparison to term the younger addict and the older alcoholic both as "chemically dependent"—a new phrasing that was to bridge the many gaps between the generations in treatment efforts.

The "chemical dependency theory" (Huberty, 1973: 342-343) contends that if persons are dependent on one mood-altering drug they will, with all likelihood, be equally dependent on some other type of mood-altering chemical if they switch to that other chemical; that once high on any other drug, they will quickly return to their drug of choice. Therefore, the common goal is total abstinence from all mood-altering chemicals as a treatment approach rather than permitting or recommending that patients cut down or control their use by changing to a so-called less addicting or supposedly less harmful substance.

AA PHILOSOPHY

These programs looked to the first five steps of the 12-Steps of Alcoholics Anonymous as an outline for residential treatment. For example, Step I, "We admitted that we were powerless over alcohol and that our lives had become unmanageable," came to include, "I am powerless over all mood-altering chemicals, not just my drug of choice!" This step took the same humility, tolerance of others, and acceptance of self for the addict as it did for the alcoholic, irrespective of age, values, past criminal record, life-styles, work experiences, family identity, or social and educational status. This emphasis forced youthful addicts to look at their abuse of alcohol, perhaps the one drug they were most inclined to overlook as they were preoccupied with a problem of heroin, amphetamines, barbiturates, or even marihuana, both in their addiction and in earlier rehabilitation programs. A didactic lecture approach—up to three formal presentations daily—presupposed an educational model largely neglected in earlier programs. Such seminars discussed the steps of AA, guilt and other emotions, family dynamics, pharmacology, physiology of drug and alcohol abuse, disease process, and other pertinent treatment concepts. Group therapy and individual counseling used a balance of confrontation and supportive techniques.

Criteria of success are based not only on the fact that the young person is drug-free but also on his or her attitude change toward life; as one program (Cull and Hardy, 1973) describes, "There is a love of self and others, community and country, and a sense of dedication to help his fellow man. . . . If the participant learns well and grasps the meaning of honesty, love, respect, discipline and affection, there is no need for him to go back to drugs."

DISEASE CONCEPT OF CHEMICAL DEPENDENCY

Once honesty, love, respect, discipline and affection are internalized, however, this is not to be interpreted as permission to return to "recreational" drug usage! The very nature of the disease concept adhered to in these programs prevents any such theoretical possibility. Heilman (1974: 29) explains why, as he characterizes the disease of drug dependency as having four universal traits:

(1) An overwhelming recurrent urge to repeat the experience of intoxication—a loss of choice.
(2) The strength of this urge transcends innate needs or learned needs. Simply, it is so powerful it achieves primacy in a person's psychology as a need that recurrently demands fulfillment.
(3) The urge to repeat the experience of intoxication becomes autonomous. This means the urge has become autonomous to

conditioning so that it needs no external or internal stimulation. It can trigger itself (the urge is automatic, not symptomatic).

(4) Once a person has become this profoundly psychologically dependent on a drug experience, there is no so-called cure. This experience becomes so deeply imbedded or indelibly etched within the person's experience that it can never be consciously or unconsciously "forgotton."

As stated by Bejerot (1972: 842), "Addiction has the strength and characteristics of a natural drive; it may be considered as an artificially induced drive developed through chemical stimulation of the pleasure center." The urge itself, then, is the disease and that urge or drive is not dependent on a particular chemical but is characteristic of all mood-altering chemicals. Therefore, any person who experiences a very exceptional pleasure in intoxication is subject to developing the disease of chemical dependency.

ADOLESCENT TREATMENT

BACK TO BOOZE

With conscription at 18 and disenchantment over the war in Vietnam came voting at 18 as a federal "mark of passage" to adulthood. Mounting youthful pressure resulted in one more "rite of passage" in nearly half of the states and several Canadian provinces as the legal alcohol purchasing age was lowered to 18 by 1973. This lowered legal drinking age correlated with (1) a significant increase in the total number of drinkers age 21 and younger—from 46 percent in 1968 to 73 percent in 1974 (Smart and Fejer, n.d.)—as well as an increase in the actual frequency of drinking, thereby increasing the "at-risk" population; (2) a 339 percent increase in alcohol-related collisions among 18 year olds over two years which often precipitates admissions to treatment programs; (3) increased access to alcohol for the 15-to-17-year-old age group and even younger (Smart and Goodstadt, 1977); and (4) increases in the proportion of first admissions of those 21 and under for treatment of alcohol problems (Smart and Finley, 1975). From 1975 to 1980 the trend has been toward alcohol and marihuana as the drugs of choice, perhaps giving a new wave of youth a drug attachment somewhat uniquely theirs and different from the polydrug abuse of their predecessors of five years earlier.

While combined addict/alcoholic treatment programs continue to proliferate, the lowered age of entry into middle and early adolescence has led to specialized adolescent treatment programs. The basic philosophy of Alcoholics Anonymous is used extensively to provide a base for group identity, a spiritual or "higher power" base, and a base for aftercare, as well as the ultimate treatment goal of total abstinence from all mood-altering chemicals. Adolescent or young people's AA groups are now in nearly every major city, even though youths felt rejected and unwanted by AA groups only ten years ago.

FAMILY THERAPY

Spouses have often been included in alcohol treatment programs. However, as the adolescent entered treatment, "family" emphasis changed to include parents, siblings, and, not infrequently, significant grandparents, aunts and uncles, cousins, and neighborhood peers. The need for total family treatment is illustrated by Smith and his associates (1974: 68-69):

> The young person's drug abuse represents merely the tip of an iceberg. For example, a 13-year old who overdosed on barbiturates was seen in our family therapy unit. After extensive evaluation of his family it was determined that her 15-year old sister was significantly depressed, her father had a major alcohol problem, her mother was using Meprobamate to deal with the anxiety and tension of the family situation and the younger 12-year old brother was developing significant psychological problems.

However, even when there is no clear psychopathology in the parents or siblings, the treatment of choice for youthful chemical dependency is still family therapy. As noted in a previous work (Huberty, 1975), the family as a unit is guided by a rational desire for stability. Its behavior can be viewed as homeostatic since it readjusts itself and continues despite reverses. Within the family construct, drug abuse evolves into an integral part of the delicate balance of the family. It serves to meet a need for equilibrium by the individual drug abuser within the family unit; likewise, the drug abuse itself and the behavior that accompanies it become a part of the family's own equilibrium. The family as a unit gradually adjusts to *any* behavior in order to maintain some sense of its own equilibrium. A sense of familiar patterns of coping and interacting develop. In other words, once the family as a unit has adjusted to or compensated for the drug abuser's behavior, it then has a major psychological investment in maintaining that member as a drug abuser so as not to upset the family pattern. Psychologically, the most effortless way for most families to respond to behavior they have an investment in is to scapegoat and chastise the adolescent for his drug abuse, conveniently failing to see that they play supportive roles in the drama.

Failure to involve the family in treatment is almost certain to result in every family member—father and mother, brothers and sisters—in some way sabotaging the efforts of the treatment staff. If change is not made in the family system which helped to produce the drug abuser and has helped to continue that abusive behavior, even "rehabilitated patients" will revert back to the same problem behaviors once they leave the treatment facility and return home to their previous role in the family environment where they and others have identified them as "*the* problem."

Circular Causality. In discussing family treatment and family change, it is important to understand causality or causal relationships. Within systems theory the family is *one* of many systems that impacts upon the drug abuser. Systems framework premises that causality is not a direct linear relationship between a cause and an effect such as is possible with the stimulus-response model. In systems theory, causality is circular: What one person says or does is the stimulus to which another responds and that response in turn becomes a stimulus evoking many more responses. This pattern of circular causality is more descriptive of what really happens when individuals interact, particularly within a system as closed and stable as a family unit. In the stimulus-response model, the stimulus is seen as the cause and, therefore, it is always possible to place blame. Within the circular causality model the emerging interaction cannot be traced to a single cause, consequently it is not possible to blame a single source.

Mutual Problem Areas. Circular causality alerts treatment personnel to several areas shared by the adolescent drug abuser and his or her family. First, ignorance of chemical dependency: Not only do families (particularly parents) feel intimidated by their ignorance, but adolescents' ignorance matches that of their parents. Their knowledge of drug effects is limited to their own experiences, which are subjective and usually limited to certain drugs. Even the thought of a developing and progressive dependence on chemicals as described earlier by Heilman (1974) is totally foreign to both sides of the generation gap.

Second, emotional denial of chemical dependency: Adolescents may typically (emotionally) deny any problem with drugs whatsoever despite their drug-taking being an obvious problem to everyone else in their network of relationships, even perhaps those friends with whom they are sharing drugs. Another characteristic of emotional denial is compartmentalizing their dependency. They may well accept that they are powerless with respect to heroin or that they have problems with barbiturates, but they fail to realize that their dependency on drugs may well encompass the full gamut of the pharmacopeia. Parents often support this compartmentalization by denying that legal drugs such as alcohol and prescription medications are problems also: "We knew he was just doing some drinking but once he started taking that LSD or THC stuff, that's when the problems began."

Third, failure to accept responsibility: When confronted with erratic and inappropriate behavior or the fact of drug-taking itself, drug abusers tend to project most of the blame onto their parents without accepting ultimate responsibility for their own behavior. Adolescents are most successful in placing blame on parents when they are able to "divide and conquer" as exemplified by one mother: "I knew my daughter was taking some pills but I decided not to tell her father because he only gets upset over such things." Parents fit nicely into this jigsaw puzzle; they defend themselves by counterprojecting total blame onto their child without examining their enabling role in the relationship. One unfortunate aspect of parents placing blame is their inconsistency in doing so. On the one hand, they verbally blame and chastise their sons or daughters; on the other hand, they repeatedly save these near-adults from the logical consequences of their behavior, thus sending a clear message that they are not to be held accountable for their actions. This failure to give and accept responsibility is a pervasive, all-encompassing family dynamic.

Fourth, anger and hostility-love and affection: Anger and hostility become repressed and denied, consciously bottled up, or expressed only indirectly or inappropriately. This tends to encourage suppression of all aggressive and assertive behavior. The result is that both adolescent and parents avoid all strong emotional expression. Warm expressions of love—a touch or tear—are as fearful to both parties as an outburst of anger and hate. Getting high provides adolescents with a mechanism by which they can experience an explosion of intense feelings whether those emotions be anger and hostility, or love and affection. This anger and hate, love and affection dichotomy is not the sole property of the adolescent. Parents frequently feel disgust and even hatred toward the drug abuser, but in "controlling" their own emotions they completely deny that they could ever feel anything but love for their child.

Fifth, ambivalence: The whole family needs help in seeing this ambivalence in many spheres as normal vacillation in the testing of new and unfamiliar interpersonal relationships as the family unit undergoes change. Even the adolescent's ambivalence of "I want to stop using drugs and I do not want to stop using drugs" is as confusing to the adolescent as it is to his parents.

Sixth, lack of honesty: Dishonesty in the parent-child relationship is another mutual-interacting problem area. Generally, adolescent drug abusers have been so used to distorting the truth and rationalizing their behavior during their active drug abuse phase that they must be all the more careful not to even slightly distort the truth once they begin their rehabilitation program. Families, too, have adapted to adolescents' dishonesty by relating to them in a dishonest fashion. Just as the adolescents have been blatantly lying to the parents, the parents have been denying and lying to friends, grandparents, neighbors, and co-workers, often covering up to protect themselves from the fear of more public embarrassment.

Seventh, role model of drug abuse: One study (Bernstein, 1973) found that for young teenagers, the most frequent source of first-drug experience is from drugs obtained in the home. A higher incidence of alcoholism has been found in the children of alcoholics and it has been estimated that approximately 52 percent of alcoholics come from homes in which one or both parents had a drinking problem (Fox, 1968). This suggests much about the marital dynamics of parents, and the possibility of active parental alcoholism must be explored and openly confronted during the course of the adolescent's treatment.

TREATING THE PARENTS

The importance of family treatment is stated succinctly by Alibrandi (1978: 115):

> The kid-fix-it-shop approach—mom and dad drop off their alco-
> holic or drug abusing young one for a carburetor tuning or tire
> patch and pick up youngster all fixed—is a myth. The entire
> family needs a healing experience. . . . At this initial stage of
> therapy, when the young drinker may not have made the decision
> of abstinence we have found that the best method of helping
> both parents and youngsters is in separate group settings.

Joint sessions with parents and adolescents seem to work more successfully later in therapy or in combination with the separate group sessions. In early stages of treatment, confrontative therapy between parents and the young drug abuser often muddies the issue, thereby giving the teen or preteen more reason to drink and abuse drugs. Separate parent group sessions help diffuse the resentment between parent and child by helping parents back away from their child's behavior. Most treatment centers for adolescent chemical dependency now involve parents in a separate group experience. This was not the common practice prior to the late 1970s, however. This attention to parental treatment is summarized in an earlier work (Huberty and Huberty, 1976), in which the primary goal was to restore the marriage relationship. In other words, the emphasis was not family therapy but marital therapy. During the *family* crisis of adolescent drug abuse, parents need encouragement to examine their changing needs as a normal process for healthy growth of a marriage. In parental treatment, it is absolutely necessary to assure parents that, in raising their children, they did the best they knew how to at the time. The notion of guilt must be deemphasized and the personal burden lessened for each partner. It is important to remind them that their adolescent's problems and the problems of the marriage do not mean failure as parents or as a couple; rather, problems represent a challenge and this view can begin to provide hope.

Support from other parents in a therapy group setting who are in, or have been in, similar situations is the strongest kind of support they can receive. By sharing their feelings of disappointment, frustration, and failure they can discover the normalcy of their feelings and problems. They can feel reassured that the anger and hate, love and affection division that they feel for their adolescent and *toward each other* as marriage partners is acceptable. Through this mutual support process, they may feel understood and are able to regain respect for themselves and each other. They may also receive specific suggestions from other parents regarding techniques to use in limit-setting and phrases to use in reestablishing communication with the adolescent and with each other.

Another technique in parental treatment and marital therapy is helping the couple to laugh *at* themselves and *with* each other. They need to begin having fun as a couple again. By the time they have reached a therapy group or by the time their adolescent is in a treatment center, the marriage has received much "leftover" time. As a couple they have not had fun together for months or, sometimes, for years. It is not uncommon to find a couple who has not vacationed together *alone*—even for a weekend—for between five and twenty years.

Their emphasis has been on the children, and their marriage has increasingly been deemphasized and ignored.

The parental approach has been more institutionalized through Families Anonymous,[3] a self-help organization started and maintained by the "hurting" family members themselves and patterned after the 12 Steps and 12 Traditions of Alcoholics Anonymous. Families Anonymous stresses early intervention for the concerned family and, in cases where the young person refuses to accept help, changed family attitudes can improve motivation and set the stage for recovery. They have chapters established in 28 states with regular weekly meetings in which "neighbors help neighbors" by sharing their own experiences, both successes and failures, and are supportive of other parents going through a particular crisis. Where Families Anonymous is not established, many Alanon groups accept or even specialize in the problems parents have in coping with their child's drug abuse and related behavior.

The overall increased interest in family factors in the genesis and maintenance of drug misuse and dependency is evidenced throughout the chemical dependency treatment field. Even therapists working in drug abuse areas which have not primarily been family focused have begun to include more relevant family information in their efforts. The literature also reflects this trend. A recent bibliography on the family and drug misuse included 370 titles (Stanton, 1978); 299—nearly 80 percent—were published since 1970 with more than one-third dealing specifically with family and marital treatment.

DIAGNOSTIC DILEMMAS

Perhaps one of the greatest inhibitors to early intervention and treatment is that, as Huberty and Malmquist (1978) point out, the diagnostic label "adolescent chemical dependency" does not appear in the American Psychiatric Association's Diagnostic and Statistical Manual and is therefore not yet entertained as a primary diagnosis by most physicians, psychologists, social workers, and other mental health practitioners. Often professionals fall victim to an enabling role in relating to chemically dependent adolescents because of their lack of training in diagnosing this disease. Since therapists are trained to respond to symptoms, they respond to symptoms with which they are most familiar. Thus, many professionals tend to interpret chemical abuse symptoms as "disturbed behavior" and view the chemical usage as unreachable or, at the other extreme, may view it as fairly normal and acceptable adolescent development. Professionals, too, may unconsciously reflect society's ambivalence in viewing intoxicated behavior either as humorous, entertaining, or enchanting—or viewing intoxicated behavior which goes beyond acceptable limits as something of a moral transgression. Many professionals simply have difficulty accepting self-inflicted chemical abuse as a disease state.

However, adolescent chemical dependency is becoming more accepted as a treatment specialty and is being annexed by institutional medicine. Hospitals have established specialized treatment programs and health insurance in recognizing this disease through payment mechanisms. This process has led to demands for more precise diagnostic skills. In order to arrive at a diagnosis differentiating among drug experimentation, misuse, or dependency, many techniques are used. As Blackmore (1977) suggests, changes in behavior and performance compared to one's past are important:

> Do not ask *why* questions, but ask *what* and *how* questions. Ask these questions as they relate to school, extra-curricular activities, new conflicts with teachers; at home check for suspiciousness, change in cash flow, obvious intoxication, defiance. In terms of peers, as friends change, check to see if their reputation is different from the reputation of previous friends and whether or not values are different. Is there police contact, changes in relationships with neighbors or church? All of these *systems* need to be compared not with other *adolescents* but with this person's past.

St. Mary's Adolescent Chemical Dependency Unit[4] uses two self-reporting mechanisms to gather a great deal of information quickly to assist in diagnosis. A 39-question self-evaluation form samples such data as "I drink to get drunk," "I use drugs to get high," "I smoke grass and drink alcohol together," "Sometimes I can't explain why I get high—I just do," and "I get angry when people say I have a drug problem." Most important is the adolescent's admission of unwanted and unplanned negative complications resulting from drug use. This Checklist of Harmful Consequences contains 34 questions in four areas:

(1) Financial Problems—i.e., "I put off buying things I need in order to get money for drugs."
(2) Family Problems—i.e., "My parents wait up for me to see if I am high."
(3) Problems with Friends—i.e., "My girlfriend or boyfriend has expressed concern about my drug use."

(4) School Problems—i.e., "My grades have gone down since I started using drugs."

Other diagnostic instruments are being researched. Alibrandi (1978) reports on a Youth Diagnostic Screening Device. One part may be used for preteens by sampling nondrinking-related items to determine the at-risk group of preteenagers whose behavior correlates with the behavior of teenagers who develop problem drinking a few years later. Another part of the screening device samples problem drinking among teenagers. Mayer and Filstead (1979a, 1979b) have developed the Adolescent Alcohol Involvement Scale (AAIS) which tests for and interprets four levels: (1) the "normal adolescent" who is either abstaining or experimenting with alcohol; (2) the adolescent alcohol user whose alcohol use is not problematic; (3) alcohol misuse with recommendations for counseling, education, and some intervention; and (4) adolescent alcoholism or dependence requiring hospitalization.

Despite greater diagnostic sophistication in chemical dependency, an earlier caution on the difficult diagnostic dilemmas in child psychiatry is worthy to note:

> Diagnostic labels for the adolescent are unreliable and often invalid. . . . The adolescent manifestations may come close to the symptom formation of the neurotic, the psychotic, or the character disorder and merge almost imperceptibly into borderline states. They may, in fact, resemble forms of almost all of the mental illnesses. . . . However, the pervasiveness of the symptoms picture more strongly suggests the accuracy of a diagnosis for the adolescent [Wallinga, 1964: 2].

ST. MARY'S HOSPITAL ADOLESCENT CHEMICAL DEPENDENCY UNIT

One pioneer in hospital-based treatment of adolescent chemical dependency is St. Mary's Hospital (Minneapolis). The Drug Unit's original goal in 1972 was primarily to provide narcotic withdrawal and other drug detoxification, but by 1974, with the rapidly changing drug scene, the unit's direction changed to adolescent chemical dependency treatment. Three separate and distinct programs developed and now operate within the overall Unit: an evaluation program, primary treatment, and the aftercare program. Goals include: (1) diagnosis and problem recognition; (2) acceptance; (3) self-assessment; (4) demonstration; and (5) maintenance. Achievement in any of these levels is significant, and the achievement of all five levels is regarded as optimum rehabilitation. However, achievement of all five levels in a short time span of less than two years is regarded as ambitious. Measurement of progress of levels of achievement include: (1) the patient's acceptance of his or her disease and willingness to comply with the treatment program; (2) the patient's growth in assuming responsibility for his or her recovery shown by changes in thinking, feeling, attitudes, and behavior; (3) the patient's willingness to change, shown by acceptance of self and others, risk-taking in showing concerns for others, growing self-esteem, developing positive peer relationships, and serious application of recovery program; (4) the patient's willingness to maintain a new life-style as evidenced by acceptance of discharge plans following a program, attendance in Alcoholics Anonymous, and successful compliance with the aftercare plan.

An intensive inpatient, locked-unit evaluation process has been developed to successfully differentiate the substance *abuser* from the *dependent* adolescent. Their director (Yupuncich, 1979) reports up to 75 percent of the admissions being in a *disease process* of chemical dependency, noting significantly greater conflicts between one's values and one's behavior in dependency. However, uncovering this value conflict is difficult as the adolescent has not developed a recognition of an identified value system. Values clarification exercises are used whereby the patient must rank in order such values as an exciting life, a prosperous life, family security, health, inner harmony, sexual and spiritual intimacy with another person, nature, peace, self-respect, sobriety, social approval, work, and so on. Such value identity with peer feedback and approval results in sufficient awareness to then recognize the conflict between values (of which the adolescent was previously unaware) and behavior (the adolescent's rejection of such values when using drugs—harmful consequences).

The Primary Treatment Unit includes a multidisciplinary team staff providing a consistent therapeutic milieu which minimizes the amount of manipulation of individual staff members. The treatment staff is trained specifically in adolescent development as well as in chemical dependency. A home-bound tutorial school program is part of the treatment modality, and didactic material on family dynamics, adolescent development, and chemical dependency is delivered in a more informal and individual way than it is in comparable adult alcoholism programs. Occupational and recreational therapy is specifically designed to meet the needs of a naturally active and energetic group of adolescents. Videotaping of therapy groups and individual interviews is used extensively. The impact of television on youth is characterized by several patients who have commented that watching themselves on videotape seems more real than the actual experience. Meditation is one tool used to lower anxiety, reduce hostility, and improve individual self-concepts. In Alcoholics Anonymous, the 11th Step of its recovery program invites the alcoholic "to seek through prayer and meditation to improve our conscious contact with God." Yoga and other systems of meditation are used in the St. Mary's program as an alternative "natural high." The aftercare phase uses a continuation of peer pressure, limit-setting, family involvement, attendance at Alcoholics Anonymous, and other techniques of the highly structured therapeutic milieu.

St. Mary's received national attention in an October 1977 ABC news documentary, "Teenage Turn-On: Drinking and Drugs." The results of the success of the St. Mary's program have resulted in assisting other medical facilities in developing and implementing units similar in design. Such facilities have been established in other hospitals in Minneapolis, Des Plaines (Illinois), Omaha (Nebraska), Columbus (Ohio), Sioux City (Iowa), Des Moines (Iowa), New York, and Baton Rouge (Louisiana). Such interest has also increased since publication of the results of research (Mitchell, 1976a, 1976b, 1977) funded by the National Institute of Drug Abuse on the attrition and follow-up of a large group of St. Mary's patients. The data obtained used a broad range of outcome measures and follow-up periods of six, twelve, and eighteen months. The St. Mary's treatment graduates who averaged 50 days in the treatment program were approximately twice as likely to show favorable outcomes as the treatment droputs. The study acknowledges that preexisting patient characteristics have a great deal to do with outcome. However,

> despite evidence that pre-existing prognostic factors have much to do with resulting treatment outcome, it will be difficult to conclude that the St. Mary's Program does not have a profound effect on many of the patients it treats. The program demands nothing less than that patients either reorganize their life-style and make a commitment to complete abstinence from alcohol and all major non-prescribed drugs or that they leave the program. Any signs of non-compliance or feigned compliance draw intensive and unrelenting confrontation [Mitchell, 1976b: 44].

Evidence is that approximately one-third of the patients who completed the program and were discharged directly to the community maintained "*continuous* abstinence for a period of 18 months and from every indication seem intent on remaining totally abstinent indefinitely." An additional group of program graduates experienced slips (relapse) after which they seemed to reaffirm their commitment to abstinence. Overall, it appeared that over half of the graduates accepted and strove for the goal of complete abstinence. The research concluded that "considering the ages of these patients and the extensive and serious histories of substance abuse which were common, it would require a tremendous stretch of the imagination to assume that this type of behavioral change in this large proportion of the patients might have occurred as readily in the form of 'spontaneous remissions' if these patients had not been treated or had undergone a simple period of confinement for a comparable period of time (Mitchell, 1976b: 45).

More specifically, at a point of six-month follow-up after discharge from the program, "A very striking finding was that more than 80% of the St. Mary's Treatment graduate group had no subsequent admissions and this rate was nearly twice as great as what was found for the St. Mary's treatment dropout group" (Mitchell, 1976b: 16). Furthermore, the difference between the St. Mary's treatment dropout group and graduate group at the one-year point could still be shown to be statistically significant. It is also significant that there was high success in locating subjects at all follow-up intervals ranging from 94.3 percent at six months to 87.1 percent at eighteen months.

FORECASTING THE 1980s

The state of the art of treatment for youthful drug use is a culmination a decades of attempts to balance treatment with control. In this new decade, youth will continue to be affected by mind-altering sub-stances perhaps no more and no less than in recent years. As in earlier decades, treatment, however, will continue to evolve and change in many predictable ways but also in some very unpredictable ways.

PREDICTABLE ASPECTS OF TREATMENT

Residential Treatment. Specialized hospital-based programs similar to St. Mary's Hospital Adolescent Chemical Dependency Treatment Unit will flourish. Availability of such treatment within institutionalized medicine will not be a major gap in treatment resources. However, similar residential programs outside of hospitals will increasingly secure payment from health insurance carriers as public financing diminishes for therapeutic communities and other nonhospital-based treatment programs. Insurance companies will respond to the comparable cost efficiency of such treatment programs outside of hospitals that do not carry high hospital overhead costs.

Techniques will not change dramatically. Confrontation and support, insight and information, meditation and relaxation, and identification of a unique value system will comprise the programming. Alcoholics Anonymous and family involvement will continue as hallmarks of treatment.

While inpatient facilities will continue to draw parent-referred adolescents in states of crisis upon intervention, more admissions to residential treatment will be elective—youths seeking to enhance their value systems, their identities, and their stability.

There may be a trend back to street drugs. If the legal purchasing age of alcohol is raised to 21, first incidence of alcohol use may again rise to age 16 or 17, but with a corresponding experimentation with "street drugs." This will not significantly affect treatment programming, however.

Locked *detoxification* and highly structured *evaluation* units will continue to be used to ensure accurate data collection and to provide for a therapeutic milieu in which acting-out adolescents can test the limits of the program prior to entering the actual treatment phase.

Treatment in the Schools. Peer attitudes will change. Kids getting straight are now true revolutionaries. This influence will result in school-based support groups and therapy groups similar to outpatient groups of the 1970s. It will become more acceptable and therefore easier for the adolescent to entertain abstinence from all drugs as a viable alternative early in life. National "Non-Drinker's Rights"[5] groups will push for support of such a freedom of choice. Peer educators trained in knowledge of drug effects, adolescent development, and alternative highs will offer such support. Successfully treated youths returning to their high schools and colleges will provide such support. University-sponsored housing or dormatories for nonusers will become available as a choice for supportive living.

UNPREDICTABLE ASPECTS OF TREATMENT

Whether a youthful drug user needs inpatient treatment, outpatient treatment, or *any* treatment will continue to be determined by the demands of the times, prevailing social attitudes, and a question of adequate control, all repeated throughout the history of youthful treatment but all unpredictable in the dawn of a new decade.

NOTES

1. Additional information on Hazelden's experience in treating addicts and alcoholics together may be obtained by writing: Literature Department, Hazelden Foundation, P.O. Box 176, Center City, MN. 55012.

2. Eagleville has published several articles on joint addict/alcoholic treatment. Inquiries may be sent to: Eagleville Hospital and Rehabilitation Center, Eagleville, PA.

3. For a complete listing of established Families Anonymous group meetings throughout the United States, contact: Families Anonymous, Inc., P.O. Box 344, Torrance, CA. 90501.

4. Copies of the Self-Evaluation Form and Checklist of Harmful Consequences may be obtained from: Director, Adolescent Chemical Dependency Treatment Unit, St. Mary's Hospital, 2414 South 7th Street, Minneapolis, MN. 55454.

5. Additional information on creating an environment in which it is acceptable not to drink may be obtained from: Non-Drinkers Rights, P.O. Box 5487, Concord, CA. 94524.

REFERENCES

ALIBRANDI, T. (1978) Young Alcoholics. Minneapolis: Comp Care.

ANDERSON, D. J. (1967) "A history of our confused attitudes toward beverage alcohol." Mayo Clinic Proceedings 42: 705-723.

BEJEROT, N. (1972) "A theory of addiction as an artificially induced drive." American Journal of Psychiatry 128 (January): 842-846.

BERNSTEIN, D. M. (1973) "Drugs and the adolescent." Minnesota Medicine 56 (February): 108-110.

BLACKMORE, G. (1977) "Diagnosing adolescent chemical dependency." Presented at the Minnesota Chemical Dependency Association Fall Conference, Minneapolis, October 17.

BOWDEN, C. L. and B. J. LANGENAUER (1972) "Success and failure in the NARA addiction program." American Journal of Psychiatry 128, 7: 853-856.

BRILL, L. (1963) Rehabilitation in Drug Addiction: A Report on a Five-Year Community Experiment of the New York Demonstration Center." Bethesda, MD: National Institute of Mental Health.

––– (n.d.) Drug Abuse Problems–Implications for Treatment. Unidentified source.

––– and L. LIEBERMAN (1969) Authority and Addiction. Boston: Little, Brown.

CULL, J. G. and R. E. HARDY (1973) Drug Dependence and Rehabilitation Approaches. Springfield, IL: Charles C Thomas.

DEITCH, D. (1971) "Evolution of treatment roles in more recent response to addiction problems." Journal of Drug Issues 1, 2: 132-140.

DeLEON, G. and G. M. BESCHNER (1976) The Therapeutic Community: Proceedings of Therapeutic Communities of America Planning Conference. Rockville, MD: National Institute on Drug Abuse.

FOX, R. (1968) "Treating the alcoholic's family," pp. 105-115 in R. J. Cantanzaro (ed.) Alcoholism. Springfield, IL: Charles C Thomas.

GOLD, R. and L. R. CHATHAM (1973) Characteristics of NARA Patients in Aftercare During June 1971. Rockville, MD: National Institute of Mental Health.

Harrison Act (1914) 38 Statutes 785 as amended in 26 U.S.C.

HEILMAN, R. O. (1974) "Common denominators: dynamics of drug dependency," pp. 27-33 in D. J. Ottenberg and E. L. Carpey (eds.) Proceedings of the 7th Annual Eagleville Conference. Rockville, MD: Alcohol, Drug Abuse, and Mental Health Administration.

HUBERTY, C. E. and D. J. HUBERTY (1976) "Treating the parents of adolescent drug abusers." Contemporary Drug Problems 5, 4: 573-592.

HUBERTY, D. J. (1975 "Treating the adolescent drug abuser: a family affair." Contemporary Drug Problems 4, 2: 179-194.

――― (1973) "The addict and alcoholic in treatment: some comparisons." Journal of Drug Issues 3, 4: 341-347.

――― (1972) "Civil commitment of the narcotic addict: evolution of a treatment method." Crime and Delinquency 18, 1: 99-109.

――― and J. D. MALMQUIST (1978) "Adolescent chemical dependency." Perspectives in Psychiatric Care 16, 1: 21-27.

KILEY, D. F. and D. J. HUBERTY (1975) "The community as a therapeutic milieu." Journal of Drug Issues 5, 2: 152-159.

KNOX, W. J. (1971) "Attitudes of psychiatrists and psychologists toward alcoholism." American Journal of Psychiatry 127, 12: 1675-1679.

LINDER v. UNITED STATES (1925) 268 U.S. 5.

LINDESMITH, A. R. (1965) The addict and the Law. Bloomington: Indiana University Press.

MAYER, J. E. and W. F. FILSTEAD (1979a) Adolescents and Alcohol. Cambridge, MA: Ballinger.

――― (1979b) "The adolescent alcohol involvement scale: an instrument for measuring adolescent use and misuse of alcohol." Journal of Studies on Alcohol 40, 3.

MITCHELL, J. (1977) "St. Mary's Hospital adolescent treatment program," in Hennepin County Drug/Alcohol Research Project. Minneapolis: Multi Resource Center.

――― (1976a) "Variables associated with attrition from a residential chemical dependency program for adolescents/young adults," in Hennepin County Drug/Alcohol Research Project. Minneapolis: Multi Resource Center.

――― (1976b) "St. Mary's follow-up study: year 02 report," in Hennepin County Drug/Alcohol Research Project. Minneapolis: Multi Resource Center.

MOWRER, O. H. (1976) "Historical perspectives," pp. 28-32 in G. DeLeon and G. M. Beschner (eds.) The Therapeutic Community: Proceedings of Therapeutic Communities of America Planning Conference. Rockville, MD: National Institute on Drug Abuse.

National Institute of Mental Health (1963) Narcotic Drug Addiction. Mental Health Monograph 2. Washington, DC: Government Printing Office.

PATTISON, E. M., L. A. BISHOP, and A. S. LINSKY (1968) "Changes in public attitudes on narcotic addiction." American Journal of Psychiatry 125, 2: 160-167.

SMART, R. G. and D. FEJER (n.d.) U.N. Bulletin on Narcotics.

SMART, R. G. and J. FINLEY (1975) "Increases in youthful admissions to alcoholism treatment in Ontario." Drug and Alcohol Dependence 1: 83-87.

SMART, R. G. and M. S. GOODSTADT (1977) "Effects of reducing the legal alcohol-purchasing age on driving and drinking problems: a review of empirical studies." Journal of Studies on Alcohol 38, 7: 1313-1323.

SMITH, D. E., D. R. WESSON and S. E. LERNER (1974) "Treatment of the polydrug abuser in San Francisco with discussion of youth and polydrug abuse," pp. 62-83 in D. J. Ottenberg and E. L. Carpey (eds.) Proceedings of the 7th Annual Eagleville Conference. Rockville, MD: Alcohol, Drug Abuse, and Mental Health Administration.

STANTON, M. D. (1978) "The family and drug misuse: a bibliography." American Journal of Alcohol and Drug Abuse 5, 2: 151-170.

――― (1976) "Drugs, Vietnam, and the Vietnam veteran: an overview." American Journal of Drug and Alcohol Abuse 3, 4: 557-570.

STEPHENS, J. (1979) "Editorial." Dawn: The SHAR Forum. (January): 3.

VAILLANT, G. E. (1966a) "A twelve-year follow-up of New York narcotic addicts: I. The relation of treatment to outcome." American Journal of Psychiatry 122, 7: 727-737.

――― (1966b) "A twelve-year follow-up of New York narcotic addicts: II. The natural history of a chronic disease." New England Journal of Medicine 275: 1282-1288.

――― (1966c) "A twelve-year follow-up of New York narcotic addicts: IV. Some characteristics and determinants of abstinence." American Journal of Psychiatry 123, 5: 573-584.

――― and R. W. RASER (1966). "The role of compulsory supervision in the treatment of addiction." Federal Probation: 53-59.

WALLINGA, J. V. (1964). "The adolescent emotional quandary." Lancet 84: 1-3.

WEPPNER, R. S. (1973a) "Forum: the role of the ex-addict in drug abuse intervention." Drug Forum 2, 2: 102-105.

――― (1973b) "Some characteristics of an ex-addict's self-help therapeutic community and its members." British Journal of the Addictions 68: 73-79.

YUPUNCICH, C. (1979) Personal interview. Minneapolis, St. Mary's Hospital, February 9.

ABOUT THE AUTHORS

G. NICHOLAS BRAUGHT is currently an Associate Professor in the Department of Psychology at the University of Denver. He received his Ph.D. from the University of Colorado. He is interested in developing interactional conceptualizations of a variety of human problems, including violent behavior, sexual deviance, suicidal behavior, and drug misuse among youth. He is also interested in the development and evaluation of prevention programs aimed at reducing these and other forms of socially deviant behaviors.

SUSAN K. DATESMAN is currently an Assistant Professor in the Center of Criminal Justice at Arizona State University. She received her Ph.D. in Sociology from the University of Delaware in 1979. Her publications include *Women, Crime, and Justice,* and several articles, chapters, and professional papers in the areas of female crime and drug use, juvenile delinquency, and juvenile justice.

DOROTHY E. GREEN received her Ph.D. in Psychology from the University of Chicago. She has wide experience in both teaching and research administration, and since 1967 has been Chief, Program Research Branch, National Clearinghouse on Smoking and Health, Communicable Disease Center. Her research interests have centered around attitudes and attitude change, program evaluation, and smoking behavior. She has published extensively on smoking and smoking-related factors, including a number of major government reports.

DAVID J. HANSON is Chairman of the Sociology department at the State University of New York at Potsdam, has received grants from federal, state, and private foundation sources for his research in drinking behaviors among youth. He is the author of over 100 publications, serves as consultant to several organizations and agencies, and is listed in *Who's Who in the East* and similar reference works.

DAVID J. HUBERTY graduated cum laude with a B.A. in Social Science from the College of St. Thomas (St. Paul, Minnesota) in 1966. He holds an M.S.W. (1968) from the University of Minnesota and is a member of the Academy of Certified Social Workers of the National Association of Social Workers. He has done additional course work at the Alfred Adler Institute of Minnesota and the University of Kentucky, College of Law.

JAMES A. INCIARDI is currently Professor and Director, Division of Criminal Justice, University of Delaware. He received his Ph.D. in Sociology from New York University and has more than 17 years of experience in the clinical and research areas of substance abuse and criminal justice. He is Editor of *Criminology* and has authored more than 70 books and articles in the fields of criminology, criminal justice, and drug abuse.

BRUCE D. JOHNSON received his Ph.D. from Columbia University and is currently a research scientist and Chief of Epidemiology and Special Projects in the Bureau of Cost Effectiveness and Research of the New York State Division of Substance Abuse Services. His areas of research interest include marihuana and other drug use in youthful and general populations, subculture theory, heroin addiction, and criminology. His publications include *Marihuana Users and Drug Subcultures, Drug Use and Abuse Among U.S. Minorities,* and numerous articles in professional journals and presentations at drug conferences. He is currently Principal Investigator of a NIDA-funded research project studying the Economic Behavior of Street Heroin users in a New York City ghetto.

MANUEL R. RAMOS (B.A. magna cum laude, Yale University; J.D., University of Virginia Law School), formerly a drug researcher for Yale University's Department of Sociology and the National Institute on Drug Abuse, is currently an attorney and freelance writer in San Diego, California.

LOUISE G. RICHARDS is Social Psychologist in the Division of Research, the National Institute on Drug Abuse. She served four years as the Chief of the Psychosocial Branch of the Division. From 1963 to 1966 she carried out government research in medical sociology and consumer behavior; since 1967, she has specialized in epidemiological and psychosocial aspects of drug abuse. She is the author of a number of articles and book chapters on drug abuse and has edited several NIDA Research Monographs. She received her Ph.D. in Social Psychology from Cornell University.

MARY E. ROHMAN received her M.A. degree in Sociology from Boston University in 1979. In addition to her current involvement in the study of drug use among college students at The Medical Foundation, Inc., Boston, her research experience includes work in human services planning and community studies.

FRANK R. SCARPITTI is Professor and Chair, Department of Sociology, University of Delaware. He is the author or coauthor of books on treatment of the mentally ill, group therapy, social problems, youth and drugs, social deviance, and female criminality. In addition, he has written a number of articles, chapters, and conference papers on these and related subjects. He served as Vice-President of the American Society of Criminology from 1978-1979 and as President from 1980-1981. In 1967, he was named cowinner of the American Psychiatric Association's Hofheimer Prize for Research.

RICHARD C. STEPHENS is an Associate Professor of Sociology at the University of Houston. He received his Ph.D. from the University of Wisconsin in 1971. He has served as Assistant Director of Research at the New York State Office of Drug Abuse Services and was a researcher at the NIMH Clinical Research Center at Lexington, Kentucky. His research interests have included the heroin street scene, the use of methadone on the streets, and the relationships between crime and addiction. He is currently Co-Principal Investigator of an epidemiological study of drug use among persons aged 55 and older.

GOPAL S. UPPAL received his Ph.D. in Urban-Environmental Studies from Rensselaer Polytechnic Institute, and is currently a research scientist with the New York State Division of Substance Abuse Services. In his present position, he heads the epidemiological research unit and is responsible for planning and implementing projects designed to assess substance use levels in the state and the unmet need for treatment services. These projects have resulted in several epidemiological reports published by the agency. In addition, he has represented the agency at NIDA-sponsored conferences dealing with substance use trends in major urban areas of the country. His other fields of interest include victim-

ization, ecology of crime, and statistical research methods, particularly
stochastic processes.

HENRY WECHSLER is Director of Research at The Medical Foundation, Inc., in Boston and Lecturer in Social Psychology at the Harvard
School of Public Health and Simmons College School of Social Work.
He has conducted research in various aspects of public health and
mental health since receiving his Ph.D. in Social Psychology from
Harvard University in 1957. He has published extensively on the epidemiology of drug and alcohol use among teenagers and college students.